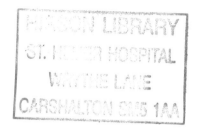
Some of the most interesting new ethnographies of experience highlight the indeterminate nature of life. *Questioning misfortune* is very much within this tradition. Based on a long-term study of adversity and its social causes in Bunyole, eastern Uganda, it considers the way in which people deal with uncertainties of life, such as sickness, suffering, marital problems, failure, and death. Divination may identify causes of misfortune, ranging from ancestors and spirits to sorcerers. Sufferers and their families try out a variety of remedial measures, including pharmaceuticals, sorcery antidotes, and sacrifices. But remedies often fail, and doubt and uncertainty persist. Even the recent commercialization of biomedicine, and the peril of AIDS can be understood in terms of a pragmatics of uncertainty.

D1351308

Cambridge Studies in Medical Anthropology 4

Editors
Ronald Frankenberg, *Centre of Medical Social Anthropology, University of Keele*
Byron Good, *Department of Social Medicine, Harvard Medical School*
Alan Harwood, *Department of Anthropology, University of Massachusetts, Boston*
Gilbert Lewis, *Department of Social Anthropology, University of Cambridge*
Roland Littlewood, *Department of Anthropology, University College London*
Margaret Lock, *Department of Humanities and Social Studies in Medicine, McGill University*
Nancy Scheper-Hughes, *Department of Anthropology, University of California, Berkeley*

Medical anthropology is the fastest growing specialist area within anthropology, both in North America and in Europe. Beginning as an applied field serving public health specialists, medical anthropology now provides a significant forum for many of the most urgent debates in anthropology and the humanities.

Medical anthropology includes the study of medical institutions and health care in a variety of rich and poor societies, the investigation of the cultural construction of illness, and the analysis of ideas about the body, birth, maturation, ageing, and death.

This new series includes theoretically innovative monographs, state-of-the-art collections of essays on current issues, and short books introducing the main themes in the subdiscipline.

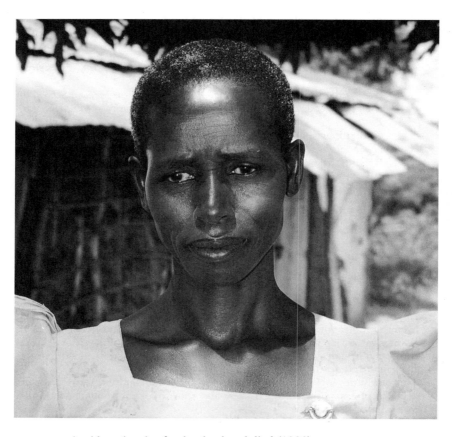

A widow shortly after her husband died (1992)

Questioning misfortune

The pragmatics of uncertainty
in eastern Uganda

Susan Reynolds Whyte

University of Copenhagen

CAMBRIDGE UNIVERSITY PRESS

PUBLISHED BY THE PRESS SYNDICATE OF THE UNIVERSITY OF CAMBRIDGE
The Pitt Building, Trumpington Street, Cambridge CB2 1RP, United Kingdom

CAMBRIDGE UNIVERSITY PRESS
The Edinburgh Building, Cambridge, CB2 2RU, United Kingdom
40 West 20th Street, New York, NY 10011-4211, USA
10 Stamford Road, Oakleigh, Melbourne 3166, Australia

© Susan Reynolds Whyte 1997

First published 1997

Printed in the United Kingdom at the University Press, Cambridge

Typeset in Plantin 10/12 pt.

A catalogue record for this book is available from the British Library

Library of Congress Cataloguing in Publication data

Whyte, Susan Reynolds.
Questioning misfortune: the pragmatics of uncertainty in eastern
Uganda / Susan Reynolds Whyte.
    p.   cm. – (Cambridge studies in medical anthropology; 4)
Includes bibliographical references.
ISBN 0 521 59402 2 (hardbound). – ISBN 0 521 59558 4
(pbk.)
1. Ethnology – Uganda – Bunyole (County)   2. Medical anthropology –
Uganda – Bunyole (County)   3. Divination – Uganda – Bunyole
(County)   4. Social problems – Uganda – Bunyole (County)
5. Bunyole (Uganda: County – Social conditions.   6. Bunyole
(Uganda: County) – Religious life and customs.   I. Title.
II. Series.
GN659.U5W59   1997
306'.09676 – dc21   97–10235   CIP

ISBN 0 521 59402 2 hardback
ISBN 0 521 59558 4 paperback

For
Zacha Mudenya
and
Tim Wamudanya

Contents

4   The pragmatics of uncertainty

Illustrations

Acknowledgements

This project began in the late sixties, and the original research was financed by the US National Institute of Mental Health and a fellowship from the Danforth Foundation. A grant from the Danish Council for Research in Developing Countries enabled me to return to eastern Uganda in 1989. Since then I have gone regularly to Uganda to work on projects supported by the European Commission and the Danish International Development Agency (DANIDA). My original affiliation with Makerere Institute of Social Research has taken on fuller dimensions as I work with colleagues there on new projects. It has also been a pleasure to establish collaboration with the Child Health and Development Centre at Makerere University. My gratitute goes to the funding institutions and the Ugandan research institutes that have supported me over the years.

Good teachers in the US set me on this track. Jim Fernandez first awakened my interest in anthropology at Smith College. Simon Ottenberg and Bud Winans were my mentors at the University of Washington. As my supervisor, Bud provided criticism, suggestions, and encouragement during those Ph.D. years. He and his late wife Patty offered us affection, hospitality, and humour that we are still trying to pass along in the generalized exchange of academic life.

Colleagues and students at the University of Copenhagen kept me going. The lively milieu at the Institute of Anthropology continues to furnish a stimulating intellectual life and a home in Denmark. I also value the collegiality of Professor Holger Bernt Hansen of the Centre of African Studies, who shares a lifelong interest in Uganda.

Of the readers to whom Cambridge University Press gave this manuscript, I can thank by name Ronnie Frankenberg, who put his signature to a declaration of support. I am also grateful to the reader who thinks I should have written a different book – for making me realize, stubbornly, that this is the one I had to write. Thanks to a third reader who understood that situation and believed in my project. Finally, my immense gratitude to the nameless person who suggested that I look at John

Dewey's *Quest for Certainty* and to Senior Editor Jessica Kuper for bringing it all to pass.

Three of these chapters are related to, or partly congruent with, articles
that have appeared elsewhere. I would like to acknowledge the *Journal of
Religion in Africa* (vol. 20: 41–62) and Indiana University Press (*African
Systems of Divination*, ed. P. Peek, 1991) who earlier published two of my
articles on divination. *Folk*, the Journal of the Danish Ethnographic
Society, published an article on clan spirits in Bunyole (vol. 29: 97-123),
written together with Michael A. Whyte to celebrate our colleague Niels
Fock. Thanks to all three for permission to use some of this material
again.

The debts to people in Bunyole are too many. When we started as green
young fieldworkers, Paulo Mbala, Grace Hasahya, Zubaire Mwidu Poya,
Silvester Mudenya, and Badiru Edube worked with us as field assistants.
With the exception of Paulo, who died in the 1980s, they are all friends to
this day. In later years, John Lyadda, Musiho Muluga Huzaifa, Polycarp
Mwima, and Tito Wamudanya have helped on my research. The diviners
Nanderiko Were, Yahaya, Abudala Hamba, and Luhonda all kept records of their work and allowed me to spend many hours in their divination houses. Since 1989 I have frequented biomedical facilities too. I want
to thank Dr Kenani Mweru, Sister Nambafu, Rachel Nerima, Michael
Mwangale, Mrs Mujalasa, Malijani Muhwana, and other staff of Busolwe
Hospital for sharing their views on the problems they face. Dr Mudusu,
the District Medical Officer, has been very supportive and we are fortunate to be able to work with him.

Siliver Musimami, then headmaster of Mulagi Primary School, was a
friend from the beginning, always ready to discuss the language and
culture of Bunyole. Other prominent people offered us perspectives on
society and development in Bunyole: the Venerable Archdeacon Zebulon
Mung'esi of the Church of Uganda; Haji Habanga, Chairman of the
County Resistance Council; Eridard Nalume, the leader of the Butaleja
Technical Institute; Wilson Birikire, local historian and Secretary of the
Lunyole Language Committee; Dan Hyuha and his wife Dorothy Hyuha,
teachers and politicians; and Sam Mutono of the Rural Water and Sanita-
tion Project. Enoch Lyadda, formerly of Radio Uganda and the Office of
the President, read the entire manuscript of an earlier version of this
book, and gave many insightful, informative, and thoughtful comments. I
deeply appreciate the seriousness with which he undertook this task and
the excellence of his contributions.

I come to those who have been our closest companions in Bunyole over
all these years. My old friend Veronica 'Namugisu' Musimami gave us,
and even our student 'Towa, the boda-boda man', the hospitality of her

home in Busolwe. Manueri Mudoto, assistant, friend, and brother over more than a quarter century, made me a part of his family in Musitu. Being involved in their struggles taught me a great deal of what is written in these pages. They have my gratitude and affection; as Tom's honorary senge, I wish him peace and wealth – may his new wife deliver twins! The late Tefiro Wamudanya insisted that we build a house on his land. His big family shares with us food, problems, laughter, grief, and a sense of belonging. They have given our children their fathers' names and have taken the names of my beloved Swedish grandmother, Selma Sophia. To mama in her kitchen, William, Apofia and the four B's in Kampala, Flora and her children, Boasi and his family, Moses whose wife recently gave birth to his father, Namulangira and the late Kenani Wapera who left us my grandmother, Tito and his wives and children – 'thanks for that heart'. We remember bbaabba's admonition to never get tired.

I wrote this book thinking of my mother Helen and my sister Anne, whose suffering and early deaths were the terrible misfortunes of my own family life. Our father John Reynolds showed us how to go on – with integrity and hard work and devotion. Now he too has died, and Tito wrote condolences to me from Bunyole: 'I counsel you to be heartedly firm.' I appreciate his advice and recognize that I share the effort with so many people in Bunyole who are trying to be just that – heartedly firm.

Our children Zacha and Tim grew up with Bunyole on their horizon, and both have spent time there as young adults. Seeing 'our branches' playing mweso and harvesting millet with people we have known for so many years strengthened the sense of continuity I needed to write this book. I dedicate it to them – not just our branches, but trees in their own right. Their vision and thoughtfulness will serve them well against the uncertainties they too will meet.

The centrepole has been their father Michael, my husband and colleague of thirty years. We shared it all – the fieldwork, the families, the ideas, the worries. He read and re-read the manuscript, contributing generously and criticizing gently. Authors often write in their acknowledgments that they alone are responsible for the faults of their books. This seems to me an unduly individualistic view of things. I would rather say that whatever is good about this book, and the years of work and learning that went into it, is as much Michael's responsibility as my own.

Introduction

One February night in 1970, a young man named Mariko called at our house in eastern Uganda. He looked frightened and asked us to hurry home with him – his mother was badly off and needed to be taken to the health centre at Butaleja. Since we had one of the two cars in that part of Bunyole County, we were used to being called out at all hours for such emergencies. But when we entered the house of Mariko's parents, we saw immediately that this was not the type of case that usually went to the health centre.

Namugwere, Mariko's mother, lay on a mattress on the floor moaning, shouting out, and trembling while her husband, Anatolius, supported her from behind. By the light of two small oil lamps, we could see the concern on the faces of her grown children. The illness had come on suddenly, they said. In the morning, when she had gone to weed millet with her husband, she felt poorly. Her heart pained her, and the smell of the gourd of banana beer her husband brought along made her feel sick. Later, in the evening after dinner, the pain increased and spread to every part of her body – her head, neck, mouth, stomach, and arms.

By the time we arrived, she was doing what Nyole call *ohusamira*: shaking, groaning, and speaking strangely. Her husband asked, as one is supposed to ask a person who behaves in this way, *Ndiiwe ani?* – 'Who are you?' 'I am Hititira,' she exclaimed, 'I want a goat. I am Walumbo, I want a cock. Again, I am Lubuya, I want a cock.' Sitting up on her mattress, she moved her shoulders as if dancing, and she kicked and flung out her arms. She called for water, and was given some in which herbal medicine had been mixed.

Returning to herself, she began to cry, 'My children, I'm dying.' She called to one of her sons: 'Siliva, don't I have your money? I'm dying – it's in my sash there at the foot of the bed – go get it.' And to her married daughter, she said likewise: 'Maria, I have five shillings of yours – go take it – as for me, my life is slipping away; I don't know if I'll recover.'

Another fit of trembling followed in which Namugwere again asserted that she was three spirits – Hititira, Lubuya and Walumbo. This time her

1

husband objected. The named spirits were *ekuni* – spirits associated with clans – and he could not see what business they had appearing so. 'I've already given Lubuya three goats – I bought them in Bugwere. As for Walumbo, I take chickens every year. Hititira doesn't yet have a medium who would be offering fowls.' He turned to his son Mariko: 'I know what this sickness is; this is fever – arising in the intestines and coming onto the heart. It makes her talk like a mad woman.'

Namugwere continued to shake and moan. 'What do you say? I am Hititira, Lubuya, Walumbo. I want a goat and cocks.' Finally her husband resigned himself, took two cocks and went out into the courtyard. Approaching the small shrine house, holding the birds, he spoke: 'If it is you Hititira, Lubuya and Walumbo, wanting to eat, I give you two huge cocks – here they are. I want you to leave my wife – let her recover.' When he entered the house again, his wife nodded gratefully: 'I'm glad, I'm glad.'

Then Mariko went and found some tablets that someone had once gotten from the dispensary for fever, and gave them to his mother. Others washed her face and breast from time to time.

At one point another man had quietly entered the room and now Namugwere turned to him – her husband's lineage brother, his father's brother's son. 'Hamala, are you here too?' she asked. 'Thank you for coming. If I die maybe you'll say that I cursed on my death bed – and yet I don't have any bad feeling toward you.' Then she turned to us and said, 'Have you white people come too? Thank you – you can take me to the health centre.'

At this her husband went to fetch his rosary and invited us all to pray for his wife. The prayers were pronounced in Luganda, the language in which the Bible and Missal were written. The sick woman joined in the prayers occasionally, then fell into silence interspersed with moaning and trembling.

We did not take Namugwere to the health centre that night; she seemed a bit better and slept until morning. The next day she said nothing about spirits, but her body still ached and her family took her to Butaleja on the afternoon bus. The medical assistant diagnosed fever and admitted her overnight, but after discharge she still did not feel well.

Ten days later, her husband went to visit a well-known Muslim diviner and medicine man. He claimed that the divination revealed a villain and his methods. Namugwere had been the victim of sorcery worked by Hamala, the very brother of her husband who had come to see her on the night she fell sick. Conniving with the wife of another lineage brother, he had scooped sand from Namugwere's footprints, and gotten hold of a bit of her hair and a piece of her clothing. These things they tied together with medicine and hid, in order to take her life. The Muslim medicine man instructed her husband to bring sand from the footprints of his brother so that they might counter the sorcery. That diagnosis was followed up by calling a specialist who found a sorcery bundle, turned back its evil upon those who made it, burned it in the bush, and gave healing medicine to Namugwere. Still her dis-ease continued off and on in the months that followed.

Marking a course

Three aspects of these events may serve to mark the course that I shall pursue in these pages. The first is the stance of inquiry and uncertainty. Misfortune raises questions: what is the matter? why is this happening? what is to be done? The second is the probing response to uncertainty. Misfortune demands action and evaluation of consequences. People try medicines, rituals, and the services of experts in their attempts to alleviate the problem and limit uncertainty. Finally, uncertainty and response are linked to broader social and moral concerns that shape and are shaped by them. The process of questioning, doubting, and trying out is about social relationships as well as individual disorders.

Namugwere's family members were active people, exploring their problems, dealing hopefully with uncertainty, suffering, and contingency. In this vein I shall emphasize the pragmatic approach Nyole take to misfortune, their considerations of consequences, their attempts at control, and their reflections on their enterprises. I shall argue, in the terms used by the American pragmatist John Dewey, that Nyole are engaged in a search for security rather than a quest for certainty. Documenting their lives in the spirit of pragmatism means describing the ambiguities and failures of their efforts as well as the effective marshalling of ideas and resources.

The dichotomy between an anthropology of practical reason in which actors are involved in solving problems and realizing values, and an anthropology of culture that examines patterns of communication and meaning in social life is a false one, because problems are always engaged in terms of social meanings (Sahlins 1976). Michael Jackson sees in the pragmatism of John Dewey (and in the radical empiricism of William James) the posssibility of an anthropology of social experience:

> It is sometimes thought that this instrumental theory of truth reduces all ideas to a matter of practical expediency or personal whim. But in going beyond the traditional empiricist's correspondence theory of truth, Dewey wanted to emphasize that ideas have to be tested against the *whole* of our experience – sense perceptions as well as moral values, scientific aims as well as communal goals. For Dewey, both the source

and the consummation of ideas lie within the social world to which we
inescapably belong (Jackson 1989: 14).

Thus I see no contradiction between an appreciation of pragmatism and a
concern to explicate Nyole notions of value, power, personhood, and
social identity as they unfold in practice and conversation. We can only
understand the experience of suffering by seeing subjects in 'local moral
worlds' and asking what is at stake for them (Kleinman and Kleinman
1991). In describing Nyole actors in their local moral world, I emphasize
the stakes in the sense of what people are striving for, and the resources,
including the meaningful ideas, with which they try to accomplish their
desires.

The Nyole ideal of the good life and the nature of adversity set the
theoretical issue of uncertainty in chapter 1. Here I praise pragmatism
for its appreciation of the embedded actor, but find it insufficient for the
task of ethnography. Cultural analysis is necessary to understand the
symptomatic and explanatory idioms that actors put into practice. The
local world in which Nyole people pursue prosperity and health is
shaped by the historical processes and family concerns described in
chapter 2. The conditions of rural life are affected by the way Bunyole
has been integrated in the nation and simultaneously left to its own
devices, as war in other parts of the country and economic decline
blighted hopes for development. But people do not experience history
and political economy directly. They live in an everyday world of social
interaction where prosperity is pursued amidst the micro-politics of domestic life. Marriage and children are both 'stakes' and matters of uncertainty.

The precarious nature of existence is a cultural phenomenon in the
sense that experience of peril and response to it are socially mediated in
ways that are shared. Chapter 3 is devoted to divination, the privileged
forum of the explanatory idiom where people confront uncertainty and
develop plans for dealing with it. There in the diviner's hut, uncertainty is
formally constructed in an attempt not to resolve it conclusively, but to lay
a course of action.

The fundamental question in the explanatory idiom is 'Who are you?', a
question that is posed about the agent but reflects upon the victim. The
following five chapters are devoted to the agents of misfortune, described
as meaningful ideas and modes of practice with distinctive social consequences. There are the agents you cannot see – spirits of clanship, ancestral shades, and 'peripheral' spirits. Dealing with the invisible might seem
to be a more uncertain proposition than interacting with tangible living
people. But assertive mechanisms such as public ritual and spirit pos-

session allow open declarations about these agents. The human agents whose hearts you do not fully know – cursers and sorcerers – are greater sources of danger and uncertainty. In the gnawing of suspicion and in the pain of recalcitrant suffering, you come to wonder about the moral ambiguity of social life.

The five chapters on spirit and human agents of misfortune are arranged in order of increasing uncertainty. I begin at home with the shades of the dead in chapter 4. These are the most familiar of the agents – your own parents and grandparents become simpler through death. The words and sacrifices shared with family are fundamental strategies for securing a home and rights to resources. The pragmatic principles of negotiation and trying out are common in dealing with shades. But there is little doubt about your enduring ties and obligations to the dead.

Clan spirits, described in chapter 5, are concerned with the fertility that should fill a home with people and plenty. Although you are also 'permanently' linked to your clan spirit, there are more uncertainties about its demands and it is less a part of daily life than the shades of your forebears. The 'little spirits' of chapter 6 have an even more random quality. They are only about affliction; they have no existence in social life apart from their threats to child survival. They are not beings with whom you ought to maintain a link as part of your kinship identity – though they tend to entangle themselves with the contingencies of family histories until you can mobilize to ceremonially bid them farewell.

Of the human agents, cursers are the more knowable. In chapter 7, I show how words and offerings are supposed to resolve the doubts about relations to senior relatives. But I emphasize the ambivalence people feel when suffering is not alleviated and when they feel unsure about the real intentions of those who have power over them. Sorcery, explored in chapter 8, is the most dangerous threat to well-being. Secrecy and silence feed suspicion; there are seldom any public declarations that could clear the air. When people speak in terms of sorcery, they relate their worst fears about malice and resentment to their experience of suffering and death.

The 1990s have brought more questions. Although biomedicine has become more widely available, it has so far failed to live up to its promise of effective treatment. Moreover, a new disease, AIDS, for which biomedicine offers little hope, has appeared in every neighbourhood. In chapter 9, I examine local experience and experimentation with biomedicine and AIDS. These recent developments can also be understood in terms of a pragmatics of uncertainty. And they provide new perspectives on Nyole ideas about human and spirit agents.

Work in progress: 1969–1996

This book is based on work in Bunyole County that has spanned twenty-five years. My husband Michael and I moved into an unused teacher's house at Mulagi Primary School, 2 miles west of Busolwe trading centre in February 1969. We lived there until April 1971, with occasional trips to Kampala where we were affiliated with the Makerere Institute of Social Research. Our house was on an all-weather road, near the Roman Catholic mission which had run the school until it was taken over by the government. As we soon found out, it was conveniently located for the curious, the friendly, and the bored. Children stopped by after school, women looked in on the way to church, and men waiting for the bus came to greet us. We enjoyed sociability as guests too and learned the Nyole art of gracious hospitality on wooden folding chairs, around pots of warm millet beer and over great mounds of steaming bananas.

Our car was an important part of our participation in Nyole life in those years. There were always things that needed to be somewhere else – sacks of dried cassava to the Bugwere canoe ferry, a goat to a funeral celebration, papyrus mats to market. Even more than things, people needed transport – for ceremonies to be held elsewhere, to visit relatives, and most urgently, in cases of difficult childbirth and sickness. Once a baby was born in the back of our Land Rover, and on more than one occasion we rushed women whose deliveries were going wrong to the hospital in Tororo. Then there were the corpses of those whom the health centre or hospital had failed to help. Those fit in the car too.

In the course of our first two years in Bunyole, we were assisted by several young men and women who helped us in our efforts to learn Lunyole, translated when we did not understand well enough, and worked on the systematic collection of information on given topics. They were all local residents and we got to know their families and neighbours. There were particular older people as well, who helped us regularly. Perhaps they could be called key informants. And there were the two families that each adopted one of us, so that I could be the daughter of one clan and the wife of another. But living in a place like Bunyole for so long, where the population is dense and people are friendly, you learn from many people, though you are more deeply involved with some.

No previous ethnographic research had been done in Bunyole, although several manuscripts had been written by Nyole who were interested in their own culture. So we tried to explore many different topics. We interviewed people on agriculture, history, kinship, and economics, and made lists of clans, market prices, and colour terms. In order to gather basic social and economic data, we carried out household surveys in two communities: Bubaali where there were twenty-nine homes and Buhabeba where there were fifty-five. Up in the bat-infested loft of the local courthouse, a helpful official found the case records for three years, 1964, 1965, and 1969, which we set an assistant to copying.

Within weeks of our arrival, several new friends suggested that if I really wanted to understand Bunyole, I should study adversity and its social causes: 'Nyole are good people, but we make each other suffer.' The cultural importance of explanations for misfortune was evident in the way themes of spirits, cursing, and sorcery were woven into accounts of Nyole history, kinship, and neighbourhood. Nyole spoke with a combination of pride and chagrin about how their neighbours in southern Uganda feared their powers and respected/dreaded their diviners and medicine men. Nyole consciousness of their own culture and the weighty tradition of anthropological research on interpretations of misfortune drew me to these topics. But equally important was the frequency of adversity itself. Sickness was a part of everyday life, and funeral ceremonies were the most common rituals.

In my efforts to understand Nyole approaches to misfortune, I 'collected' cases that I heard about through acquaintances and our field assistants, where possible following them as they unfolded, and sometimes getting involved by taking people to the hospital or attending divinations and therapeutic rituals. I worked closely with three diviners who kept records of their cases or had them recorded by someone else over several weeks. In all, I accumulated information on about 300 divinations. I went regularly to discuss the cases with these three men, occasionally sitting in on consultations and tape recording a few sessions. In time people got to know of my interest in misfortune and the rituals intended to alleviate it. They invited me to attend funerals and offerings, and they told me of events and issues and rumours that they thought might interest me. It is the results of these people's generosity that form the content of this book.

We left Bunyole four months after Amin's coup in 1971 and years followed in which our contact with friends there was limited to very sporadic letters. We managed to visit them for a week in 1979, but it was not until the end of the 1980s that we really went back to Bunyole. I spent two months there in 1989 and 1990, and five months in 1992–3. In 1994 we embarked on a long-term research training project on health in Tororo District that takes me to Bunyole two or three times a year. So this book is a kind of progress report.

Going back in the late 1980s, we took up old friendships, whose value seemed the greater for having survived so many years. At first, we stayed in Busolwe, the trading centre, with former neighbours who had moved

0.1 The author and friend Veronica Musimami on the
papyrus-choked Mpologoma River (1992)

to 'town'. The man who had jokingly claimed Michael as his child during our first period of field research, together with his sons, urged him to put up a house on their land, as a son should do. In time our game about being members of local families was translated into bricks and corrugated iron sheets. When we finally formally 'entered' our own house in early 1993, with help from my adopted family as well as Michael's, it was with a sense of increasing engagement and, I think, mild wonder on all parts, at the way 'playing' at relationship has become increasingly serious.

When I started going back to Bunyole in 1989, I concentrated on the local appropriation of biomedicine, whose presence in Bunyole had been strengthened by the building of a hospital at Busolwe. But the continuities in the 'explanatory idiom' I had studied two decades before intrigued me too. I visited diviners and even got one to keep a record of his clients (forty cases) for a one month period. I attended ceremonies, interviewed mediums, and followed developments in the lives of family and neighbours, as well as sitting in drug shops and talking to health workers.

Re-studies by anthropologists often concentrate on transformations in social life and economic conditions (Colson 1971; Wilson 1977). There have been changes in Bunyole that we too have documented (M. Whyte 1988; S. Whyte 1991a; Whyte and Whyte 1992). However, the changes have been additive in the form of more variety, rather than revolutionary in the sense of essential transformation. When we resurveyed the villages of Bubaali (now forty-seven households) and Buhabeba (fifty-two households), we found that rural life had changed very little in terms of social and economic fundamentals. In fact, the lack of 'development' was a constant theme in conversation. The roads are worse, and many people are poorer now than they were then, despite the new hospital and the increased trade in food crops.

The chronology of our fieldwork, and the patterns of continuity and change, raise more than the usual problems about what tense to use in writing. Much of the material presented derives from dialogues more than twenty years old. Clearly this should be related in the past tense, as Harris (1978) and Fernandez (1982) chose to do in their publications of old fieldwork data. Yet many of the concerns and practices I studied then are still current, and recent inquiries have allowed me to fill out points that I started to explore long ago. This sense of continuity reflects my own continuing position as listener, analyst and author, making the ethnographic present an honest choice (Hastrup 1992: 127–8). But to conflate everything in the present is to miss the opportunity for time depth that comes of keeping touch with a place over many years. So I have chosen to follow the practical advice of Davis (1992) in choosing tenses as they seem appropriate, letting present (1989–96) and persisting patterns be present, and events and past patterns be past – as best I can separate them. In the text I date events and dialogues as they appear.

Spelling and grammar are easier to deal with. I have used the orthography agreed upon by the Lunyole Language Committee (M. Whyte and LLC 1994). The Lunyole language has seventeen noun classes. In order to simplify the matter for readers unfamiliar with Bantu linguistics, I use the root 'Nyole' for people and as an adjective in English. Following Ugandan conventions, I retain prefixes for the place (county), Bunyole, and the language, Lunyole.

The people whom I was able to ask said they would like to have their real names used in this book. I have followed their wishes except in cases where conflicts and secrecy were involved (as in sorcery matters). I have also used pseudonyms where I feel it would be a breach of confidence to identify individuals.

Part I

An uncertain world

1   Misfortune and uncertainty

Some thirty years ago, Clifford Geertz declared that the problem of suffering, as a religious problem, is how to suffer, not how to avoid suffering (Geertz 1965: 19). For people in Bunyole, however, the issue is neither the one nor the other. Suffering is not necessarily a problem at all until it is too late to avoid it. Then the challenge is how to deal with it. It is not a question of making affliction sufferable, but of engaging it in order to change it. This is an uncertain enterprise. My analytical task is to examine this chancy business as a cultural and social problem. Let me begin by introducing some Nyole and some theoretical perspectives on adversity and on the cultural resources for managing it.

The failure of the good life

Nyole express a vision of the good life when they address ancestors and spirits. Though they improvise prayers on the spot, they always mention certain standard themes that constitute an image of good fortune. These prayers provide an introduction to the 'stakes' that are important in Bunyole and to the dangers and uncertainties with which Nyole people are trying to cope.

As sacrificial animals were dedicated to the ancestors at a second funeral ceremony in 1970, a man implored them to bless their descendants:

> We are begging here for getting [wealth], we are begging here that all the children may study and learn. Here we too would like a motorcar to drive. Wherever we plant millet, wherever we plant sesame, wherever we plant sorghum, may it come quickly and soon. Here let us elope with women; we are begging here for facility in bringing wives. We are begging here for fertility: let us strike two by two, that we may hold a twin ceremony everyday. Let us be well; you give us life [health] and let us be free from cold [illness].

At a ceremony for removing a curse in 1971, the curser spoke of the curse victim:

> He is crying for his house, that it be put right. He is begging well-being; he is begging wealth; he is begging abundance in the gardens. May the home be well and these small children bounce happily on their mother's breast.

At another curse removal ceremony from the same period, the curser invoked blessings on a woman:

> You also, go and get a husband, and let your father get bridewealth. Bring cows, cows without end. When you are settled in that home . . . may you have fertility . . . you deliver a child, deliver females and males, deliver twins.

In 1993, when Tefiro Wamudanya offered cocks to his ancestors to bless our new bicycles and later, our house, he spoke with a twinkle in his eye, adjusting the blessing appropriately:

> Let these bicycles move well, and may they soon be replaced by motor-cycles . . . May the children of our children study well in university and come driving to this house in Bugombe, each one in a motorcar . . . Next time our children come from Europe, may they come in their own airplane and it will land here in our courtyard.

To be blessed is to have prosperity; the terms used mean 'picking things up' (*obwangasi*) and 'getting' (*obusuni*). It is marriage: men speak of 'the ability to pull, or elope with, women' (*olubang'iso*). Childbearing (*olusaaye*) is a blessing too: a friend once explained to me that 'children are our resurrection', using the Luganda word from the Catholic mass, because after death we live through them. People want the blessing of peace (*miyaaya*) – that is, tranquillity, well-being and freedom from worry. They desire health (*obulamu*) – a word which also means life, and in a broader sense, comprises all the other blessings. It is the failure of these things which makes people suffer (*ohuwonaawona, ohudamba, ohung'ata*) and which raises questions and demands action.

'Problems are for knowing', as John Dewey said, emphasizing the process of purposive action. If people reasoned from given truths as mere spectators, then problems would be objects of knowledge – phenomena to be simply re-cognized (Dewey 1984: 143). Nyole know misfortune by engaging it – using social resources and experience to deal with problems and then judging the consequences. To ignore problems, or to be silent about them, instead of joining in the conversation that would provide terms of action, is foolish in Nyole eyes. If someone is sick, for example, you are obligated to speak out so that the situation can be known – deliberated and dealt with. Several proverbs stress the dangers of waiting too long to speak up:

1.1 Dedicating a sheep for the spirit Seja. Michael Whyte, trying to be
discreet behind a tree, tape records the request for blessings (1969)

The one who keeps quiet – he too cries for his mother.
The one who always hides sickness is revealed by [the sound of]
mourning.
'I had wanted to speak,' he says at the grave.

Some people always reply to greetings by saying, 'We're fine at home', even
when someone is sick. And some people suspect the cause of sickness, but
never say a word. Their silence is broken by wailing at the grave when it is
too late to help.

The site explicitly devoted to conversing about suffering is the diviner's
hut. Through working with diviners in 1970 and 1971, I assembled a
picture of what constitutes misfortune – what people ask about – as well as
what kinds of reasons they find. Two diviners kept records of their consultations for me in Lunyole; they noted basic information on their clients, the
problem examined, the reasons revealed in the divination, and the suggested course of action. Each week I visited these diviners to copy out the
Lunyole records and discuss the cases with them. A third diviner had so
many clients that he did not have time to write journals; a research assistant
sat in his divining 'office' and made notes about his cases. The 300 consultations documented in these ways provide both illustrations and a basis for
generalization. Work with diviners in the early 1990s indicates that the
patterns that emerged in these records from 1970-71 still hold.

The misfortunes that brought people to the diviners' huts can be
grouped in four categories. *Failure of health* is by far the most frequent
misfortune about which people go to divine. More than 80 per cent of cases
were attempts to establish the reason for sickness. In the diviners' records,
the symptoms were not usually given in detail: 'at home a child was sick' or
'the woman had pain in her stomach'. In the divinations I attended and in
the cases I followed closely, the symptoms of sickness were not accorded
careful attention, once the misfortune was defined as attributable to 'reasons'. Certain symptoms tended to be noted however. Any swelling of the
body or of parts of the body was remarked, whether it occurred in children
or in adults. Likewise, splotches on the skin were mentioned – they were
suspect as signs of leprosy. Both swelling and skin discolouration suggested
the possibility of sorcery; they were aetiologically marked symptoms,
though sorcery was not the only possible diagnosis.

Failures of health also encompass strange behaviour, fits, fainting, signs
of possession, and insanity. The diviners' records included cases of a
schoolgirl who removed her clothes in public, a young man who climbed up
on a high rock and refused to come down, people who talked madly or did
not speak at all. The groaning, trembling, and strange speech that Nyole
call *ohusamira* is sometimes associated with other physical symptoms, as in

the case of Namugwere with which this book began. Sometimes the strange behaviour itself is the sickness, as in this journal entry from 1971: 'I divined two men. . . [who] have their sick one, a woman. She's ill with a sickness of running. You'd think maybe she has fallen into spirits. And in speaking, she speaks Luganda.' In such cases, the word *obulwaye*, sickness, was consistently used, just as it was when the symptoms were fever or swelling.

The second category of misfortune might be called *failures of prosperity*. They included a few consultations concerning poor crop yields and the once important activities of hunting and trapping animals. The death of cows and goats was a more common topic of investigation. More frequent still were analyses of employment, business and financial problems, especially by the two Muslim diviners. Thus a woman came to ask why 'money did not stay in her working children's pockets'. A man inquired why business was so poor in his shop; a parish chief came to learn who was trying to make him lose his job; another man had been fired and could not find other employment. School problems can also be included as failures of prosperity in that parents invested in their children's education and hoped that, if they did well, they might be able to get a job. Why did the girl's eyes fill with tears every time she picked up a book? Why did a man's four children all have to repeat classes regularly?

Failures of gender include problems of marriage, reproduction and sexuality. There were people who came to find out why their daughters refused to marry. In one case, a mother came to ask why her daughter ate the letter sent by a suitor 'asking to be born' – that is, asking her parents to become their son-in-law. (A certain appropriateness was discovered in this behaviour; she had 'eaten' the money of an earlier suitor, promising to marry him, and then refusing. The divination showed that he had given her medicine never to marry, 'for her cheekiness in eating men's money'.) A man wanted to know why his two married daughters had returned home and were refusing to go back to their husbands.

There were women who inquired why their husbands neglected them, as in the case recorded by one of the diviners in 1971: 'I treated a woman whose co-wife had bewitched her – she smells like a latrine. The husband doesn't enter her house or come to her doorway. He only goes to the house of the other woman, but not to hers.' In another case, a bride was sent home 'because her vagina was blocked'. There were women who wandered (*ohugendahugenda*) and 'did not stick in marriage' (*ohutagumya malya*), whose brothers or husbands came to ask the reason why. This was considered a misfortune not only for the men who were loath to pay or accept bridewealth for such women; it was sometimes also felt to be an affliction by the wandering woman herself. As one put it, 'I suffer because I never harvest what I sow, and I will die on the road.'

Men's marital situations can also be unfortunate. Inquiries were made about men who could not get wives, and others who could not keep them, in spite of the fact that they were 'healthy' (*balamu*) – that is, not impotent.

Reproductive problems of women include menstrual disorders, vaginal discharges, bleeding during pregnancy, and miscarriages. There were a few inquiries about why girls got pregnant in school or gave birth in their fathers' homes. But the more common concern was barrenness, that a woman was 'a dry tree' which did not bear fruit. Men were not seen as sterile, but the problem of impotence (*obufirwa*) was common. The word means 'loss by death'. In the diviners' records, there were about half as many men suffering impotence as women suffering barrenness.

A final type of misfortune comprises puzzles or portents indicating conflicts and *failures of personal safety*. Lightning that strikes a person, crops, or house belongs in this category; so do snakebite and being hit by a motor vehicle. Nyole reckon that such things do not happen by accident. Other examples from the records were a whirlwind which destroyed a roof, and a bird entering a house.

Aggression or signs of aggression are puzzles too. Finding medicine was fairly common – and sometimes people felt ill immediately they stepped over it on the path or tasted the beer. A person goes to weed millet and finds a dead jackal 'which has been worked upon', or uncovers the banana beer fermenting in a hole and discovers a dead bird, seven incubated eggs, and the head of a sheep. Obviously sorcery, but who did it and why? In the same way, theft and house burning were attacks that demanded explanation and could be analysed in divination.

The greatest puzzle of all is death; a mourner cries, 'This is a wonder – we're puzzled.' Families always look for a reason behind death, even when an old person dies after serious illness. Although people not close to the deceased may say he died of sickness and old age, close relatives do not accept that the failure of life itself is simply that. There is a reason.

A pragmatic view of uncertainty

John Dewey takes as fundamental the fact that the world is 'precarious and perilous'. Experience is characterized by uncertainty, ambiguity, and contingency. It has been said that Dewey celebrated rather than deplored uncertainty, because he believed that through interacting with our ambiguous and troublesome surroundings we refine our abilities to imagine, plan, and control (Diggins 1994: 223). His vision of mankind is not one of people alienated or helpless in a risky, uncertain world; humans are actively and intelligently engaged in creating a degree of insurance despite the lack of assurance.

In his Gifford lectures, published in 1929 as *The Quest for Certainty*, Dewey contrasted two modes of dealing with the uncertainty of experience: being and doing, or thought and action. The 'spectator theory of knowledge', concerned with being, envisions an enduring, timeless, transcendent reality of certainty beyond the contingencies of ordinary experience. It re-cognizes order, examining reality in terms of given antecedent truths. It sees intellectual and spiritual concerns as separate from and superior to the practical ones of health, wealth, and the control of the conditions of life. In contrast, practice, doing, is concerned with the apparent, the particular, the empirical, the changing, perishable, contingent and chancy. Practice looks to the consequences of commitment and action. The key words here are belief and intelligent inquiry, rather than knowledge and reasoned recognition of existing order.

Dewey argues that the spectator theory of knowledge ('the doctrine that knowledge is a grasp or beholding of reality without anything being done to modify its antecedent state') is an illusion: 'If we see that knowing is not the act of an outside spectator but of a participator inside the natural and social scene, then the true object of knowledge resides in the consequences of directed action' (Dewey 1984: 157). Likewise the quest for certainty, with its conviction of enduring ideals beyond experience, is pathetic (ibid.: 27).

Uncertainty is not to be denied, but acknowledged as a characteristic of both the experience of misfortune and the process of dealing with it. 'It signifies uncertainty of the *issue* of present experiences; these are fraught with future peril as well as inherently objectionable. Action to get rid of the objectionable has no warrant of success and is itself perilous' (ibid.: 178). Uncertainty has to do with the outcomes of events and actions. It is not a vague existential angst, but an aspect of specific experience and practice.

For Dewey, the very definition of mind is response to the doubtful. Mental life, in this sense, has three phases or aspects. Responses can be emotional – the immediate quality of concern for what the present situation may become. They can be volitional – tending to modify the ambiguous situation in a preferred direction, moving purposefully in terms of what is at stake. Finally they can be intellectual – which for Dewey means responding indirectly, by delaying action, defining the situation as a *problem* to be explored methodically (ibid.: 179–83).

It is central to Dewey's understanding of the mental response to uncertainty, that indeterminateness or uncertainty is not just in people's heads, but is a property of natural existence. Mental activity involves changing both the situation and the self. Moreover, the precarious nature of existence and our responses are not private individual confrontations with natural dangers. As Sidney Hook points out, Dewey's notion of experience is a cultural one (Hook 1981: xii). Both the perils we undergo and the responses we undertake are mediated by the context of meaning we share with others.

Dewey writes as well of the means by which people attempt to control consequences. We use antecedent ideas; Dewey defined an idea as a plan for action. And we select the data from our experience that are relevant to the problem at hand. The Latin word data means 'givens'; Dewey wishes that we instead should think of them as 'takens', discriminated and chosen for the purpose of locating and resolving a problem (Dewey 1984: 142–3). Dewey's steadfastly social view of mankind means that all problem solving relies on the use of ideas from our social experience. Richard Rorty sees as a central feature of pragmatism this realization that our point of departure is contingent on our social situation: 'To accept the contingency of starting-points is to accept our inheritance from, and our conversation with, our fellow humans as our only source of guidance' (Rorty 1991: 166). This philosophical position is congenial to many anthopologists because it recognizes the cultural without being deterministic. It speaks of starting points and not finalities, pointing towards a more naturalistic (Barth 1992), lifelike (Jackson 1995: 163), open-ended and inconclusive (Lambek 1993: 405–6) anthropology.

Dewey contrasted two modes of dealing with uncertainty: denying or transcending it (the spectator theory of knowledge) and attempting to hedge against it through action. A parallel distinction has been made by Maurice Bloch who distinguished ritual knowledge communicated as unquestionable truth, from empirical knowledge arising from practical experience (Bloch 1989). He accuses anthropologists of having focused only on ritual knowledge: 'they have confounded the systems by which we know the world with the systems by which we hide it' (1989: 18). Clifford Geertz's paradigmatic definition of religion (Geertz 1966) rested on something of the same distinction between religious conceptions of ultimate reality and common-sense concern with practical action. For Geertz, religion was concerned with the problem of recognizing suffering while denying that the world is randomly perilous. Bloch's ritual knowledge and Geertz's problem of meaning are related to the spectator theory of knowledge that Dewey argued against. Applied to ethnography, his pragmatic approach requires that we see people as actors trying to alleviate suffering rather than as spectators applying cultural, ritual, or religious truths.

For the study of misfortune in Africa, this is a particularly suitable approach because of the way troubles demand intervention. Evans-Pritchard recognized this early on in passages that emphasized Zande pragmatism in matters of witchcraft: 'The Zande actualizes these beliefs rather than intellectualizes them, and their tenets are expressed in socially controlled behaviour rather than in doctrines' (Evans-Pritchard 1937: 83). He spoke of witchcraft as 'the socially relevant cause' that allows intervention (ibid.: 73) and claimed that 'A Zande is interested in witchcraft only as an agent on definite occasions and in relation to his own interests' (ibid.: 26). But much of the succeeding work on witchcraft and other interpretations of misfortune has been concerned with the structure and function of knowledge and ritual, rather than with agency and action in response to suffering and uncertainty.

No warrant of success

When Nyole speak of agents of misfortune, make sacrifices, carry out rituals, and manipulate medicines, as did the worried family of Namugwere, they are neither adjusting their social structure, constructing narratives, staging performances, expressing the nature of personhood, nor exercising their symbols. At least these are not their primary intentions. They are dealing with agents in order to alleviate misfortune. In many anthropological works on witchcraft and spirit possession, affliction is merely the occasion for a cultural analysis, an examination of social/political organization, or a revelation of symbolic structure. There are good reasons for this. When conceptualizations of misfortune are deeply social, when bodies are seen in terms of their surroundings and vice versa, then we cannot understand suffering and health without seeing them in social and cultural terms. Yet in doing so we often fail to appreciate the reality of misfortune. As Victor Turner remarked: 'It is not sufficiently recognized how closely witch beliefs are associated with the high rates of morbidity and mortality which afflict most tribal societies' (1964: 315). We skip quickly over morbidity and mortality figures, if we have them at all. We describe healing rituals, and the effectiveness of symbols, without going back three weeks later to learn how the patient is doing. We are entranced by the logic of ritual, the form, the assertions, but we tend to ignore the logic of affliction when it resists efforts to shape it. As Marc Augé put it: 'All exclusively symbolistic interpretations of diagnostic and therapeutic procedures overlook their most important characteristic – the fact that they are subject to reality and the demands of the ailing body' (1985: 5).

The point is not the simple positivist one that rituals do not work, or that science provides better answers. Rather I am suggesting that scholars have tended to ignore the significance of affliction's stubborn resistance, because they have ignored the actor's perspective. Nyole people acknowledge the possibility of failure to alleviate misfortune. Not only does curing sometimes fail in the sense that a patient does not recover, but healing also fails when doubt, stress, and hostility are the outcome of questioning and treating misfortune (cf. Kleinman 1980: 82).

Nyole ask about misfortune because they are uncertain. They negotiate answers that form the basis for treatment, which may be followed by further uncertainty both about how to deal with the affliction and about the agents and the social world they represent. Indeed, they know they may spend large sums of money, sacrifice animals, and inconvenience themselves in vain. Affliction may overtake them anyhow. Although I realized this during my first fieldwork, I did not think systematically about it until I went back to Bunyole many years later. People whose misfortune treatments I had followed had succumbed to greater troubles in the interim. My friend and brother Manueri Mudoto had been deserted by his wives and gone lame, and our younger sister had lost her sight. My favourite 4-year-old died, they say of AIDS, at 23. Mariko, who fetched us out on that February night in 1970, died in his thirties, slowly and painfully of throat cancer, leaving eight young children. Within a few years, his father and his mother Namugwere and the most prosperous of his brothers had also died. Going back through all my notes, I came upon a piece of bitter ironic encouragement which the famous diviner Yahaya had given to one of his clients: 'Let us struggle and we'll see where things end, when I've done for you that which doesn't prevent people from dying.'

The fact that affliction can have its own unrelenting logic is not something that Nyole hide from themselves, even in their most non-empirical ways of knowing (Bloch 1989: 18). In a setting of poor health, uncertain livelihood, and shortage of resources, people realize that more misfortune is about as likely as alleviation. In practice, uncertainty is often expressed, as if to comment at another level on efforts being made to interpret and treat misfortune. Yahaya was not just saying that we all must die in the end. He was speaking from experience of frequent illness, the death of children and young people, and treatments that fail, suggesting that the diagnosis was wrong. What Yahaya and other specialists know is that their efforts are often unavailing. Pragmatically, they look to the consequences realizing that action has no warrant of success.

Alternatives, trials, and hope

Richard Rorty's formulation of Dewey's work is influenced by the 'linguistic turn' of contemporary philosophy (Diggins 1994: 410); he speaks of our *conversation* with our fellow humans and explains that Dewey 'sees *vocabularies* as instruments for coping with things' (Rorty 1991: 198, my emphasis), whereas Dewey himself spoke of *antecedent ideas* as plans of operation. Other scholars, following Michel Foucault, have proposed the rather awkward 'discursive practice' (Abu-Lughod and Lutz 1990) emphasizing that talk is only one kind of practice; injecting chloroquine or sacrificing a goat are also forms of discourse. In this work I use the term idiom, as Evans-Pritchard did when he wrote of the explanatory idiom that Azande used to understand misfortune. But I should like to extend its meaning beyond the strictly linguistic sense. I see idioms as guides to action that are in common currency in a community (shared, like a dialect), that convey meaning and are understood like a vocabulary, and that constitute a situation in a particular way, as Foucault meant that discourse does. I shall distinguish between idioms as general ways of defining and dealing with a situation, and specific terms or ideas within an idiom. It is important to emphasize the meaningful aspect of idioms and terms. We do not have to choose between semantics and pragmatics, for the consequences of using a given idiom or term have everything to do with its meaning – and meaning is imbued and revised through practice.

There are two common idioms for dealing with misfortune in Bunyole. The symptomatic idiom brings the power of substances (in terms of pharmaceuticals or African medicines) to bear on problems. The explanatory idiom identifies a personalistic agent as a cause of affliction: terms in this idiom include human cursers, sorcerers, shades of the dead, and spirits. A third idiom, of individual responsibility, is being promoted by biomedical professionals and religious organizations, but is not as significant as the other two. This book focuses mainly on the explanatory idiom; the relation between it and the medicinal means to which Nyole have increasingly turned in recent years is examined in chapter 9.

Whether people deal with problems medicinally or in terms of causal agents, they have at their disposal a diversity of possible treatments. Some, like clan spirit ceremonies, are considered traditional Nyole culture; others, like combinations of capsules, are attractive by virtue of recent experience. In Dewey's terms, there is a variety of antecedent ideas with which people try to secure their existence when it is threatened by misfortune. The existence of alternatives is important for the issue of uncertainty. Afflicted people 'try out' (*ohugeraga*) a plan of action to see if it works. Diviners say frankly that if the line of treatment they are proposing does not help, the family should go and divine elsewhere. In view of the stubborn resistance of affliction, alternative courses of action are welcome, even necessary. But the existence of alternatives in itself promotes some uncertainty in that there are no standard treatment guidelines for choosing a correct response to a particular problem.

When Nyole try out an idea, they are not convinced it is going to work. As Mary Douglas wrote thirty years ago, rites hold no magic promise of efficacy. Rather they serve to focus attention on hopes and intentions, thus modifying experience and permitting new knowledge (Douglas 1966: 63–4). The qualities of purpose, possibility, and hope are central in Nyole dealings with misfortune. I was often struck by the way people spoke conditionally of the agents of affliction: 'Perhaps the spirit touched this child...'; 'If you are the one ... then may she go in peace.' Byron Good has written of this quality as 'subjunctivity', citing Jerome Bruner: 'To be in the subjunctive mode is . . . to be trafficking in human possibilities rather than in settled certainties' (Good 1994: 153). My dictionary defines the subjunctive as: 'that mood of a verb which represents an attitude toward, or concern with the denoted action or state not as fact but as something either simply entertained in thought, contingent, possible . . . or emotionally viewed as a matter of doubt, desire, will, etc.' If we understand subjunctivity not just as a form of language and narratives, but as an attitude informing people's responses to affliction, then we are close to Dewey's vision of the search for security, and to a better understanding of Nyole efforts to try out terms of treatment.

The approach to the study of misfortune in terms of pragmatism, possibility, and hope is a key to understanding the position and intentions of healers as well as sufferers (M.-J. Good et al. 1990). Consider the following extract from a focus group discussion held in 1994 with 'traditional healers' at the county headquarters in Bunyole.

> Now the biggest problem we get is when a patient is brought to you and you fail to treat and cure that person. That is a big problem because they will have wanted that patient to get well and you will have promised to cure that disease. And this person will have . . . paid you the money for treatment and yet you fail to cure the disease and you have 'eaten' the money. . . . (With) *silimu* – AIDS – this patient will have gone to several traditional healers and failed. So when he comes to you who doesn't know, he will tell you, 'My friend, this disease is paining me very much. If you can only cure it, I will offer even a cow.' So you give in, and yet you will not cure it. Even medical doctors have failed.[1]

The healer feels himself pressed (and tempted) by the hopes and desires of an afflicted person. Yet he has no illusions of success.

Subjunctivity is a mode of sociality as well as an individual mental posture. Interacting in the subjunctive allows people to avoid confrontations with one another and with unpleasant information. As we shall see, Nyole civility is preserved by 'perhaps' and 'maybe' rather than direct accusation and blame.

The emphasis on intentions, hopes, and doubts, like the pragmatic focus on action to counter uncertainty, has the virtue of attending to the actor's situation. We are drawn to the practices of people positioned in the midst of the desires and difficulties of their actual lives. This is fundamental for a humanistic and open-ended anthropology. It allows the researcher and the reader to experience the sense of resonance that allows understanding (Wikan 1992). It opens important questions about intentionality (Rosen 1995) and fits well with the concern of late-twentieth-century anthropology and sociology to recognize agency (Giddens 1979; 1987, Ortner 1984) and the creative self (A. Cohen 1994). Yet we must take care not to lose sight of that which has been fundamental to ethnography – the analysis of the worlds in which agents act. If we subscribe to the idea that local moral worlds are continually created by the practices of situated actors, we need to describe the patterns they produce and reproduce. Cultural resources of meaning, particular perspectives and idioms, are used by Nyole. They are tied to social relations and institutions. They reinforce or undermine relations of power, authority, and solidarity. The explication of these is the task of ethnography.

Symptomatic and explanatory idioms

In the flow of life, affliction does not usually strike, so much as it reveals itself. Things start to go wrong in a mild way and that in itself is not peculiar. Troubles (*ebigosi*) are a normal part of life and you deal with them symptomatically. Parents of children doing poorly in school admonish them to study harder. Men who have lost jobs apply for others. Sick people are given herbal or European medicine at home or taken for treatment. Difficulties are no more than they seem to be. This *symptomatic* idiom concentrates on the phenomenal aspects of problems and entails attempts to change unpleasant characteristics that are 'obvious' to the senses. The kinds of experience that are taken as data are bodily conditions, failures, and losses.

Symptomatic treatment is most developed for the kind of affliction that is most common: sickness. All families have knowledge of some herbal and manufactured medicines which they use as a first resort. If they want more specialized advice, it is usually close at hand. In every neighbourhood, there are people who know herbal medicine for particular symptoms. They are sometimes called *abagangi*, people who treat, but they are not healers, or even herbalists, as these terms are generally used in English. Someone may know medicine for one or two kinds of symptoms; one treats diarrhoea, another menstrual problems. The knowledge is often secret and the owner may be paid a small fee 'for going in the bush' to find the plant medicine.

There are also local people who are knowledgeable about European medicine (*obulesi bw'ehisungu*). In 1970 'needle men' (*abahubbi b'episio*) treated symptoms by injections of penicillin. These men had no biomedical training, but were in great demand because of the popularity of injections.[2] With the increase in biomedical facilities and consequently of staff, most people know someone who has acquired experience with the various types of tablets, capsules, and injectables available locally. A more educated person, or one who has worked in town, may function as advisor within a family.

If home treatment is not sufficient, you can go to a government or private facility. This is also a form of symptomatic treatment, in that people see it as a treatment for the symptoms rather than the underlying cause of sickness. The word for hospital (*egangiro/edwaliro*) is used of all kinds of facilities from store front clinics to government health centres to the national hospital in Kampala. Medical staff, no matter what their training, are called 'doctors' (*abasang'o*), but they can also be referred to more generally as people who treat (*abagangi*). They ask about symptoms and prescribe medicines. At the government facilities, the patient has to be brought in person, but at private clinics and drug shops, treatment by proxy is common. The customer describes the symptoms and buys medicine to take home for the sick person.

Symptomatic treatment is cheaper and simpler than dealing with causes, and it is usually the first resort in cases of sickness. Sometimes, however, it does not help. The quality of biomedical care is often poor, full courses of treatment are seldom taken, and people are not willing to return for further treatment if the first one or two attempts fail to bring relief. Many diseases cannot be effectively treated with the medical resources available. When sickness becomes worse or spreads to others in the family, it is taken as an indication that dealing with symptoms is not enough and people begin to take other aspects of experience as data relevant to the problem at hand.

Many kinds of problems are subject to such a shift in perspective. When the condition does not resolve itself, when years pass without a bride becoming pregnant or a man getting a wife, people say 'there is a reason' (*ng'aling'o esonga*). The move from a symptomatic to an aetiological idiom means that causes have to be considered and dealt with; the power of an agent is imagined to lie behind the symptoms and addressing that agent is seen as imperative for the alleviation of the symptoms. The symptoms are no longer mere phenomena in themselves; they are signs indicative of problems in relationships to people or spirits and it is these aspects of experience that become relevant.[3] People begin to review the offerings they have made, just as Namugwere's husband did on the night of her sickness in 1970. Identifying the 'reasons' is usually, but not always, done by going to a diviner. 'Let us go to ask' (*hwenda ohwebuusa*) or 'get hold of a divination fee' (*ng'ambe omuhemba*), people said. Once a cause has been established, treatment can be directed to that, either instead of, or together with, symptomatic treatment.

The distinction between symptomatic and explanatory (aetiological) idioms resembles dichotomies in styles of reasoning suggested by several anthropologists. In one of the best known discussions of 'African traditional thought', Robin Horton speaks of the 'jump' from common sense to theory. He sees common sense as the direct apprehension of the everyday empirical world by the senses. Theory is the positing of causal relations not immediately obvious to common sense that 'link events in the visible, tangible world (natural effects) to their antecedents in the same world (natural causes)' (Horton 1967: 54). Common sense and theory have complementary roles: 'common sense is the handier and more economical tool for coping with a wide range of circumstances in everyday life. Nevertheless, there are certain circumstances that can only be coped with in terms of a wider causal vision than common sense provides' (ibid.: 60). A problem with this formulation is that common sense is not common, but culturally determined (Geertz 1983). The appropriation of phenomena by the senses is highly variable; I noticed things that Nyole friends ignored and they observed signs that I did not see. When I commented that a child's hair was thin and light (to me, an indication of kwashiorkor), Manueri replied that it was normal for children that age. When people said a child was vomiting *in the morning*, I thought it peculiar to mention the time of day (to them a sign of the sickness called *enyuni*). Likewise I wondered at the description of some fevers as feeling hot in the body and cold in the legs, which did not quite correspond to my common sense notion of fever and chills. Despite the difficulties of common sense, however, Horton's emphasis on two ways of knowing is valuable; Nyole themselves marked a difference in approach when they talked about 'reasons'.

The danger is that such a dichotomy may be taken out of the unfolding of practical experience and placed in the pure and static realms of cognition and classification. Horton's dichotomy and my distinction between symptomatic and explanatory modes of relating to misfortune overlap with that between 'natural' and 'supernatural' disease categories. Eva Gillies (1976) has pointed out that anthropologists have systematically neglected 'natural' views and treatments of sickness, in their enthusiasm for more exotic supernatural ones. She pointed out that even the Azande, famous for their concern with causes, recognized some 'natural' sickness categories. Decontextualizing symptom sets and making classifications are part of a spectator approach to knowledge and Nyole are not on-lookers in this matter. What is important for them is not so much a system of classifying diseases or symptoms as 'natural' or not, but a running evaluation of a person's condition and how it is developing. Symptoms do not exist in isolation; they are seen in the context of other symptoms and of social and ritual relationships. Most important, they are continually assessed in relation to what measures have been tried. This means that perspectives on what biomedicine would consider one disease, can shift from 'natural' to 'supernatural', from symptomatic to aetiological and also back again.

On what grounds do people make the shift? They often do so on pragmatic grounds, in most cases on the basis of a therapeutic trial. If people are not satisfied with the results of symptomatic treatment, they take its failure as an indication that causal agency needs to be addressed. Once I asked a man why some sicknesses had a cause and others not. He replied that all sicknesses probably had causes (*esonga* – meaning agents who sent them), but that in most cases it was not necessary to deal with the causes. The ability to cure by symptomatic treatment is thus more important than the nature of the symptoms in determining what perspective is adopted.

Modes of power

Notions of power are central in Nyole dealings with misfortune. By power, I refer to transformative capacity – the ability to affect the human condition for better or for worse, with affliction, alleviation, and prosperity. The powers that cause and ease affliction are conceived in two ways – as relational and substantial.

Substantial powers are inherent in concrete things, substances, that can be acquired and exchanged, hidden, eaten, or injected. The word for medicine in Lunyole, *obulesi*, has a broad range of meanings, as in many African languages (S. Whyte 1988: 218). Almost any substance that has the power to change something can be called a medicine, including shoe polish.[4] Substantial powers can be used to cure, to harm, to counteract, to protect, or to influence an outcome. They may be inherent in herbs, pharmaceuticals, brake fluid, battery acid, bodily exuviae and effluvia, amulets, dissolved words, fertilized eggs, dead animals, and pipe smoke. Whether ingested, inhaled, tied or rubbed on the body, stuck in the thatch, or buried where someone will 'jump' them, materia medica do their work because of their innate powers. Power to effect a change is inherent in the thing itself.

In contrast, relational powers are understood in terms of the positions occupied by two beings. Cursers and spirit agents transform human conditions by virtue of the *relationship* they have to the victim. They have power because of who they are *vis-à-vis* the victim – that is, they have 'power to' because they have 'power over'. In treating affliction caused by this type of power, you address the agent directly and publicly through negotiation, gift giving, and ritual. Words must be spoken so that all, including agent and victim, are conscious of the nature of the suffering, the relationship involved and the transformation desired. Alleviation involves a demonstration and declaration of relationship.

Although sorcerers who use harmful medicines have a relationship to their victims (co-wife, brother, colleague), the power they have to harm derives not from who they are, but from what they use. There is no open statement of intent or identity. In treating sorcery, you do not openly confront the agent, but secretly apply medicines that can counteract his medicines.

Nyole believe that misfortune agents are aware of what they are doing. A sorcerer means to cause harm to a certain person. But because the power used is inherent in a medicine, accidents can happen in a way they never can with relational powers. Medicine buried to affect one person can be unwittingly 'jumped' by someone else, who then falls ill instead. A love potion wrongly concocted might make the object of desire run mad instead of turning affectionate. Medicine can even be 'turned back' by more powerful medicine, striking the sorcerer with the affliction he intended for his victim. By contrast, a curse or a spirit's displeasure can never fall on the wrong person by mistake, nor can it work in a way the agent did not intend. (The biblical story of Jacob tricking his father into blessing him instead of Esau goes against Nyole principles in this respect.) Nor can the power of such agents be turned back upon them. Nyole think of such relations as asymmetrical; you find out what the agents want, negotiate perhaps, and try to satisfy them.

These two kinds of power, substantial and relational, may be seen as two different means for securing the uncertain outcome of a perilous situation. Put into practice, these two kinds of measures have quite different possibilities and implications. Because substantial powers are concentrated in things, they are transactable (Parkin 1968). They can be acquired and exchanged, diffused and adopted in ways that relationships cannot be. As objects, these powers can become commodities. By a simple effort of acquisition, you can possess a means of control that you can use according to your needs. Medicines are empowering in the sense that you, the possessor, obtain the 'power to' influence outcome, without having to depend on the willingness of a person or spirit that has 'power over' you. If the practice of substantial power is medicinal, the practice of relational power is ritual. Ritual always involves others and it always involves spoken acknowledgement of relationships and 'power over'. That is why therapy that uses the modes of relational power is more socially embedded than medicinal treatment. Of course one acquires materia medica through social relationships, but using them does not require reviewing relationships and putting them in order.

How does the distinction between medicinal and ritual practice fit with the contrast between symptomatic and aetiological modes of approaching a problem? When symptoms are the relevant 'takens' of experience, when the problem is the symptom itself, then practice is very often medicinal. Use a powerful substance to transform the unpleasant experience. When symptoms are indications of underlying causes, when the real problem is an agent and the relevant experience is of disturbance in relationships, then ritual may well be the prescribed plan of action. But not always. If you think that the agent used medicine against you, you may decide to counteract with substantial powers. You may even try to use materia medica to avoid doing a ritual, as we shall see. Thus a medicinal measure may be used in an aetiological perspective.

Who are you?

The aetiological perspective invites deliberation and examination of evidence (antecedent experience) in order to take action. We need to be very clear about the nature of this deliberation in order to understand the kinds of uncertainties that Nyole are working with. Since the publication in 1937 of Evans-Pritchard's milestone work on Zande witchcraft, it has been accepted wisdom that when misfortune falls, Africans (and other peoples who see the cosmos in personalistic terms) seek an answer to the question, 'Why me?' (Good 1994: 11). However, the question I hear Nyole people ask is not 'Why me?' but 'Why you?' Their immediate focus is not on the self, but on the other: who are you behind this affliction and why are you doing it? The people gathered around Namugwere were concerned to know the identity and motives of the external agents, spiritual and human, that had encroached upon her person. It is through dealing with those others that her own position is defined. 'Why me?' suggests introspection. The Nyole question involves *extrospection* – an inquiring gaze focused upon the beings outside your self. Deliberation is other-directed. You must fathom the motives and requirements of other agents in order to take action and adjust relations appropriately. In this way uncertainty of the outcome of suffering is tied to uncertainty about others.

These others are personalistic agents: human beings, living or dead, or spirits that resemble humans in certain ways. The causes of misfortune are *agents* in that they are seen to act and their actions are thought to be motivated or purposeful (Foster 1976). Their existence as agents is confirmed through exchange and counter-action. However, the nature of agency, and the possibilities for relationship, communication, and mitigation depend on whether the agent is a spirit or a living person. Spirits are person-like agents but they are not persons. The concept of *person* entails 'a certain standing (not "status") in a social order, as agent in society . . . To be a person means to be a "somebody" who authors conduct construed as action' (Harris 1989: 602). Being a somebody involves the incorporation of social features – being a certain kind of somebody, having a set of social identities, being at a given point in a social life cycle.[5] Spirits are not somebodies because they have no bodies, and no set of identities.

Of spirits, people often say: 'What you cannot see – what looks at you over the shoulder – don't quarrel with it!' They thus emphasize the asymmetry in the mutual regard of people and spirits. The seeing is mostly one-sided. Spirits look askance ('over the shoulder') at oblivious humans. Shades and spirits manifest themselves in human affairs by 'touching' people with suffering; occasionally they possess individuals and speak through them. Only then do you see them. For the most part, you deal with invisible beings through the mechanisms of negotiation, exchange, and reciprocation. You listen to their messages when they speak through diviners or possessed people. You speak to them in return and offer to them in the hope that they will be moved to cease their affliction. In these exchanges, there is a tendency towards formalism and mechanical treatment. The animal offered to a spirit is always mentioned in the noun class that makes it huge, no matter what its actual size. People say that you can't quarrel with a spirit, implying that you must accept its demands. But once they take the step to offer something, they often express themselves insistently, charging the spirit to reciprocate, or instructing it to leave them alone. Sometimes they coax spirits with promises of more substantial offerings in future: 'Whence comes a small thing, thence comes a big thing.'

When the agent is a human being, the seeing is two-sided and so is awareness. Though spirits are treated as purposeful and capable of communication, they are simple in comparison to living people. With a human agent, you must try to guess the details of sincerity, capability, and feelings, as these are revealed through a myriad of subtle indications. You go on living with human agents in the coincidences of daily life, and new clues are continually revealed. The words 'You'll know me', like 'you'll see' in English, carry a veiled menace; the truth is that it is difficult to really know the heart of another person. Spirits lack the nuances of feeling and complexity of motivation that people have. They are not conceived of as having the reflective ability that we associate with a *self* – the essential quality that makes human beings so complicated. The notion of self concerns 'the human being as a locus of experience, including experience of that human's own someoneness' (Harris 1989: 601). Nyole imagine the human agent as a self, ruminating on experience, resentful, angry, or grieved.

In deliberating about agents Nyole deliberate about relationships. The assertion of the agent's causal intervention is a statement of relationship between agent and victim; the misfortune demonstrates that the agent has a connection to the victim which needs to be adjusted in order to alleviate the suffering. Moreover, this negative or disturbed relationship is seen in the context of still other relations, both to spirits and to human beings. Treatment dramatizes these relationships, either reconfirming or breaking them off.

Determining the cause of a misfortune always involves a consideration of the possible motivation of the agent and this in turn involves moral reflections not only about the agent, but about the victim and the people responsible for the victim. Are there obligations which have not been met? Has the father of the bride distributed shares in the bridewealth to those who have rights in it? Has the victim aroused anger in the agent by spurning his sexual advances? While the intervention of the agent is the focus of concern, the past actions of the victim and others have to be considered as well. They are evidence 'taken' from experience. It is because moral qualities are attributed to all these relations and actions that a divination bears certain resemblances to a court trial.

Some negligence or affront moves the agent to afflict the victim. Yet it is not necessarily the victim who has annoyed the agent; the actual sufferer may be a dependent of the person whose relation to the agent is disturbed. Thus Namugwere's husband divined that she was suffering because of the conflict he had with his lineage brother. The agent had afflicted her in order to strike at her husband. The suffering of children and women is often interpreted this way. I have called this the 'innocent victim' pattern (S. Whyte 1981), but it is questionable whether Nyole see it that way. To the extent that children are extensions of their parents, they are not innocent of their parents' problematic relations to the agent of misfortune. The issue of the innocent victim is really an issue of social identity and the definition of persons, as we shall see.

The link between misfortune, social relations, and social identity means that uncertainty about affliction is mirrored in uncertainty about the relations, agents and motives behind affliction. Uncertainty about the outcome of adversity involves exploration of the nature of personhood, identity, and morality. The ambiguities and uncertainties that people are trying to control in order to secure their values are not only about bodies, but also about the relations and agents that affect them. The question of who you are is intimately tied to the concern about the course of the suffering. This means that purposes and deliberations are more complex than the ones that seem to form the paradigm for Dewey's pragmatism. The purpose of Namugwere's husband was not simply to insure her physical health, but also to pursue a quarrel with his lineage brother. The relevant experience from which data were taken was social as well as physical. The scientific method that inspired Dewey, requires that problems be detached from other aspects of existence in order to be subjected to intelligence. But in real life, neither problems nor purposes exist singly.

2   The pursuit of health and prosperity

The failures of fertility, health, and prosperity that I introduced in chapter 1 occur in a place and a space that I set out in this one. The place is geographical – a location where people work at particular tasks and get sick from specific diseases. And it is historical – a locus where political economy, world religion, and state institutions have had a characteristic course. The space is a moral one dominated by the social relationships of kinship and marriage. This chapter takes up aspects of the good life: economic security, health, religion, education, marriage, and children. I contextualize these pursuits and describe the difficulties of securing these values in rural Bunyole.

Bunyole is a county in Tororo (formerly called Bukedi) District, which lies between the sprawling mass of Masaba (Mt. Elgon) straddling the Kenya–Uganda border on the east, and the papyrus-choked Mpologoma River on the west. The land is high (3,500 feet) and gently rolling, cut by swamps, both seasonal and permanent. In 1970, the swamps were largely uncultivated; now many of them have been planted to rice as this area has become the leading rice producer in Uganda. Trees grace the landscape – mvule stand majestically amid fields and fallow, and spreading fig trees collect banana groves about them. Here and there great granite stones are interjected in the tall grass and sandy soil.

Although it is rural, Bunyole is densely populated and the landscape is heavily marked by people. Round or square mud-walled houses with thatch roofs are scattered everywhere. More permanent brick buildings with corrugated iron roofs appear too and cluster in small trading centres. A network of paths criss-crosses the landscape, easily negotiated by bicycles, which are ubiquitous. Tracks large enough for motor vehicles branch off regularly from the main roads. An important road connection runs east to west, connecting the trading centre of Busolwe and the county headquarters at Butaleja with the region's most important town, Mbale; another road runs southeast from Busolwe to Tororo, the District headquarters. The roads are unsealed and rough, but passable in all but the worst rains for the daily buses and heavily loaded pickups.

The Kenya–Uganda Railway passes through the southern part of the county with stations at Busolwe and Budumba, where a bridge carries the tracks across the Mpologoma. On train days, bicycle taxis (*boda boda*) vie for customers, carrying people and goods to and from the stations. Sacks of rice and charcoal, and bulky bundles of baskets are piled into the wagons, while fresh and smoked fish are unloaded.

The people of Bunyole consider themselves to be a distinct ethnic group. The original administrative division of eastern Uganda was meant to reflect ethnic grouping; in Bukedi, each county corresponded to a 'tribe' and this pattern has carried through to today. The Gwere have their county; the Adhola have theirs. Although some non-Nyole live in Bunyole, and very many people who identify themselves as Nyole live elsewhere, Bunyole County is the territorial focus of Nyole identity as one of the 'tribes' of Uganda.[1] The county itself has a population of just over 100,000 people (1991 Census) and there may well be that many again living outside Bunyole who think of themselves as Nyole.[2]

Nyole speak a distinct language, Lunyole, which is classed by linguists with the Luyia family of Bantu languages (Morris 1963; Eastman 1974; Ladefoged et al. 1972). For Nyole the distinctiveness of their language is confirmed by the broadcasting of regular Lunyole radio programmes, as part of Radio Uganda's regional service. There are no books published in Lunyole, except a small collection of proverbs (*Engero ja Banyole*) which was privately printed in Mbale in 1936. However, Nyole writers have produced a number of manuscripts on their own culture written in Luganda, English, and Lunyole (see list of manuscripts in reference list). The importance that people attach to their language is reflected in the work of the Lunyole Language Committee which, in collaboration with Michael Whyte, has completed a Lunyole–English Word List (M. Whyte and LLC 1994); they plan to produce school materials so that children will be able to learn to read in their own language.

Nyole contrast themselves with their neighbours to the south, the Luo-speaking Adhola (whom they call Badama), who share a history of settlement (Ogot 1967: 82; Packard 1970) and conflict with the Nyole (Ogot 1967: 92ff.). In the formation of Nyole identity the most important 'others' were not Adhola, however, but Ganda, the people of south central Uganda whose powerful kingdom was the nineteenth-century focus of Arab and then British interests in the interior of eastern Africa. Ganda presence and Ganda dominance came to eastern Uganda in the person of the legendary Ganda general, Semei Kakungulu, at the turn of the century. With British approval, he moved into what was then known as Bukedi, literally 'the land of the naked people', between Lake Kyoga and Masaba (Twaddle 1993) and divided it into counties on the Ganda

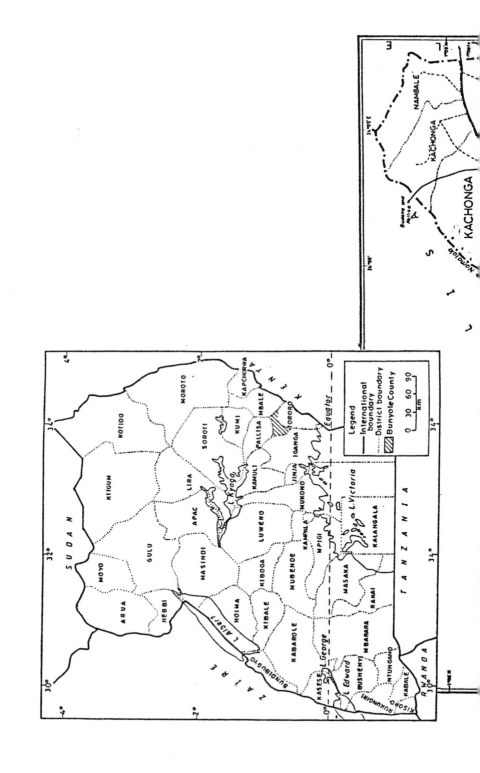

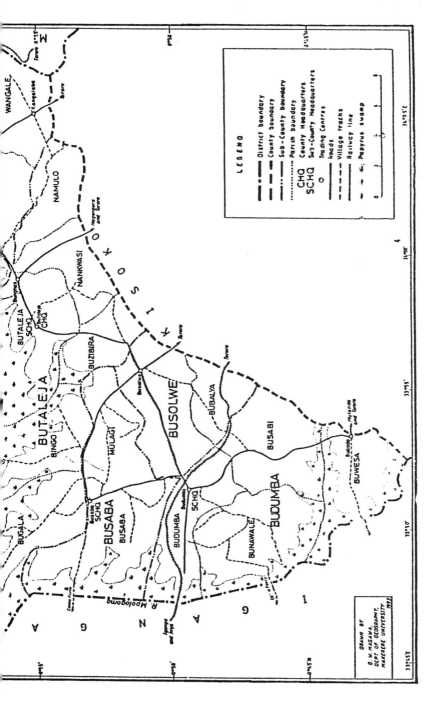

2.1 Uganda showing Tororo District with Bunyole County (shaded) and Bunyole County with main roads and trading centres

2.2 Celebrating the joy of twins at the *erongo* ceremony, the parents take on a serious mien for the camera (1970)

model, each with a chief chosen from among his followers (Gray 1963:47). In 1904 the first road was built through Bunyole from Budumba to Mbale, linking it physically as well as administratively to the colonial state. In a very real sense, Kakungulu and his Ganda followers brought civilization to Bukedi. In his wake came economic changes, world religions, and state institutions of education and health care.

The fundamental hoe

Agriculture pervades daily life in Bunyole in 1996 as it did in 1969. Every family produces food; although the ideal is to be self-sufficient, people with regular cash incomes sometimes buy food for consumption, as do many families in times of drought. Selling crops provides cash for payment of taxes and school fees, and the purchase of household goods, clothes, bicycles, radios, and perhaps a corrugated iron roof. Crops and livestock are the necessary basis for a good life, blessings always mentioned when addressing spirits and shades: 'Give us prosperity. Wherever we strike a hoe for cotton, wherever we cast millet seed, may it flourish. From there we'll get many goats.' Hoes are the tools of survival. Few families own ploughs, and tractors are hardly seen in Bunyole.

Nyole speak of subsistence crops in terms of 'food' (*ebiryo*) and 'vegetables' (*eriani*). Starch dishes are food, of which the most important is finger millet. Ground by hand into flour and cooked into a thick mush, shaped into sacramental portions, or fermented for beer, millet is significant for subsistence, ritual, and sociability. Bananas are somewhat 'finer' because of their association with the Ganda and Soga people. Many homes have a banana plantation with varieties for cooking and for 'squeezing' beer. Other common foods are sweet potatoes, cassava, and maize. Rice used to be prized as luxury fare to be offered to guests; it is now far more common in family kitchens, but is still produced more for sale than for home consumption. 'Vegetables' form the relish or sauce with which starch dishes are eaten (thus chicken and meat are also 'vegetables'). They include cowpeas, groundnuts, beans, soya, sesame, pumpkins, and green leafy vegetables. Papaya, mango, jackfruit, and citrus trees provide snacks. Wild fruits and vegetables, including the beloved mushrooms, are gathered in their seasons as are termites, which are appreciated fresh, lightly fried, or boiled.

Cotton, first grown in Bukedi in 1910 (Ker 1967:71), was so firmly integrated in Nyole agriculture in 1970 that it was hard to imagine life without it. Cotton was the crop which 'opened' a new field in the short rains of September–October. Sprayed (sometimes) and weeded (several times), it was harvested in December and January, providing cash for everyone at once, and leaving a fine seed bed for millet which ripened in the long rains of April and May. During the era of 'regimes', the troubled years between 1971 and 1986, the cotton marketing system degenerated severely and many people gave up cotton altogether. Although Museveni's government has attempted to encourage farmers to go back to cotton, low prices and delays in payment have discouraged all but the most devoted cotton growers.

As cotton declined, rice boomed. The Chinese initiated a rice scheme in eastern Bunyole at Doho in the mid 1970s, which involved water control measures and 600 acres of swampland. Nyole who got plots in the scheme sold their rice on the open market, which boosted trade, especially in Busolwe. People began to plant swamps all over the county to rice, and today more is grown outside of the Doho scheme than in it (M. Whyte 1990a: 125). Like cotton, rice is grown primarily as a cash crop, but it differs in important ways. It is not grown by every family; people who have money to rent a plot and to hire labour are more likely to grow rice. Thus it reflects and encourages economic differentiation. Nor does it fit into the cycle of crops as cotton does; it is grown on land used only for rice and competes with other crops for labour.

The real agricultural transformation in Bunyole is not the switch from cotton to rice, but the move from one dominant non-edible cash crop to a variety of foods with a variety of markets. 'We have no cash crops anymore,' people say, because nowadays any crop can be sold (M. Whyte 1990b). Planners and administrators believe this has negative consequences for food security, in that cash needs may press people to sell too much of their harvest. Nyole are conscious of this danger and women are particularly sensitive to the need to keep enough food in the granary.

Nyole men and women both do agricultural work, yet women more than men are seen as providers of food. Thus a blessing invoked upon a man at a curse removal ceremony said: 'May your food ripen at home where you work with your wife . . . Go and bring a wife, give her a hoe that she may cultivate food.' The identification of women with hoes was even more explicit in the special speech of divination where a woman was sometimes referred to as 'the handle of a hoe'. Women are responsible for feeding their families; particularly in a polygynous home, each wife has her own granaries, from which she prepares meals for her children. People used to say that a man should not take from his wife's granary without her permission. Nowadays women complain that men demand a share of the harvest to sell. But ultimately, men own the land and women only use it, so male rights in agricultural matters are very strong.

Cattle remain the most important objects of symbolic exchange with other people (as payment to affines at marriage and death) and with shades and spirits (as offerings at clan spirit ceremonies and second funeral celebrations). In addition they are part of a lively activity in investment and trade, of which the number of butcher shops is one indication. Goats are used for the same purposes of trade, bridewealth and sacrifice. Sheep are kept more rarely and are sacrificed on certain occasions but can never be included in bridewealth. In addition, every household has a few chickens for feasting visitors, trading, selling for ready cash, sacrificing, or gift giving.

One of the greatest problems of agriculture in southeastern Uganda is the growing shortage of land. In 1935, Budama District (which roughly corresponds to the present Tororo District) was said to have the highest population density of any district in Uganda (Thomas and Scott 1935: 439). Bunyole County's population increased from 45,712 in 1948 to 60,734 in 1969 (Republic of Uganda 1971), with a corresponding increase in density from 86 to 114 per square kilometre. By 1991, the population was 106,700 giving an overall density of 201 per square kilometre (Republic of Uganda 1991). In some areas, the density is extreme. We estimate that it is currently 640 per square kilometre in Buhabeba village; people say that living there is like living in town!

A geographer assessing Bukedi in 1971 considered the soil of the district as a whole to be of only moderate fertility and pressure on the land to be heavy, given existing agricultural techniques. In the past, fallow periods had at least equalled periods of cultivation; but already by 1959 a ratio of 1:1 rest to cultivation was impossible to achieve (Langlands 1971: 28–30). Since his study, the amount of usable land has been effectively increased by water control and swamp drainage, and agriculture has been intensified in connection with the cultivation of wet rice (see M. Whyte 1988). Still land pressure continues to grow as the population expands. The average land holding for a household in Buhabeba was about 3 acres, while it was about 5.5 in the less crowded village of Bubaali. Farms of these sizes do not permit much fallowing.

For many years, the solution has been migration to Busoga, particularly to areas that were depopulated by outbreaks of sleeping sickness early in the century, and to Buganda, especially Bugerere (Robertson 1978). The 1959 census (Uganda Protectorate 1961: 51) shows that half of the Nyole in Busoga District were born in Bukedi, indicating considerable migration. The 1969 census does not give figures by tribe, but shows that 54,284 inhabitants of Busoga were born in Bukedi. This would of course include Adhola who also migrate heavily and others besides Nyole.

Conflicts over land are common between both agnates and unrelated neighbours. Although land is not registered by title deed, it is considered to be owned by individual men. Distributions to sons are witnessed by village clan leaders. Land can be sold, though it is felt that agnates should be offered the first opportunity to buy it. In the early part of this century, when land was readily available, men often allocated portions to friends and affines. By 1970, this was no longer the case, and there was sometimes pressure on people who were not patrilineal heirs to relinquish land which had been given to them. Land conflicts frequently come to court and, as Sharman suggests for neighbouring West Budama County, a court decision is one way of gaining official recognition for land rights in the absence of title deeds (Sharman 1974). Land quarrels are commonly behind accusations of house burning and of sorcery. The bitterness of Namugwere's husband toward his brother Hamala, in part the fruit of land disputes, was symptomatic of a fundamental problem that worsens year by year.

'Thanks for earning . . .'

When people give gifts that have been bought (as opposed to presents of food), or even when people purchase an item to keep themselves, others express their appreciation by saying *webale hupakasa*, which could be translated as 'thanks for jobbing' or 'well earned'. Strategies for getting cash and the commodities cash can buy are an integral part of rural modernity. Money is needed for everything from matches and medicine to blankets and bicycles.

Cloth, basins, paraffin, salt, tea cups and a myriad of other durables and consumables are available in markets, trading centres and small shops throughout the county. The early association of trade with Islam, established by Swahilis and Arabs, continued as Nyole Muslims opened shops. Disadvantaged as regards education and government positions, they concentrated on trade, sometimes earning far better incomes than the rural salariat. Their main competition was from South Asians. The first Indian trader settled in Busolwe in 1930. Their numbers had increased to fifteen by the time restrictions on Asian businesses in smaller trading centres forced them to leave in 1970 – even before Amin's expulsion of Asians from the country.

In the following two decades, Busolwe boomed (Whyte and Whyte 1992). The building of the hospital was good for trade, and the milling and marketing of rice encouraged other commercial activity not only by Muslims. A video hall opened, and a small hotel where rice traders could stay. Busolwe became a town, boasting a bank, fresh bread daily, and cold bottled beer. New shops have opened with a wider variety of goods than ever was offered by the Asian shopkeepers. Yet despite this pocket of growth, most Nyole are no better off today than they were twenty years ago.

Taking bicycles, radios, and corrugated iron roofs as measures of prosperity, we found that there was no improvement in the standard of living from 1970 to 1993. According to our village survey there was a slight decline in ownership of these desired commodities. In Bubaali in 1993 about 80 per cent of homes had no structure with an iron roof and no radio. Less than half had even a single working bicycle. In the somewhat more prosperous village of Buhabeba about one home in two owned these items.

Durable goods are only the most visible of the reasons for which people want cash. Men must pay taxes; every year at tax season roadblocks are set up to catch those who cannot show receipts and they are detained until their tax is paid. School fees are a major expense, especially considering the number of children in many families. Secondary school fees are prohibitively high for ordinary farmers. It is very common for children to drop out of school or to sit home a year for lack of fees.

Paying bridewealth and staging a ceremony that requires the slaughter of animals are also essentially cash expenses. Cattle and goats are the equivalent of money in an increasingly commoditized rural economy. A serious bout of illness is likely to require cash outlays for both biomedical and other kinds of treatment. All of these needs, together with the desire for a minimum of clothing, a new hoe, and perhaps the small luxury of tea with sugar, mean that ways of earning money, or getting help from someone who is doing so, are a basic theme of rural life.

From the time of the First World War until the 1980s, cotton was the most important source of cash for Nyole families, but it was never the only one. It overshadowed other items of trade which have flourished since its decline. I have mentioned food crops and livestock, which earn money for traders and middlemen as well as producers. Shopkeepers buy up produce; in the 'little famine' of 1992 they did such good business that several in Busolwe were able to buy used vehicles at the end of the year. In addition to food, Bunyole produces hides, charcoal, papyrus mats and palm strips for weaving baskets and mats, which traders bring to Mbale by road and to Tororo, Jinja, and Kampala by rail.

These forms of trade are dominated by men. Moreover, men earn money as tailors, tinkers, butchers, and bicycle repairmen; they make pots (especially in Buwesa where good clay is found), distil alcohol, build houses, and weave granaries. They run shops, bars, and tea stalls. Women help to serve customers, and a few own small businesses in the trading centres. But in general, their opportunities for earning cash on their own are far more restricted; they sell cooked food at markets and wayside stalls, and brew millet beer for sale from their homes.

Wage labour opportunities exist within Bunyole but they are limited.[3] The ginnery, the rice scheme, and the hospital are the largest employers of unskilled and semi-skilled labour. Civil servants include chiefs, clerks, police, health workers, agricultural officers, and teachers. Whereas this rural salariat was relatively well off in 1970, they cannot now live on their salaries and all farm and have other sources of income as well. While the majority of salary earners are men, some women work in the health services and as teachers. Even in schools, however, male teachers out-number female by about three to one. In our household surveys, there were practically no women with paid employment.

Long-term labour migration has not been common here in contrast to western Kenya (Whyte and Whyte 1985) or parts of northern Uganda. Men with insufficient land and no source of income in Bunyole prefer to emigrate with their wives and children to settle in other rural areas, rather than to leave their families behind while they take up jobs in town.[4]

In a situation where most people are chronically short of cash, the successful businessman, the person with some income or a job, is under a great deal of pressure, as more fortunate Nyole know all too well. The expectation is that if one person in a family does well, he will be able to pull his relatives through their difficulties and educate all his nieces and nephews; this puts a heavy burden on someone trying to run a business or progress in a career. He should never forget his poorer kinsmen; through his gifts and assistance he must give them opportunities to thank him for earning (Whyte and Whyte 1997).

Reading and religion

'We're all readers' (*Huli basomi hwesi hwesi*) remarked the master of ceremonies at a recent event in Busolwe, as he introduced both Christian and Muslim religious leaders to give invocations. To read, *ohusoma*, also means to study religion, or to attend a religious service. Followers of religion, whether Christian or Muslim, are readers (*abasomi*), regardless of their actual literacy. Religion and education form important parts of Nyole people's lives and sense of themselves in the context of modern Uganda. To be a citizen of the nation is to be a 'reader', to share in the universalist values of the religions of the book. But religion and reading have more specific relations to the pursuit of prosperity; parents hope that education will help their children not to be totally dependent on the hoe.

The Nyole word for religion, *ediini*, refers to the world religions of Christianity and Islam and is itself a word which came into the language through Luganda and Swahili, from Arabic. Like so much else, religion came into Bunyole in the wake of Kakungulu; the first Nyole conversions to the three religions occurred between 1901 and 1905. There are three kinds of *ediini* in Bunyole: Protestant, Muslim, and Catholic. Nyole concepts of spirits and ancestral shades, and communication with them through invocation and sacrifice are not seen as religion, as the term is commonly used. The explanatory idiom for dealing with misfortune does not belong to the realm of Nyole religion as Nyole understand the word *ediini*.

There are no figures for religious adherence in Bunyole as a whole, but there is general agreement that Protestants are most numerous, Muslims second, and Catholics third. The importance of Islam makes Bunyole unique in eastern Uganda; no other county in the old Bukedi District (or the present Tororo District) has such a high proportion of Muslims. Separatist and fundamentalist churches have had limited importance in Bunyole. The Malaki sect found support in the decades after the First World War (Welbourn 1961: 31ff; Twaddle 1993: 262–91), but it has now disappeared. Although there seems to be an increase in evangelical (*abalokole*) activity (some of which is centred at the hospital in Busolwe), the overall significance of revivalism and pentecostal sects in Bunyole is still small. The vast majority adhere to the mainstream of the three major religions. In 1970 there were still Nyole who 'had no religion'. In one of the villages we surveyed, Bubaali, 26 per cent of adults, almost all women, were identified as *abakafiiri*, 'pagans'. When we resurveyed the same village in 1993, there were none at all. Today, everyone in Bunyole is a 'reader'.

The association of religious differences with politics is a well documented theme in Ugandan history (Welbourn 1965; Hansen 1984; Mudoola 1993; Hansen and Twaddle 1995). But religion has an individual and social significance far beyond its unfortunate marriage with national and local politics. It is a part of personal identity rather like clanship. As there are contrasting clans of people, so are there different religions of people. Religion is a means of identification in an immediate way because a Protestant, Catholic, or Muslim 'reading name' is given in addition to the inherited ancestral name. Tuma, writing of neighbouring Busoga, says that the Christian name was an 'identity card' which was desired even by people who were uninterested in Christian teaching, because it brought respect and recognition in the community (Tuma 1980: 61).

There is considerable marriage across religious lines in Bunyole, and inasmuch as *ediini* is part of identity, it is significant that women often switch to the religion of their husbands. The reverse is seldom the case.

People are very much aware of these shifts. Once when we were driving some members of a bride's family to a wedding, they composed a song for the occasion that ran: 'He made our girl change religion, but they don't have a motorcar like we do!' Thus marriage can involve a change of name for a bride in that she might take a new name appropriate to the religion of her husband. We puzzled over why our friend Jaini was called Joisi by her father, until we learned that Joyce was her Protestant name from before she married a Catholic and became Jane. Later she married a Muslim and changed her name to Fatima.

The churches and mosques of Bunyole play important roles in promoting progressive values and a sense of wider community. However, they have not been as successful as religious leaders might wish in changing some aspects of local social life. Polygyny and divorce are common among Christians despite the ideal of lifelong monogamy. In 1969 schoolteachers remarked that since the government had taken over from the churches responsibility for schools, teachers were able to live openly as polygamists. Under church supervision they would have been fired for doing so.

All three of the world religions require that believers leave aside practices associated with spirits and ancestors, divination, cursing, and sorcery. In the early days, the Christian denominations campaigned strongly against these 'pagan' practices. In Busoga, there were a series of incidents of burning of 'lubaale houses' (spirit shrines) by both Catholics and Protestants (Gale 1959: 222–6; Tuma 1980: 53). Such actions were carried out by Christians in Bunyole too, but by 1970 they were things of the past. The Dutch Catholic priest said that he simply did not address issues of cursing, divination, spirits, and sorcery: 'I leave the negative side and teach the positive message of Christianity. If that gets across, people will naturally leave the other things. I even baptize babies who are wearing amulets. If we try to preach against those things, people will say you don't really know anything about them. And that's true.'

A Nyole Anglican pastor interviewed in 1971 had a more complicated view. In his sermons, he used the example of his own rejection of spirits when he began to study for the ministry. He no longer burned spirit shrines, saying that interest in spirits (he was thinking especially of clan spirits) was declining in any case. However, he felt that cursing and sorcery were more difficult for the church to deal with. 'A curse depends on the individual who speaks the words in anger and causes trouble. As for sorcery, it is difficult to stop because it is a business from which people make money.' He knew that many members of his church did not seek help from him, or the Bible, or prayer, when troubles befell them – especially if they related those troubles to conflict-ridden interpersonal relations and the transaction of dangerous substances.

Islam affirms the power and will of Allah in all things, including suffering. Muslim leaders are adamant that sacrifices should be offered neither to the shades of the dead, nor to spirits; in 1970 Sheikh Njalira said that he burned down spirit shrines if he found them in Muslim homes. We heard several stories of the struggles of good Muslims to oppose the demands of clan spirits. Learned Muslims agree that people do not have the power to bring evil; only God has that, just as God alone can heal. Yet many Nyole believe that Muslim specialists are particularly capable of dealing with evil.

More than Christianity, Islam – in its local version – has contributed to the pool of cultural resources upon which many Nyole draw in order to understand and control suffering. Jinns (*amajini*), like other 'foreign spirits', may affect anyone including non-Muslims. Even more important are the Muslim diviners and medicine men who use techniques brought to Bunyole by Swahili and Arab traders right after the turn of the century. Many eastern Ugandans fear and value their reputed skills with sorcery medicine. Arabic books and amulets are used by practitioners in their treatments; the Bible and Christian prayer are not offered as part of healing services in the same way.

The significance of *ediini* was tied to education and books from the outset. Christian churches taught converts to read the Bible (in Luganda), and they established the first schools. During the colonial period, the actual financing of education was increasingly done by the government through grants to religious bodies (Oliver 1952: 277ff.; Hansen 1984: 224–58). In 1965 the government assumed full responsibility for administering schools. Nevertheless, people in Bunyole strongly associate schools with denominations, and speak of Protestant, Catholic, and Muslim primary schools, even today when they are all formally government schools.

In 1970 there were twenty-six primary schools and one secondary boarding school in Bunyole (Mwima-Mudeenya and Wafula 1977: 145). As the population expanded, so did the number of schools. By 1990 there were seventy-one primary schools (Akello and Bawubya 1990: 9), eleven secondary schools, and a technical school in the county. But the standard of education is thought by many to have declined along with the morale of teachers, whose real salaries have fallen drastically like those of other civil servants.

Education is keenly desired in Bunyole. 'May our children go to study and open their eyes to learn', was a phrase I often heard addressed to ancestral shades. But school fees are high and only about half of all school age children are actually attending school. According to our recent survey, male heads of household have an average of four to five years of education, an increase from an average of two years in 1970. The average education of wives, however, was only half that of their husbands.

In the 1950s and 1960s, it was widely accepted that individuals could get ahead by going to school and getting a job. The rural salariat enjoyed moderate prosperity. The old prayers that children should open their eyes and learn were first formulated in a time when civil servants had a steady cash income and provided a model of local success. But even then the really successful men were those who managed to get a job that gave access to resources outside Bunyole. Individual Nyole men who reached high positions in the East African Customs, in the President's Office, in ministries and parastatals, were prototypes for young men struggling to pass their exams with distinction. In this scenario, individual achievement was tied to educational accomplishment.

By the late 1970s this connection was no longer self-evident. Hyperinflation and the inability of the state to pay a living wage meant that the position of the rural salariat deteriorated sharply (Jamal 1991). Those who had advanced to influential positions could still parlay a government job into individual wealth. But they did so more as entrepreneurs than as educated civil servants. By the end of the 1980s, university graduates unable to find work in Kampala were coming back to try to scrape out a living as teachers in local secondary schools. As one educated woman explained bitterly: 'Unschooled traders ask what advantage education brings (*Abasomi batusinga hii?*). They say we learned to read the sign that shows which bus is bound for Busolwe – but the bus is owned by an uneducated man.'

For women who are fortunate enough to go to school, the chances of getting employment are even less than those of educated men. In Buhabeba, the survey village with the highest level of education, only 8 per cent of female school leavers had paid work. The others were married and farming, like their uneducated sisters.

As means to securing a good life, and as tools for dealing with adversity, religion and education in Bunyole have not lived up to the promise they seemed to hold. Christian churches today speak of development, encourage women's groups, and promote AIDS education (M. Whyte 1996), but development seems woefully slow in coming to Bunyole. Charismatic Christianity, which constitutes a means of struggling against adversity through healing and protection against human and spirit agents of misfortune, has not taken firm root in Bunyole. Only some elements of popular Islam have been directly enrolled in the struggle against affliction.

Struggling for health

Death and disease are all too common features of Nyole life today as in the past. If Nyole seem to be preoccupied with misfortune and its treatment, they have long had good reason from a medical point of view. Early Protectorate records report the health disasters that struck eastern Uganda at the end of the First World War. In Bukedi District alone, more than 100,000 people died from famine and the influenza epidemic in 1918–19 (Low 1965: 110–11). On the basis of the 1959 census, Bryan Langlands estimated that Bukedi had the highest death rate of any district of Uganda at 30 per 1,000 against a national average of 20 per 1,000. Although the birth rate in the period 1948 to 1959 was one of the highest in the country (50 per 1,000 when the national average was 42), so was the infant mortality rate (death in the first year) at 200 per 1,000 births against a national average of 160 (Langlands 1971: 29). Today Tororo District still has one of the country's highest infant mortality rates at 138 per 1,000 compared to a national average of 122 per 1,000 (Barton and Wamai 1994: 65). However, such figures give no indication of local familiarity with child death. In our household survey we found that it was part of the experience of most families.

In 1970, 39 per cent of all the children born to mothers living in Bubaali had died. That is, mothers experienced the loss of more than a third of their children. This is quite a different measure than the infant mortality rate, because it combines mothers of all ages, births in different years and deaths of older children as well as infants.[5] But I would suggest that this is the meaningful figure, if figures like this can be meaningful at all, in that it reflects the community experience of how commonly children die. Most women knew what it was like to bury a child. Many older women, the generation who were helping to interpret the misfortunes of younger women, had lost half of their own children within the first few years of life.

By 1993, in the same village, mothers reported that 27 per cent of the children they had borne were dead. This seeming decline probably reflects the fact that the older women who had borne children in the era of much higher mortality are no longer living. Yet if we consider community experience, child death is still extremely familiar. Given the increase in population density, there are probably more burials in any given neighbourhood than there were twenty years ago. Indeed, when we asked mothers in our survey whether they had lost any children, they did not say 'no', but rather 'not yet'.

No figures are available on maternal deaths in Bunyole, but childbirth itself was, and still is, dangerous. The greeting to a newly delivered mother is: 'Welcome back from the trap.' Most women give birth at home, with the assistance of a relative or neighbour. But their concern about the risks of pregnancy and childbirth is reflected in the fact that attendance at ante-natal clinics is quite high. In every neighbourhood there are women who know herbal medicine to speed delivery. Such medicine, common throughout Uganda, is considered dangerous by biomedical experts who relate ruptured uterus, the most common cause of maternal death, to the use of 'traditional medicine' with oxytocic properties (Grech et al. 1975: 128). There is no local treatment for complications of childbirth, and women die if they cannot be brought to a hospital.

General health conditions, affecting adults as well as children, were acknowledged by researchers and health authorities to be poor in Bukedi District during the time leading up to our first field research. Malaria was hyperendemic, the many swamps affording excellent breeding conditions for mosquitoes. In a sample survey made in 1966–7, the crude parasite rate was found to be among the highest in the country. Malaria is a major cause of child death and is associated with anaemia in pregnancy and low birth weight (McCrae 1975: 30–2). Childhood malnutrition was a recognized problem; the Bukedi Food and Nutrition Project which ran from 1960 to 1963 apparently had little impact (Sharman 1970: 86; see also Burgess 1962). A survey showed that hookworm was more common here than in any other district, present in 50 per cent of schoolchildren (Bradley 1975: 19–20). The prevalence of leprosy was high in relation to the rest of Uganda (Brown 1975: 28–9) and a leprosy camp had been opened near Butaleja in 1959. Trachoma was also unusually common in the district, and the US Peace Corps had posted volunteers for a trachoma project, four of whom were working in Bunyole from 1969 to 1971.

By 1993 many features of the disease picture remained unchanged. National figures show that the infant mortality rate was actually slightly higher in 1991 than in 1969 (Barton and Wamai 1994: 18) reflecting the instability and breakdown of health services in those two decades. Malaria continues to be a major health problem, accounting for the largest number of hospital admissions and out-patient treatments. Malaria is also commonly treated at home with medicine bought from local shops. Respiratory tract infections are the second most common diagnosis at the hospital. Together with malaria they probably account for most child deaths. Severe diarrhoea is a third grave problem according to hospital records, a killer of children here as in the rest of Uganda. Hookworm is still common; though not deadly, it, together with the high frequency of malaria, contributes to the anaemias common in women and children.

Eye diseases sometimes lead to blindness. In addition there are the less grave, but frequent, skin infections – from ringworm to tropical ulcers. Gonorrhoea and syphilis are still present, as they have been for many years. Untreated gonorrhoea in women may lead to chronic pain and sterility, and is probably the biomedical reason for some of the 'dry tree' misfortunes which found their way to the diviner's hut.[6]

Two important trends in the disease pattern in Bunyole are emerging in the 1990s. One is the decline of immunizable diseases in children: measles, whooping cough, tetanus, tuberculosis, and polio. Immunization coverage is far from universal; some health workers reckon it is not more than 30 per cent in the county as a whole. Yet it has been enough to make some impact. When I first came to Bunyole in 1969, there was no vaccination of children, except for occasional campaigns against smallpox and polio. The other important change is the advent of AIDS. While Bunyole has not (yet) been struck as hard as some other parts of Uganda, cases are increasing. The hospital now sees about ten cases a month, and there have been deaths in every neighbourhood attributed to AIDS, 'this disease of ours', 'the persistent one'.

In these conditions of high morbidity and mortality, biomedicine has been welcomed. In 1926, a government health centre was opened at Butaleja, the county seat. By 1970, there were also two sub-dispensaries in smaller trading centres. All three units provided free care, and only rarely ran out of medicines. The health centre was supervised by a Medical Assistant, provided in-patient and out-patient care, and had a maternity unit with two midwives. An ambulance was attached to the centre from 1950 for the transport of seriously ill patients to the government hospitals at Mbale or Tororo. The two sub-dispensaries were staffed by medical auxiliaries and provided only out-patient services.

There were always crowds at these facilities. In June 1970, following the relatively cool weather of the long rains, the health centre at Butaleja was receiving 500 out-patients a day, with every bed full, 4 children to a bed. This was a peak season, but even under normal circumstances, the sub-dispensary at Busaba treated up to 300 patients a day. With one to three people on duty, no patient got more than a few minutes of staff time. And most people had to wait several hours to be seen.

Treatments were limited to dressing wounds and dispensing antibiotics, anti-malarials, painkillers, and worm medicines. Many patients could not be helped; they were given aspirin or told to go to the hospital in town. The transport of very sick people was a constant problem. In order to get the ambulance to fetch someone from home, it was necessary to have a letter from the village chief and the sub-county chief. Having such letters did not guarantee that the ambulance would come, however. It had often broken down or was otherwise engaged. Failing the ambulance, there was the bus or the back of a bicycle. The fact that government health facilities were so heavily used despite these problems reflects the severity of the health situation and the importance in people's minds of 'hospital medicine' as a resource in dealing with disease.

In the two decades between 1970 and 1990, there were major changes in the health services. A 100-bed hospital was opened at Busolwe, with a staff of 300, trained and untrained. Several new government sub-dispensaries were established, as well as two clinics run by religious organizations. At Kiyeyi on the border between Bunyole and West Budama County, the government health centre became a facility for community-based training of various cadres of health workers. There, and at Butaleja Health Centre, groups of 'traditional birth attendants' were taught to help women delivering at home and to act as extension workers for institutional maternity care. Thus the formal, public sector of health care expanded considerably. Yet there were and are problems in its functioning. The government is unable to pay health workers a living wage, supervision is weak, morale is low, and supplies often run short. Fixed fees have been introduced in the hope of counteracting demands for under-the-table payments. But in Bunyole, as in Tororo District and the rest of the country, patient loads at government health units have fallen off drastically (A. Hansen 1995; Mwesigye 1995).

At the same time, private and informal biomedical care has grown exponentially (S. Whyte 1991a). In 1971 there were no private clinics or drug shops in Bunyole County. By 1989 there were eleven; today there are many more, mostly owned by government health workers who need to supplement their meagre salaries. These storefront clinics and user-friendly shops, together with the lively business in pharmaceuticals carried on in homes and market places, have made manufactured medicines available on a far wider scale than ever before. Pharmaceuticals have become folk medicine (S. Whyte 1992); they are no longer associated primarily with government health units – in Lunyole people now refer to 'European medicines' rather than 'hospital medicines'.

The conditions of rural life

After the cataclysmic transformations of the Nyole world at the beginning of this century, a set of structures developed that was well in place by the 1920s and that lasted with very little change until the early 1970s. Cotton allowed Nyole to remain subsistence farmers, pay taxes, and buy cloth. It rarely made anyone rich, however, and the District as a whole was poor compared to Bugisu, Busoga, and Buganda.

Amin's coup in 1971 made no immediate difference to life in Bunyole for most people. There were local small-scale refractions of the brutality and terror for which his regime became infamous: Muslim aggression against their Christian neighbours near Busolwe and attempts to settle personal scores by reporting enemies to the barracks commanders in the next county. But Bunyole was for the most part mercifully spared the atrocities, battles, state terror, and looting that occured under Amin and during the second Obote period (1980 to 1986) in Kampala, West Nile, and Luwero (Mutibwa 1992). There was no bush war here; even when Alice Lakwena and her followers came through Tororo District in 1987 (Behrend 1991), there was no fighting in Bunyole. In these years some Nyole living in less secure parts of the country sought the relative safety of Bunyole, as did refugees from Teso.

News of war and terror in Uganda appeared in the international media; the mounds of skulls in Luwero appeared in newspapers and on television screens around the world. Outsiders imagine that life throughout Uganda was marked by grim violence. But for ordinary people in areas not directly caught up in political conflict, the struggles of those times were economic ones. The fifteen years from Amin's coup in 1971 to Museveni's accession in 1986 saw the collapse not only of cotton, but of national marketing patterns and structures. While the horrors of war unfolded in other parts of the country, Nyole continued farming. Some people went into rice cultivation and many tried new crop strategies and marketing patterns appropriate to the new situation. The fact that Nyole remained farmers, producing for their own subsistence and for more diversified outside markets, meant an intensification of kinship ties, since they constituted the social relations of production. The continuity of many social and cultural forms over the twenty-five years since we first came to Bunyole must be seen in this light.

In 1986, Yoweri Museveni and his National Resistance Movement acceded to power. Security was reestablished throughout southern and western Uganda, ensuring the safety of trade and travel. The government implemented a new political structure based on elected representation in Resistance Councils (recently renamed Local Councils) at the old village, parish, sub-county, county, and district levels. Local initiative, privatization, and decentralization are the new policies, partly a gesture towards democracy, economic liberalization, and self-determination – and partly a recognition of the reality that the central government is unable to provide services and control to the extent it did before 1971. Museveni inherited a national economy in shambles and a civil administration that was weak, demoralized, and sometimes corrupt. The economic and social consequences of fifteen years of misrule have not been alleviated in the ten years since the NRM took power. The signs of hope – new tarmac roads between the main cities, acronyms of development projects stencilled on new Pajeros in Kampala – have not dispelled the sense of impoverishment and stagnation among most rural people. Everyday life in Bunyole is as much or more concerned with the struggle for prosperity and health in 1995 as it was in 1970.

People as wealth

The word for poverty in Lunyole, *obutahi*, also means being without relatives. Conversely, people are wealth. In different ways for men and women, marriage and children are what life is all about. While the political economy of eastern Uganda structures overall conditions of rural life, the promise and uncertainties of kinship and marriage are the immediate experiences relevant to people struggling for a good life and dealing with adversity. In the chapters to come, we will see how clanship and descent are brought into play in terms of spirits and shades. But first I must introduce the fundamentals of prosperity, the spouses and children that make a home.

An individual is not a complete social person until he or she is married and can begin the process of forming a new household. People speak of marriage in terms of cooking, as in the question, 'Where is your daughter cooking?' 'To marry' for a woman is to 'cook for' (*ohufumbira*) and for a man is to 'be cooked for' (*ohufumbirwa*). Men without wives tend to attach themselves to other households, where their mothers or their brothers' wives cook for them. Unless they are attending secondary school, Nyole girls begin 'cooking for' a husband at about 16 years of age. Most boys do not marry for the first time until they are 25 or so. Thus, even for first marriages, there is often a ten year age difference. When men are marrying for the second or third time, the difference is often much greater.

Most marriages do not start with weddings. For nearly three-quarters of the women who had married men in Bubaali, and just over half of those who married into Buhabeba, married life began when they moved in with their husbands, 'eloping', as people translate the Lunyole word *ohubang'ira*. Eloping is not less expensive in terms of bridewealth, as Elley Wesana-Chomi (n.d.) writes; 'but it hurries things' if the parents of the bride are reluctant or the groom lacks sufficient bridewealth. If the bride is pregnant, it is a solution which allows her to give birth in her husband's home; no bridewealth payments can be made while a woman is pregnant. Eloping is not simply a modern phenomenon. Some older men told with satisfaction how they had 'eloped' many wives; one explained laughingly that he had medicine for 'eloping' women.

The main component of the bridewealth is livestock: five cows and five to seven goats are still the usual amounts named. The animals can either 'walk on legs' or be paid as a cash equivalent; several goats can be given as a cow or a cow as several goats. The number of livestock is fairly standard because, in 1950, Bukedi District By-Law No. 259 was passed specifying five cows, five goats, and 21 shillings as the amount of bridewealth which could be litigated in government courts. In fact, the number of goats and the amount of cash agreed upon often exceeded this in 1970. But even then it was unusual for all the bridewealth to be paid at once. At least one cow was usually left to be paid years later when the first daughter of the union married. (This is in addition to the cow 'of nieceship' which the mother's brother receives as his share of his sister's daughter's bridewealth.) Today two or three cows is a good bridewealth, though the amount agreed upon remains five cows and five to seven goats.

Although hard times have led to a decline in the amount paid, there is still strong support for bridewealth, also on the part of women. For in spite of the fact that women sometimes say that bridewealth is the means by which men control them, they want it to be paid because it affirms their ties with their own families. By bringing bridewealth, women make possible the prosperity of their fathers' lineage; they give wives to their brothers. This is conceptualized very concretely in cases where a sister is paired with a brother as his bridewealth loan (*ehihowa*). The wife her bridewealth brings is hers; she can address her as 'my wife' and ask her to warm bathing water when she goes home to visit. When the daughter of her 'wife' marries, she should be given a goat from the bridewealth as a 'repayment' of the loan.

Marriage brings respect for both men and women, but children are the fruit which gives meaning to marriage. 'Give us births (*olusaaye*)', goes a common prayer to ancestors. 'Give us male and female, let us deliver two by two, that we may always hold twin ceremonies here.' Children are keenly desired and dearly loved; they should be many, both boys and girls. Although a man may abuse and even beat his wife if she delivers only girls, it is also bad to have only boys. How will they marry if they have no sisters to bring bridewealth? At birth, the midwife should acknowledge God as she cuts the umbilical cord by repeating 'God the Provider, provide' (*Hasahya Namugaba, gaba*). In the old days, the stumps of umbilical cords were preserved by the family's male head in a gourd called *embeehero*, which represented the children of the lineage.

People value women who have many children. In our household survey, we found that the average number of children born to mothers who had completed their childbearing (over 45 years) was between 8 and 9.[7] This average figure covers a wide variation in fertility – from a woman who had borne twenty children to those who had only one. In addition there are women who have never had a child (they are not included in this average). Given the strong desire for children, the range of variation encompasses a group of unhappy women at the low end of the scale, who compare themselves unfavourably to their more fertile neighbours. A barren woman, or one with few children, can be almost certain that her husband will take a second wife. Even if he himself is not keen to do so, his family will put pressure on him to bring a woman who will bear them children. A woman who does not deliver is a 'dry tree' while children are sometimes referred to as 'branches'.

The problems of marriage

A woman's relationship to her husband is perceived by both men and women as being one of subordination. She kneels when greeting him or offering him something. She washes his clothes, heats his bathing water, and prepares food even if he comes home late at night. If there is a load to be carried, she carries it – since it would be undignified for a man. She has to ask his permission to go to visit her family, to attend a funeral, or to join a women's group (of which there are a growing number in Bunyole). If she fails to obey him, he can beat her.

'Men rule their wives because they pay bridewealth', explained a woman friend. 'If a woman tells her husband to do something or complains about his behaviour, he asks, "Were you the one who paid bridewealth for me?"' A young man who was marrying for the first time explained: 'It's good to pay bridewealth because otherwise you cannot own a wife. If she comes only for friendship, she can leave easily. You can't beat her because she'll leave, whereas with bridewealth she must stay unless her father repays you.' A man who wants to insult his wife in an argument can say, 'Keep quiet, I bought you', using the word *ohugula,* to purchase, rather than the more usual *ohuhwa,* meaning to pay bridewealth. I once asked a woman whether she ever earned money by doing day labour for others. 'I hardly have time for that', she said. 'Because my husband paid bridewealth for me, I am a day labourer on his land.'

Men recognize that ruling women depends on maintaining control over crucial resources. I heard men say: 'Always marry a woman who is less educated than yourself – otherwise she may rule you'; or 'A woman may never own land; if she has money and wants to buy it, she must have her brother or husband do so for her.' Male control over property seems as firm today as it was in 1970. Household heads are almost invariably male. The 'owner of the home' (*omwene mago*) is a man, even if he is actually staying with another wife elsewhere. In our household surveys, in both 1970 and 1993, the only female household heads were widows who had not remarried, but stayed on their husbands' land 'to keep it for their children'.[8] Women practically never owned cattle. Sometimes they had goats of their own, but even this was rare. When we asked about this during our survey, some men pointed out that 'everything my wife owns is mine'. One woman told me quietly that if a wife says she owns some animals, she would be 'despising' her husband, 'because the husband owns the wife'. Given this prevailing attitude, it is understandable that women who do own animals prefer to keep them at their natal homes and not to mention them to their husbands.

Marital disagreements about property tend to revolve around the products of a woman's labour and household commodities. As food producers, women are unhappy when their husbands appropriate their work. Recently when I asked at a women's group meeting about the main problems women face, I was told: 'If there is any food to sell, your husband sells it and doesn't give you the money, though you did the work. It's his home – even if you work, it's his work. Women don't own things.' In fact, there is variation and room for negotiation in these matters, which is why they are contentious. In the cotton era of 1970, a woman might grow her own cotton, and her husband, selling it for her at the Society, occasionally kept the proceeds or gave her only a small portion. She would quarrel with him over this, and complain to his parents. If he did it in the following seasons, she might go home to her parents in protest.[9] Yet at that time, there were even women teachers whose salaries were paid to their husbands as household heads.

Insofar as men control cash, a woman expects her husband to be responsible and a good provider of commodities – to buy sugar and cooking oil, blankets and above all, gowns. It is these demands upon men which have pushed some husbands to accept and even encourage their wives' efforts to earn cash on their own. Women's desires to have control over the products of their labour, to have money and buy things for their homes, thus sometimes fit with men's inability or unwillingness to provide for them and allow, or force upon them, a modest degree of economic autonomy. Issues of gender, rights over food crops, and responsibility for household expenses have become considerably more fraught as cotton has been replaced by food crops as the major source of cash.

The rule of husbands is often an attempt to manage more than one wife at once. Our household survey showed that in both 1970 and 1992 about 20 per cent of men in Bubaali were currently polygynous; in Buhabeba 31 per cent of men had more than one wife in 1970, falling to 25 per cent in 1992.[10] The number of married women living polygamously is much greater of course: in Bubaali about 42 per cent of wives had co-wives in both years; in Buhabeba the proportion was 57 per cent in 1970 and 49 per cent in 1992. Even more women had lived with co-wives at one point or another; conflict between wives is a common reason for leaving a husband, rendering him a monogamist again. A majority of married women are likely to have the experience of living in a polygynous home at least for some period in the course of a lifetime.

In a polygynous home, each wife should have her own house and kitchen in her husband's compound. He is the 'owner of the homes' while she is in charge of her house. Normally the houses of co-wives lie in a single compound; sometimes excessive quarrelling leads a husband to move one farther away. Each wife has her own fields and granaries and a husband should take turns helping each in her fields. A polygynous man sometimes has his own fields upon which his wives also work and an older, ideal pattern was for him to have his own granary (*ehy'epongo*) of food to be kept in reserve in case of shortages.

Polygyny usually implies greater independence for a wife. In a monogamous marriage, husband and wife are more likely to have common property which in effect means that the husband controls it. In polygyny, each wife's house has property allocated to it and competition between co-wives fosters a woman's concern with her own economic rights and those of her children in opposition to the other house. In his manuscript, Y. Nyango also remarks upon the irony that a man's authority over his wife is actually restricted by polygyny, in that he must respect the autonomy of each wife's house (Y. Nyango n.d.: 16).

Even so, women seldom see the acquisition of a co-wife as an advantage. Although they may gain a degree of autonomy, it is at the price of having to share their husband's land, livestock, cash income, labour, and attention. The very word for co-wife (*omung'alihwa*) is related to the word *eng'ali*, meaning jealousy. The conflicts of co-wives are one of the main reasons for women leaving their husbands.

Divorce is common in Bunyole; about one-third of all marriages reported by men in our survey had ended in divorce. A man can dismiss his wife (*ohumubbinga*– to chase her away), she can go off with another man (*ohupaala*), or she can leave on her own initiative (*ohunoba*). In reporting the termination of their marriages, Nyole men, like Nyoro men (Beattie 1958: 11), seldom see a reason for discontent. Their wives simply left, they say. Wives have other views. Asked why women leave their husbands, women gave answers such as: 'Men don't respect their wives–just because they paid bridewealth, they rule them like animals'; 'A man loves one wife more than the other and the co-wife hates you'; 'Some men are bad mannered when drunk and keep on beating their wives'; 'Some husbands don't help their wives – they don't buy them clothing, bed sheets, or cooking utensils.'

No matter what the reason for leaving, and no matter how long they have been married or how many children they have, a husband always has the right to a refund of all of his bridewealth up to the legal limit. This can be difficult of course; a father has often used his daughter's bridewealth to obtain a wife for his son. In that case, he asks his daughter's ex-husband to be patient until she marries another man who can pay bridewealth anew so that he can repay the first husband.

Fathers and brothers are not pleased to see their daughters and sisters leaving their husbands to come home. But though they usually try to encourage a reconciliation, they do not, or cannot, force a woman to remain with a husband she does not want. If she does not remarry immediately, she can go to stay with a 'parent', for example a mother's sister, or she can use land at home to cultivate until she finds a new husband. This last arrangement is particularly attractive if her mother is still living in her father's home. The allocation of land to a woman of the lineage is always seen by the men as a temporary arrangement while she is between husbands. In fact some women spend years at home.

The other option for women who leave their husbands is to go to town where they can earn money to support themselves. It is supposed that such women become prostitutes (*malaaya*). Prostitution is so firmly associated with urban rather than rural life that the presence of commercial sex workers in Busolwe is taken as an indication that it has indeed become a town. A daughter or sister who refuses her husband and goes to town cheats her father and brothers of the exchanges upon which their own position depends. With the advent of AIDS, there is even greater sensitivity about women leaving their husbands. A few Nyole women, living independently in towns, have come home to die of AIDS, exemplifying what people claimed in 1970: that 'walking about with men' is a form of affliction. Indeed, 'not sticking in marriage' is considered a misfortune that may be caused by an agent.

It is within this everyday lifeworld of marriage and children, hoes and land rights, schooling and earning, that adversity arises. When misfortune puts its questions, people work out answers that have consequences for the relations they maintain in this moral space. But they do not usually jump to conclusions. They acknowledge their uncertainty about what to do by going to ask.

3   Going to ask

When Nyole go to divine, they say they are going 'to ask' or 'consult'. The word they use, *ohwebuusa*, is a reflexive form, also used of the question one puts to the agent incorporating a person who trembles, dances, swoons, moans, and stares, as possessed people do. When Nyole say they are going to ask the reason in divination, they mean they want to ask the presumed agent of misfortune to reveal itself, to say who it is and what it wants. Although agents are sometimes identified without consulting a diviner, divination is the formal occasion for making uncertainty explicit and for developing the ideas that form plans of action for dealing with it. This chapter examines the process of discussing uncertainty and shows how it inheres in Nyole notions of personhood, as they are expressed in divination.[1]

As often as not, the sick or afflicted individual does not attend the divination. Older men or women divine on behalf of their dependants; men go to ask about their wives or sisters. From a Nyole point of view, this is not a form of domination, but an expression of responsibility, care, and concern for someone whose personhood is not separate from yours. Affliction is not seen as an individual matter. As a grandfather said in a divination about the sickness of his granddaughter, 'When it catches the child, it has caught you' (S. Whyte 1991b: 162). Seeing people as extensions of yourself means that in divination their afflictions are often associated with your conflicts and your uncertainties about agents and relationships.

Diviners (*abalagusi, abafumu*) are specialists, who are paid a standard (modest) divination fee (*omuhemba*) for each consultation. The divination (*endagu*) consists of an identification of cause and prescription for treatment. Most diviners specialize in some form of treatment as well; treatment is always arranged separately and the cost varies widely. Those who deal with little and foreign spirits and administer herbal medicines call themselves *abagangi*, emphasizing their role as healers. Others protect people and homes against sorcery and sell powerful medicines, including, it is said, sorcery medicine. They are called *abang'eng'a*, from the verb meaning to 'to protect through countermedicine'. Such 'medicine men' often refer to themselves as 'healers' since 'protection' of the sort they engage in carries ambivalent connotations of sorcery.

At the time of our first fieldwork there were two principal methods of divination in Bunyole: spirit possession and examination of Arabic books. 'Those of the gourd rattles' (*ab'esaasi, ab'enyengo*) had a working relationship with teams of spirits who possessed them and spoke through them to reveal the causes of a client's misfortune. *Lamuli*, who were always Muslim, used a folk Arabic technique of performing calculations and consulting books. Although their method was exotic, they manipulated the same aetiological model of misfortune used by the spirit diviners. Both men and women could be diviners, but of the thirty-eight concerning whom I obtained information in 1970, less than a third were female. While nearly half of the spirit diviners were women, there were none among the book diviners. As this Arabic form of divination has become increasingly popular since the 1920s, divination as a whole has become a male-dominated speciality.

In addition to these two techniques, there was a scattering of special methods, including *mayembe* divination, said to be from Buganda. The Nyole notion of *mayembe* is that they are Ganda spirits, kept in or fed from a horn, which dance about in a darkened hut wearing bells. By 1990, this form of divination had gained in popularity, so that many gourd rattle diviners also had *mayembe*.

Spirit colleagues

In the Nyole view, gourd rattle diviners are caught not taught. Even people who are familiar with the work through a close relative do not think of becoming a spirit diviner in terms of apprenticeship. Spirits take the initiative in sending some affliction such as impotence, illness, or strange behaviour to show that they want to 'settle' and to work with the person they have chosen. Not everyone who receives such an interpretation of misfortune becomes a diviner; it is possible to 'say goodbye to' divining spirits with a sacrifice, thus refusing the call. But those who accept establish a long-term relationship to their spirits.

A divination house, *amasawo*, is built in the compound for the spirits and they are thought to stay there. Some diviners seem to conceive of their relationship to their spirits as similar to marriage. Two women mentioned that their spirits were like husbands; they had to sleep in the divination house with them.

Two experienced spirit diviners, a man and a woman, called 'midwives' (*abalerwa*) initiate the new diviner. First they come to plant a pole (*ohuhoma ehisiiro*) as a kind of acknowledgement to the spirits that their demands have been heard. When the initiate has accumulated the necessary resources, the installation itself can take place; this is known as encouraging or inviting (*ohutendeha*) the spirits. First, chickens are killed at a crossroads 'to open the way' for the spirits to come in. Later, more chickens and goats are offered to each spirit. All night long, people drink beer while the 'midwives' beat their rattles to please the spirits. When they possess the initiate, they cause him or her to tremble, fall, speak strangely, and occasionally to run into the bush. One diviner told how his spirits had caused him to go into the bush and eat leaves like a goat, coming back with some in his mouth. In 'settling' the spirits, Nyole seem to be domesticating them, bringing them from outside, from the road or the bush, to live in a home. They are straightening the paths from wilderness, in the terms used by Parkin (1982).

The fact that the officiating diviners are not seen as teachers fits with the conception of gourd rattle diviners as mediums for their spirits. The spirits are the authorities, the active agents. When I asked one diviner what his 'midwives' had taught him about divination when he was initiated, he replied, 'Those people didn't teach me anything – they just got drunk. The spirit is what taught me to divine.'

Who are these spirits which enter into such active and useful relations with human beings? The most important spirit of divination is Hing'ira or *ehifumu*, literally the 'divination thing'. Nyole say that *ehifumu* is composed of the spirits of people who died long ago. These spirits come from the 'mother's brothers' of the diviner's mother and father. Thus they are related (from grandparental clans into which you cannot marry), but they are not named individuals.

There is an androgynous quality about 'the divination thing': it comes from both the maternal and paternal sides and is composed of the spirits of both men and women. Therefore, it has to be settled by both a male and a female diviner. Some diviners have two sheaves of grass in the divining hut, one for the male and one for the female aspects of 'the divination thing'. Peek (1991: 196–7) suggests that this kind of androgyny is widespread in African divination and he relates it to the fundamental characteristics of divination as a non-normal mode of cognition that both marks differences (such as gender) and synthesizes. Perhaps it is significant that the most common reason suggested for impotence is 'the divination thing'.

In the old days, people said, diviners used only *ehifumu*. But, by 1970, virtually all gourd rattle diviners had 'foreign spirits' as well. One diviner told me that these spirits came to Bunyole on the roads built by the Europeans. Unlike the 'divination thing', the foreign spirits have individ-

ual proper names. They are male or female, come from a particular place
and cause their mediums to speak in appropriate foreign languages. Most
of them are said to be Ganda; others are Soga, Swahili, Gwere, and Gisu.[2]
They are settled in the divining hut at the same time or after *ehifumu*.

Divination sessions, which are private, take place in the divination
house with the diviner seated upon a skin (*ehyambi*), sometimes behind a
partition. The clients, also seated, are always more clearly visible to the
diviner than he or she is to them. The diviner begins by shaking the gourd
rattles rhythmically; in the small hut, the sound is deafening. Sometimes
he or she sings special songs to please the spirits. Then the diviner may
begin to make strange noises – snorting, growling, belching, crying. After
a few minutes the spirits speak. One diviner explained that 'the spirits
come like a cold wind and stay in my throat and I don't know anything, I
just speak'.

Often the client cannot understand what the spirits are saying; either
their voices are indistinct or they speak loudly and rapidly in incompre-
hensible words that are said to be other languages. The diviner tells the
client, in a more normal voice, what the spirits are saying. The spirits can
speak through the diviner to the client or they can speak to the diviner
who then passes the message on to the client. Some diviners apparently
use ventriloquism; some seem to be carrying on a conversation with other
voices that are drowned out by the noise of the gourd rattles.

Sometimes the potential agents of misfortune themselves seem to speak
to or through the diviner. Sometimes it is 'the divination thing' that
addresses the clients. In either case, the special quality of the spirit diviner
is the ability to speak as another being. Listening to seances, you have the
sense of at least three participants: the client, the diviner, and the spirits or
potential agents, with the diviner mediating between the client and the
unseen beings.

Spirit divination is considered the traditional Nyole way in contrast to
the Muslim method. But even here, innovation and borrowing are evident. I have heard the foreign spirits that are part of the divination team
referred to generically as *emandwa*, a Nyoro term for spirits (cf. Beattie
1967: 222–3). Even the 'divination thing' itself keeps up with the times.
Recently I visited a diviner in Doho who had rigged a rope as a telephone
wire from the centrepole of the divination hut, out through the roof,
around a 'telephone pole' stuck into the ground outside, and over to the
spirit shrine for the 'divination thing' in the courtyard. He explained that
when he shakes his gourd rattles, the spirits come from their shrine,
through the wire and down the centrepole to catch him and speak
through him.

More evidence of the openness of 'traditional' practice can be found in the increasing popularity of *mayembe*, a Luganda word meaning 'horns'. Most diviners say that you have to buy *mayembe* from someone who has them. All agree that they are Ganda spirits. Even the diviner who claimed that he had bought his *mayembe* from a Samia man (at an astronomical price) added that they came from Bukunja in Buganda, home of the most powerful *mayembe*. They are consulted in a hut which can be made completely dark. In the blackness, a ring of bells, of the kind that is worn around the ankle when dancing, moves about and voices seem to come from it. People say that it can emit sparks, and that it can climb onto clients in order to examine their problems. In the demonstration I experienced in 1993, the moving bells and sparks were very convincing; the diviner conversed from his place on the floor with two spirits: one with a deep gruff voice and the other with the higher pitch of a woman.[3]

Like the 'divining thing' and foreign spirits, *mayembe* can be used for divination. Some diviners have two divination 'offices': one for each team. But *mayembe* are more mobile than other divination spirits. The diviner can carry them in their horn in his bag of medicines when he travels on curing missions. And they have functions in addition to divination. They can be sent to find things, such as hidden sorcery medicines or wives who have gone away. They can also be dispatched to harm people. Indeed, they seem to be favoured in dealing with sorcery cases. The fact that they can be purchased likens them to medicines, and several diviners told me that, like medicines, they can be used to alleviate problems caused by curses, spirits, and shades, without directly addressing the agent.

Arabic books

The system of divination by calculation and examination of Arabic books is widespread in East Africa (Trimingham 1964: 124; Bloch 1968; Swantz 1990). The *lamuli* (Swahili *ramli*, from the Arabic *Khatt ar-raml*) are Muslim, but in Bunyole a majority of their clients are Christian. Of 101 persons seen for divination and/or treatment by the *lamuli* Yahaya in 1970, 37 were Roman Catholic, 34 Protestant, and 16 Muslim (religion was not recorded for 14). *Lamuli* attract clients from other ethnic groups; the fact that there are more Muslims in Bunyole than in neighbouring areas enhances the reputation of Nyole as people with access to special powers.

The method of 'examining books' seems to have been introduced into Bunyole by the Omani trader, Ali bin Nasoor, who settled in Busolwe around 1915. He and other Swahili or Arab traders taught it to local Muslims, and patterns of apprenticeship continue, often involving contacts elsewhere. *Lamuli* working in Bunyole today have lived or studied with Kenyans or people from other parts of Uganda. One learned from a Swahili man at a trading centre in the next county; another in Mombasa where he lived for a time. A *lamuli* interviewed in Bubalya in 1992 mentioned two teachers from Buganda, one from Busoga, and one from Nairobi.

The *lamuli* see their work as a science, based on calculation and written knowledge. Numbers are an important input in their consultations, and they note the time at which the client arrives. For this purpose, Yahaya, a well-known *lamuli*, had a fancy clock in the 'office' where he received his clients. Each letter of the client's (and/or the sufferer's) name had a numerical value, and the sum of these as well as the arrival time figured in calculations made upon a slate. Clients who came at a 'bad' time were asked to return later. Yahaya said: 'My science is that of the seven days, I know how every hour is called and what can be done at that time.'

After initial calculations, the *lamuli* refer to their books. Yahaya used *Sa'atili Habari*, 'for examining the time' and *Abu Mashari Faraki*, for revealing the causes that operate at a particular time. He explained that this latter book helped him to know what kind of person had caused the client's troubles, where medicine was buried, and what type of sacrifice was needed. While these two books are common, others are used as well: the Koran, or that portion of it called *Yasini*; *Elimu Fasiru* ('like a thermometer', it can be used to determine a number that shows whether the patient will live or die); and *Wafaaki Imamulu Gazaali* (for examining the days and what can happen on each day).

Book diviners proceed by looking up appropriate passages and reading phrases aloud in Arabic.[4] But since their clients do not understand, they have to translate for them and explain the relevance of the passages to the client's problems. As the client comments and conveys more information, the *lamuli* may refer to other passages in his books. As in divination by spirit possession, there is a three-way conversation, with the diviner mediating between the client and the authoritative book.

Both *lamuli* and their clients contrasted the sober examination of books with the boisterous, sometimes chaotic consultation of spirits. As one regular client put it: 'They do not deafen you with gourd rattles and strange noises – they just examine their books quietly.' The emphasis on measurement, counting, the division of time as measured by clocks, writing, reading, and books is part of a powerful, modern way of ordering the world. Although writing came to be associated with mission education and the colonial regime in Uganda, it was in fact the Arabs who first introduced it (Twaddle 1974) and it was Muslim *lamuli* who usefully applied it to the analysis of life's problems in Bunyole.

Book and spirit divination in Bunyole fit oppositions proposed by various scholars between 'possession' and 'wisdom' divination (Zuesse 1979: 212), 'mediumistic' and 'interpretive' (Devisch 1985) or 'revelatory' and 'analytical' divination (Turner 1975: 15–16). The contrast between revelations made by spirits through a medium and the implementation of a complex system learned through long years of study seems great. Yet in practice, there are common elements. Both kinds of divination relay a message that must be analysed; both involve a revelation of information which must then be interpreted by the client and diviner (Peek 1991: 12). In both there is an authoritative third voice (of spirits or texts) which the two parties must relate to the realities of the client's situation. The 'high tech' methods of Nyole book diviners open the way for the same kinds of considerations about affliction and agency that occur in spirit consultations. They reveal the same types of spirit and human agents found in mediumistic gourd rattle divination.

There is an important difference, however, which arises not from the form of divination, but from the fact that the two kinds of diviners tend to specialize in different kinds of treatment, with corresponding biases in their patterns of diagnosis. Many gourd rattle diviners also perform ceremonies for getting rid of bothersome little and foreign spirits or for settling divining spirits. Having spirit colleagues themselves, they are more aware of all types of spirit agencies, including ancestor and clan spirits. *Lamuli* diviners are often also 'protectors' or medicine men who deal with sorcery and even claim to be able to 'tie' curses by medicine, thus obviating the need for a family ritual of reconciliation.

Book diviners are very aware of human agency in their clients' misfortunes. In analysing the records kept by two book diviners and one spirit diviner in 1970, I found that the spirit diviner diagnosed human agents (cursers and sorcerers) in 28 per cent of his cases, while the two *lamuli* found human agency in 80 per cent and 63 per cent respectively. The human agents which the spirit diviner did find tended to be cursers (who invoked the power of ancestors) rather than sorcerers. The book diviners, who used modern technology and had learned their skills as medicine men from 'outside', were far more oriented toward sorcery as an explanation.

Of course these divergent patterns reflect selection on the part of clients as well. Aware of the differing skills and orientations of spirit and book diviners, they choose their specialist in terms of their own suspicions about the cause of affliction and their own therapeutic biases.

The construction of uncertainty

Nyole divination is governed by principles that set up uncertainty as a point of departure. The first of these is relative privacy. The client usually comes alone, sometimes accompanied by one or two relatives or friends. Consultations take place in the divining house while other clients wait outside. This means that not only uncertainties, but also suspicions and conflicts can be discussed openly and in detail. Werbner (1973: 1423) has pointed to the importance of examining 'the context of communication between specific sets of persons' in order to understand the rhetoric of divination. Kalanga domestic divination tends to involve a congregation of neighbours and this, together with the fact that the diviner himself is a neighbour who knows the people involved, has important implications for the content of the exchange. While the Kalanga diviner addresses, and tries to convince, a congregation, the Nyole one is dealing with one or two individuals whom he invites to express fully their doubts and suspicions.

The second principle is that the client does not know the causes of the misfortune being considered; he comes to get help with what he cannot manage on his own. This ignorance was often expressed. In one consultation I recorded, the client remarked at the beginning of the session: 'I do not know about the case – if I were wise, I would not [need to] come.' In another seance, the consulter said: 'The case is bad . . . because thoughts fail us – that is what we want you to tell us, where it comes from and where its source is, where it is going and where it ends.' This same consulter subsequently refused to accept the first five or six suggestions as to the cause of the misfortune, pushing the divination in the direction of the curser she and her son suspected to be the cause of her daughter's barrenness. Yet, in spite of the fact that consulters sometimes had definite preconceptions, they declared their uncertainty and their desire that the divination should help them resolve it.

A third principle of Nyole divination is that the diviner as an individual does not and should not know the details of the case beforehand. These are to be revealed by the divination. For this reason, Nyole say that to get the truth, you should not go to a diviner near home. He or she might be influenced by previous knowledge or local gossip, so that the 'neutral' other voice of the spirits or Arabic books cannot come through clearly. It is these authoritative sources, not the diviner as person and neighbour, that must make the revelation. The records kept by three diviners showed that people did not in fact divine in their own neighbourhoods. Some clients travelled considerable distances for consultation. So diviners generally confronted people about whose background and current situations they knew little or nothing. The information needed in order to formulate a relevant diagnosis had to be supplied by the client. Some people used the same diviner regularly, so that he or she presumably knew something about the client's affairs. But even here I believe that the clients supplied substantial and new information at every consultation.

Thus both client and diviner should begin a seance in a state of uncertainty. This uncertainty is not simply 'there'. It is constructed and emphasized. The declarations of ignorance and confusion are artificial in a sense: the client might well have his suspicions, and the diviner's uncertainty is imposed by the convention that he or she should not ask directly for the facts of the case. In his seminal article on how divination creates clarity out of confusion, Parkin uses the terms simultaneity and sequencing in describing the process of working out a precise interpretation from a simultaneous chaos of possibilities. Speaking of how order is brought out of disorder, he says, 'We see this as man at his most creative. A point I want to make is that this creativity consists not simply in answering the puzzles posed by cognitive simultaneity, but in setting up the simultaneity in the first place' (1982: 71). I take Parkin's point to be that uncertainty must be dramatized in order for clarity to be created; disorder must be demonstrated so that order may triumph.

In Nyole divination, uncertainty is emphasized by several forms of obscurity. The diviner speaks incomprehensibly part of the time – either reading Arabic, pronouncing indistinct words in the growling or shrill voices of spirits, or drowning out mystical conversations with the deafening noise of gourd rattles. Even when the diviner speaks to the client in audible Lunyole, the meaning of the words is often elusive. He or she generalizes, uses circumlocution, ambiguities, confusing idioms, metaphors, and allusions, and regularly suggests that the statements being made might be untrue. This resembles Werbner's characterization of Kalanga divinatory rhetoric: 'Ambiguous understatement is the essence of a diviner's art . . . he makes explicit comment about equivocating . . . or about the indirectness of his speech' (1973: 1421). In the tape recordings I made of consultations, it is possible to follow the rise and resolution of misunderstandings between client and diviner.

Yet from such perplexity a consensus must emerge. It does so through a dialogue in which diviners make (often) vague suggestions upon which they encourage their clients to comment, affirming that the line of reasoning seems plausible. One diviner confided to me that the most difficult clients were those who were not used to divining and did not realize what role they must play. In one of the consultations recorded, the client initially sat silent, remarking, 'You are the one to speak to us, we have come so that you tell us.' The diviner corrected this misapprehension saying, 'Don't you know that I speak to you, and you also speak to me? I

don't speak while you sit silent like one who cannot talk . . . Even if you go
to a book diviner, he'll ask you and you also answer.' In this and other
sessions, the diviner urged on clients who were not forthcoming enough:
'Answer!', 'What do you say?', 'How do you see it?', 'Do you know this?'
In one session, a diviner corrected a consulter who had missed a cue,
causing the diviner to proceed on the wrong track: 'So at that point you
should have said to me, it's true, that is the matter we are looking for.'
Throughout the consultation there is always a meta-level of communication through which information is sought and given concerning the
quality of the other messages: 'Is this true?' 'Am I right?' 'Do you agree?'
'Should I go on?'

The diviner usually begins by establishing the nature of the problem,
and the relation of the sufferer to the clients. In the following case of the
Dry Tree, the diviner began by shaking the rattles and then saying: 'That
little noise [the moaning of a sick person] should be chased away.' 'We
should chase it away', replied the clients. After more rattling, the diviner
said, 'That little dry tree should be removed', and the clients replied, 'Ah,
that small dry tree – we don't know how we shall remove it – what can we
do to remove it?' The diviner asked in effect whether it was a case of
sickness and was told no. Then he asked whether there was barrenness in
the home and the client affirmed that he should proceed in that direction.

In opening another session, the diviner, trying to establish who was sick
in the home, spoke as follows:

> The spirits are saying that a house keeps three bodies. The first body
> truly is called the centrepole – if it has a matter [reason], it can cause one
> to get hold of a divining fee . . . The body called 'little ash sweeper' also
> makes one take a divining fee – a body called 'umbilical cord container'
> also . . . Shall we send away the little [moaning] sound if it is not on the
> umbilical cord container?

Here the diviner was saying that there are men, women, and children in a
home, and asking whether it was a child who was sick.

If it was not clear whose child was sick, that also had to be clarified, as in
a consultation for an older man (presented more fully in S. Whyte
1991b), when the diviner said: 'Children are of many types. There is a
real child who came from your body. There is also the child who came
from the child you produced. Do you send this one away too?' Here the
diviner paused so that the client could confirm that he was inquiring
about his grandchild: 'The child who is removed [the child of your child]
is also your child.'

In cases of sickness, the diviner does not necessarily discuss symptoms,
and since the sick person is frequently not present, the profile of the disease

often remains vague. When symptoms are discussed, the diviner might mention a number of very different ones, as in the example below of Somebody's Wife, so that the consulter can indicate roughly what sort of phenomenon is being considered. The focus is not on symptoms but causes, and they are not related to symptoms in a strictly determinate way.

Establishing the cause of suffering is the central act of divination and it is a dramatic creation which may take some time to unfold. People speak of 'reasons' appearing in the divination – either in passages being read or in the spirit world of the gourd rattle diviner. The reasons must then be evaluated as to their likelihood, and the claims and obligations involved. One experienced consulter, comparing the seance to a legal proceeding, challenged the reasons to appear in the divination: 'This is a court, come and we argue, he himself [referring to the diviner perhaps] is the one to judge.' In fact, the diviner did often seem to weigh the evidence, reminding the client of norms and expectations regarding relations with other people and spirits. But the client also weighed and judged, and decided which arguments had merit. The word 'legal case' (*omusango*) was often used.

The rhetorical device used by Nandiriko Were, the spirit diviner with whom I worked most closely during my first field research, was that he heard and could speak to the 'reasons' and conveyed their messages to the clients. But he frequently commented that the agents might not be speaking the truth, that they might be appearing without any just claim. In this way, he could allow the client to volunteer more information, or reject ('chase away') the agent.

The matter of the Dry Tree

In 1970, the mother and brother of a barren bride, a 'dry tree', came to consult Nandiriko Were at Lwamboga, in western Bunyole. At first, the diviner was barely heard talking to 'someone' over the noise of the gourd rattles. Then he stopped rattling and spoke:

> DIVINER: This one has begun by giving us lies. He is the one to start taking sides here saying, 'I want to argue with them – if I am defeated soon I shall leave, but if I defeat them, then it is I who have won . . . I am the one called the senior relative, I am the one arguing with these people because maybe they gave what is mine to eat . . .' This relative is called the mother's brother [of the barren woman].
> CLIENT: Does he say that they gave nothing to the mother's brother?
> DIVINER: That's what he says. Perhaps they gave him and he is [still] coming here . . . there are those with quick heads who rush into a divination for nothing [without grounds].

Interval of rattling gourds

> DIVINER: He says it's true, they gave me the cow, I'm not going to deny the cow. They gave me the last cow of the bridewealth [the last cow owing for the bride's mother] but they haven't given me the cow of nieceship [the one a mother's brother should receive from the bridewealth paid for his sister's daughter] . . .
> CLIENT: (After more discussion) Yes. We've heard his case, but let him be patient and go aside.

Gourds are rattled again

> DIVINER: These little spirits that are quarrelling, perhaps they go on quarrelling even though you dealt with them and finished with them . . .

After more discussion of this possibility, the line of questioning moves back toward a suspected curse and other potential cursers appear.

> DIVINER: Do you have a father's sister? She's here quarrelling . . .
> CLIENT: Yes, let her come too and we hear her reasons.

Each agent in turn is rejected by the clients with explanations as to why they do not think that person is cursing: for example, 'I was the one who killed the goat and they divided it among themselves right there.' On several occasions the diviner tried to insist that a particular person must have cursed, because the clients admitted that they had not given that one the rightful share of the bridewealth. But the clients would not accept the interpretation.

> CLIENT: . . . it's true we did not give to them, but we also want to look at another place where there are other reasons . . .
> DIVINER: So you wanted to ask in every corner to make it clear . . . But there is nothing with the father's wives, the grandmothers are refusing, her fathers are refusing.
> CLIENT: . . . No, no, her grandmothers are the ones upon the heart [whom we suspect] . . . There, go there in that very place . . .
> DIVINER: They are refusing.
> CLIENT: They refuse, but no. For us, we're still with them. Just try to find out. I think if you go along those lines, you will bring them back.

First the maternal grandmother appears and the clients admit that she did not receive her rightful share of the bridewealth. But 'because of her softness' and because she died saying that her son-in-law, the bride's father, had always loved her, they did not believe that she had cursed. At last a decision was reached; it was established that the father's mother of the barren bride cursed her before she died. The mother of the bride remarked that she suspected this woman, *her* mother-in-law, because they used to quarrel a lot. The clients wanted to offer a goat at her grave and have the curse removed by the dead woman's eldest daughter, the bride's father's sister. But before doing so, they wanted to be sure that this was the real reason for the barrenness. The diviner gave them detailed instructions from the dead woman about how the ceremony was to be carried out, and the clients asked her questions which were conveyed by the diviner during intervals of rhythmic beating of the rattles. As the session ended, the clients, having been confronted by so many different causes, most of which they refused to accept, said that they did not know the truth – perhaps the ceremony of curse removal would be for naught.

> CLIENT: Ah, there are many matters – again there are her mother's brothers, there's her grandmother, there's her father's sister . . . There's the one grandmother, and the other grandmother.
> DIVINER: The fertility is going to be difficult.
> CLIENT: Among all those cases, ah, we do not know where the truth is and where there is no truth.
> DIVINER: You go and do those things [the curse removal ceremony]. There is where God can give you luck. You, when you divine through so many spirits [use different diviners], don't you go on touching this [case], touching that, touching another [trying different explanations and treatments]?

Earlier in the session, the diviner had made the same point, saying 'Let them do the ceremony. And if she does not get any benefit, let them go and divine elsewhere. A single divination does not heal a person.'

These selections from a consultation that lasted nearly an hour illustrate the way uncertainty is structured and explored through dialogue in the explanatory idiom. The client puts questions to the diviner and through him or her to the spirit agents who appear. In turn, the diviner, in the double role of human interpreter and Another (in this case, the agents of misfortune), questions the client about social and ritual relationships.[5] Here we see the methodical exploration of a problem that Dewey called intellectual – the careful deliberation of possibilities. Dealing with uncertainty involves the selection of evidence (the 'takens') of prior experience – in this case, the old quarrels with a mother-in-law. There is the formulation of the curse idea as a plan of action – the offering of a goat at the grave and the ceremony of curse removal. Finally there is the anticipation of consequences – the hope for fertility and the realistic acknowledgement that it will be difficult.

Resistance and decisions

George Park (1967: 238) speaks of divination as providing 'resistance' to a client's proposal; such resistance is inherent in chance-like mechanisms (such as the unpredictable effect of poison upon fowls) and also in the professional independence of the diviner who cannot simply label as truth every idea a client comes with. In Nyole divination there appears to be a kind of double resistance. The diviner resists the client's proposals, although they may eventually win through as happened in the case of the Dry Tree. And the client resists some of the diviner's proposals by denying their relevance or likelihood. To the extent that both sorts of resistance operate, divination is both a joint venture and a creative one, for neither party knows exactly what conclusion will be agreed upon. The way in which they provide resistance for one another's proposals enhances the impression of a process in which doubts are confronted and cast aside, one by one, so that decisions can be made about plans of action.

Not all clients resist the proposals appearing in the divination as rigidly as the consulters in the case of the Dry Tree. Age and experience as well as the particular circumstances of the case being considered determine the attitude of the client. But all clients retain a degree of autonomy in relation to the diviner, who solicits and respects their opinions. The diviner has to convince the client; he or she has to have the client's understanding and agreement in their joint venture. It is tempting to contrast this situation with that of the biomedical doctor making a diagnosis for his patient. The doctor has a monopoly on knowledge which the diviner does not. The diviner is analysing social and ritual identity in relation to misfortune; in this matter, he or she is not wiser than the client, whose subjective experience is legitimate knowledge. For the doctor, as Kleinman (1980: 72) has stressed, the main concern is the objective analysis of pathological processes; the client's (patient's) experience and interpretation of them is not necessarily of interest.

The volition and relative autonomy of the client was brought home to me in discussing the causes of death with Nandiriko. I asked him why sorcery was always said to be the cause, and whether spirits could not kill people. He replied that they could indeed, but that his clients would not believe him if he found that their relative had been killed by spirits rather than human enemies. 'They will just go to divine elsewhere', he said. Apparently clients could be very stubborn. A man once told me how he had gone to consult a gourd rattle diviner on a certain matter. After two hours, he still had not found an explanation that seemed acceptable to him. So he left, refusing to pay the divination fee. On another occasion, this man remarked that if you wanted the truth from a diviner, you had to accuse him of lying.

The importance of the client's agreement to the decision was clearly illustrated by the records kept in Lunyole by Nandiriko Were. I had asked him to record basic information about number, provenance, and gender of his clients, the type of problem and what the divination revealed about the cause and treatment. I did not mention the client's attitude, yet in nearly all of his entries, he noted the consulter's acceptance of the divinatory conclusion: 'They replied, true, this is the second time we have divined [the agency of] the clan spirit', or 'They replied, true, that's how it is.' Just as many clients declared their uncertainty at the beginning of the consultation, the diviner announced certainty at the end. This movement from puzzlement to decision is the intention of divination. By emphasizing that his clients were convinced, Nandiriko was engaging in a creative attempt. This is not to say that certainty was established once and for all. It was also Nandiriko who said, 'Sometimes God can give you luck' and 'One divination does not heal a person.'

The case of Somebody's Wife

In 1970, a man went to divine about his new second wife, who was suffering severe pain after her recent childbirth. The diviner he chose used a special technique of sprinkling medicine and sand into a basin of water. Then he read words which only he could see written on the surface of the water. Like most texts with which an older generation of Nyole were familiar, this one was written in Luganda, the language of Christianity and education. The source of obscurity in this case was not the language; the client understood Luganda well. But he could not read the invisible text, which was a source of knowledge available only to the diviner. The diviner read aloud, pausing from time to time, to talk to his client about what he was reading.

> DIVINER: This boy's reason – actually he's really worried – that which brought him here to look – the reason why he's worried – he has worries of one type. The reason he has – the sickness of a certain kind – which has come as a joke in the stomach, which pains greatly, and it pains the heart, burning, and it feels cold in the legs. This sickness, do you know it?
> CLIENT: Eeee, you go ahead.
> DIVINER: And it makes one feel cold in the legs and dizzy and badly off. This sickness was sudden. And it makes the head heavy and it brings darkness and dizziness in the eyes. Especially the real illness is in the stomach – very strong – and on the heart – and that is the reason which has brought this one to see the cause that has sent this sudden illness of the stomach and eyes, which almost wanted to prevent this person from seeing. Do you know this sickness?
> CLIENT: I don't know this sickness – I want to know the reason which has brought the sickness.
> DIVINER: And it started with illness – this is very strong and it is not

peaceful, it is very great indeed. There was a day when it came and seized, as if going into a trance. Do you know?

CLIENT: I know.

DIVINER: As if wanting to go into trance.

CLIENT: Yes, s/he did act as if possessed a bit.

DIVINER: She did that? If this sickness was sorcery – in different types of people – if this person was suffering, she would die. But it is different from sorcery and because it came by day and she suffered a lot and she had much pain. The illness first left her a bit, and then afterwards again, another sickness came, of coldness and shuddering, as if going into trance and that was thought to be like spirits. Do you know this clan spirit?

CLIENT: I don't know whether it is of her home.

DIVINER: It's of her home.

CLIENT: Because this wife – I haven't stayed long with her.

DIVINER: Was she married somewhere else?

CLIENT: Yes, she was somebody's wife.

DIVINER: There's sorcery in this matter – what a pity for you! My child, it's bad for you.

CLIENT: Her husband is doing sorcery?

DIVINER: Yes – did you pay the bridewealth?

CLIENT: There's not much bridewealth.

DIVINER: But will you pay it?

CLIENT: Yes.

DIVINER: Do you like [want] her?

CLIENT: Yes. The clan spirit is true, but there's sorcery. Now what does the clan spirit want?

DIVINER: The clan spirit is easy . . . It attacked her where she was first married. And it attacked her so she suffered and nearly died. It wanted them to do a ceremony, to take a cock and the spear. So these things – that man was somehow proud and those things were not very fine and he didn't care about them. That sickness caught her in her first house and now here she first ran and escaped and ran. In this escaping, she hid herself and went again to her first home. Did you know it?

CLIENT: Yes.

DIVINER: You have to understand.

CLIENT: It's very true.

DIVINER: And this one escaped and afterwards she went to her own home. And when she went back to him, that man became wise and started to be clever and when he became wise, he knew what to do and then he knew that, 'this wife of mine seems to refuse me in my marriage'. And he took her things, the saliva, the old clothes, faeces, and footprints. And on that day, they fought and it rained in the evening and he told her that even if you are proud, you will die. And that is the reason which has brought this sickness. This woman – in the house where she is going to stay, perhaps it will be peaceful or it won't be peaceful. We don't know. And so, see – she has been happy and pleased to come [to your home].

He was preparing to bewitch her bleeding in the womb which shows her fertility. And I see the cleverness, how he is proud, and the girl, now she has to be careful. First she seems to have finished here about three months in this house. This is the fourth, but three full ones, but she seems – her body now is different [pregnant] . . . Answer me, answer!

CLIENT: Read – go on.

DIVINER: How do you see?

CLIENT: It's like that, but is there something more coming?

DIVINER: These things, now –

CLIENT: It's the husband doing this?

DIVINER: There is sorcery.

CLIENT: What can I do?

DIVINER: How many months has she finished in this home?

CLIENT: Now she has finished a month – because – there is – she finished about two months and left and returned. She delivered the child.

DIVINER: At yours?

CLIENT: Yes, it is now the third month.

DIVINER: Why haven't they refunded to him [repaid the bridewealth to the first husband]?

CLIENT: I haven't taken the bridewealth, and there is very little money, only 60 shillings.

DIVINER: Which you have paid?

CLIENT: No, which he paid.

DIVINER: And he bewitched her child?

CLIENT: And she produced a girl for him.

DIVINER: Is she there?

CLIENT: Yes.

DIVINER: He's very stupid. The girl you haven't married and you bewitch like that. And her body, how do you see?

CLIENT: The woman's body is now getting thin.

DIVINER: In the womb is where there's sickness. He was going to bewitch her bleeding, but in her monthly period, how do you see her? In delaying?

CLIENT: She has much pain in her womb.

DIVINER: Is the husband very near?

CLIENT: Yes, he's at Nawanjofu.

DIVINER: Ah, here, that one will be cured. But use wisdom, she's very badly off.

. . .

CLIENT: Again, find other things, other things, perhaps in that house.

DIVINER: Perhaps there might be a reason. The co-wife, perhaps she bewitched her comrade. Perhaps there's another kind of reason in those matters in the home. There may be a lot of quarrelling, and there must be jealousy because you like her. Go there in the home – don't go there.

CLIENT: Which home?

DIVINER: I've told you, there at the man.

CLIENT: Is that where the trouble is?

DIVINER: You, son, she came at yours and bore a child?

CLIENT: Yes, and she went when she was pregnant.
DIVINER: And she came back here. That's what you've said.
CLIENT: So when she was about to deliver, she came back.
DIVINER: And she came back – now she's badly off in the womb. Ah, for those, don't think of the home, there's no case. Have they told you about this clan spirit themselves?
CLIENT: No – perhaps they are the things which have come [referring to clan spirits, I think].
DIVINER: For that you'll do a ceremony – for her home, you will take a cock and a spear, but it's not alright – the sorcery is coming. What made her go back there?
CLIENT: Herself, perhaps it was her heart.
DIVINER: And she wants to be like foolish people?
CLIENT: She went as if taking that child.
DIVINER: When taking that child? But this one should let you go and get roots of *emilandira ejoluhandira*. Dig it quickly. Again, don't be on government medicine. Dig that medicine and go to prepare it. Let her drink a cupful without sugar and she should drink everything at once. And in the evening again, she can bathe with it.
CLIENT: With this very medicine she has drunk from?
DIVINER: No, the remainder. She should put it in a basin and bathe. And then tomorrow she should drink some with sugar. Afterwards, when there is peace, you will come back and see what will happen. But he has started to bewitch the woman. It can be stopped if you get [earth from] the footprints, his footprints, and you drink.
CLIENT: Of that man?
DIVINER: But don't worry. We only want this sickness to decrease. These things are finished.

This diviner's technique involves less relaying of information from his esoteric source of knowledge, and more direct questions to his client. Still, he is to some extent bound to his Luganda text, and has to elicit the client's reactions to it: 'Do you know?' and 'Answer me, answer!' The diviner's uncertainty is great at the beginning and his description of the symptoms is a 'simultaneity' precisely parallel to those described by Parkin. He mentions a great variety of symptoms all at once, but does not begin the sequence of logical steps until the mention of trance elicits confirmation from the client. The diviner may not even have known whether the sick person was a man or a woman at first (the third person singular marker in Lunyole is neuter), but trance behaviour is much more common for women. Once it is clear that the woman is 'somebody's wife', the diviner moves through a set of questions that will clarify the situation. In this case, the client does not seem to have a suspicion which the diviner has trouble guessing, as in the divination of the Dry Tree. But the client wants to examine every possibility, so even after the diagnoses of clan spirit and sorcery have been established, he asks if there is anything more.

Analysing persons

Both of the divinations reported here illustrate the ways in which a suffering individual is analysed as a person. They indicate some of the central elements of Nyole personhood, but they also show its complexities and uncertainties.

It is fundamental that a person is a body. The moaning of a sick person and the barrenness of a young woman were points of departure. But the details of the body's pathology were not relevant to the analysis of the suffering person in the aetiological perspective. In the divination about Somebody's Wife, physical malfunctioning was mentioned, but the client immediately moved from symptoms to cause: 'I don't know this sickness. I want to know the reason which has brought the sickness.' In divination there is a tendency to see the body as directly affected by relations to agents, rather than as a system unto itself. In Harris's (1989) terms, Somebody's Wife was not seen as an individual biophysical entity, but as a person whose condition was determined by her social situation.

A woman's fertility is a central part of her existence, because it creates the relations to other people that are so important in the Nyole notion of person. This was beautifully expressed in the diviner's closing words in the matter of the Dry Tree. Addressing the curser who had appeared in the divination, he said:

> If you are the one, I would like all of you to have a good heart – ah, you remove the curse from this person, that she may go and become a woman where she is [living], so that she may be respected in that home. And when you call to visit there, a little child will go to fetch her from the garden saying, 'Ah, grandma has come' . . . They'll look for her and she'll come. A door does not show us a person nor where the person has gone.

When visitors come, it is the children of the home who go to call their mother from the garden. In a home without children, the visitor finds only a closed door, which can never show her a person.

Much of the dialogue of divination is devoted to going through the relations whose disturbance might explain the misfortune. The suffering person is cast as a niece or a granddaughter or an ex-wife of a possible agent. Norms and obligations are checked through as part of an assessment of the person. Senior relatives have a right to shares in the bridewealth received by a woman's father – because she is their 'child'. And as their 'child', she can be cursed if they do not receive their due. Such relationships define her as a person to the extent that she can be wracked with pain, or bear dead babies, if they are not recognized. A

3.1 Children ready to greet visitors at the entrance to a compound (1969)

man's wife belongs to him if he has paid the bridewealth, and should she run off with another man, she might be made to suffer for it. Even the assertion that Somebody's Wife was affected by spirits of her clan, was an assertion about her social identity as a member of her father's clan, with its own unique spirit, as we shall see in chapter 4.

In divination this normative aspect of social identity is problematized. If bridewealth has not been repaid to the woman's first husband, does she still belong to him? Even if he has only paid 60 shillings? Is a bride a proper 'child' of her mother's brother if the cow of nieceship has not been given to him from the bridewealth paid for her?

It is not only a matter of uncertainties within specific relationships. Indeterminacy arises from the fact that an individual is involved in many relationships, and has different identities depending on context. The mother and brother of the 'Dry Tree' exclaim, 'Ah, there are many matters', and name a number of relatives who might participate in the person of the barren bride. The diviner agrees: 'the fertility will be difficult' – her situation as a person is multifaceted. Which aspect of her social identity is the relevant one?

As agents of misfortune, human beings are conceived as persons, with a certain standing, and selves, who have feelings. In the case of the Dry

Tree, when the diviner insisted that the maternal grandmother must have cursed because she had not been given her share of the bridewealth, the bride's brother explained that the old woman had been similarly neglected at the marriages of other granddaughters, but 'because of her softness', her other granddaughters were bearing children anyway. She was not just a grandmother who had certain bridewealth rights; she was a person whose affection for her son-in-law might be expected to incline her to gentleness towards his daughter, the barren bride.

In analysing persons, the divinatory gaze is upon those agents who affect the victim's condition. It is their characters and feelings that are examined, more often than those of the suffering person. This is extrospection, rather than introspection – an examination of the agent, rather than of the victim. In the case of Somebody's Wife, the diviner raises the possibility that the client's first wife is jealous of the new one. He speaks of her ex-husband, who is 'stupid' and 'clever' and 'somehow proud'. In divination, agents are found to be envious, angry or greedy, indignant or just plain malicious. They are imagined as loci of experience, feeling love towards a granddaughter or disinterest in the spirits of a wife's clan. Very seldom are the feelings and dispositions of the victim or the client so directly addressed.

The analysis of misfortune involves a consideration of what may have moved an agent to act. In probing into the personal sources of action, Nyole recognize that there are hidden aspects of the person; the theme of concealment and revelation is woven through their discourse about agency and misfortune. When the brother of the Dry Tree said that he doubted their maternal grandmother had cursed, because she was soft and affectionate, the diviner was cynical. 'Perhaps she talks like that while hiding something. Perhaps she is ashamed to reveal herself.'

Lienhardt has warned against too much emphasis on the 'collectivist orientation in African ideas of the person'. He speaks of 'the importance, no matter how much store may be set by social role and status, of individual, private, intellectual and emotional activities: the private self ... that acts and is acted upon and where that action is located' (1985: 146). The recognition of the part of the person from which action springs, the part which is least accessible to others, is essential in Nyole divination. The secrets of the heart are an element of personhood too. Other people are recognized as being selves, reflecting on experience and acting on the basis of feelings and private purposes. The other person, the agent of misfortune, is not just a somebody, but a self. It is for that reason that one can never be certain about people.

In the case of Somebody's Wife, somewhat untypically, the analysis turned to the victim herself when the diviner questioned the client about his new wife, who moved in while she was pregnant with somebody's child and then left. The diviner wondered what made her leave, but the only answer her husband could offer was, 'Herself, perhaps it was her heart' – that is, some motivation of her own must have prompted her. He speculated that she may have wanted to bear the child at its father's home, but neither of them seemed sure that that was the reason, especially since she came back before her delivery. In the course of the consultation, she had been considered as a member of her clan (subject to its clan spirits), as somebody's ex-wife, and as a co-wife. Yet there remained aspects of her person that were opaque. The reference to her heart as a reason for her behaviour was not really an explanation, but simply a way of 'paraphrasing the unexplainable' (Ramløv 1986: 132).

Uncertainty resolved?

Many excellent studies of divination have emphasized the way in which it helps the consulter to bring order out of confusion, to make a decision. Michael Jackson, writing of Kuranko divination, says:

> The diviner's analysis transforms uncertainty into a conditional certainty and his instructions . . . enable the consultor to move from inertia to purposeful activity (praxis). He regains his autonomy; he acts upon the conditions which are acting upon him. And this autonomy precludes anxiety. I have argued that these psychological and existential changes are immediate and positive, and that the ultimate outcome of any prognostication or sacrifices does not necessarily inspire retrospective interest in the truth or falsity of the diviner's original propositions. The reassurances that follow from and the activity enabled by the consultation entail a suspension of disbelief. (1978: 134)

Much of this description could also be applied to Nyole divination. Not only is uncertainty transformed, but it is emphasized in divination in order that it may be diminished. The consultations show the movement towards clarification and the final recommendations for action with which the client leaves the divining hut.

Yet we must take care not to mistake the intention of divination for its result. Both the client and the diviner want to create certainty, but they are not naive about the difficulty of their task. The analysis of persons does not involve the application of some clear model, but the working out of at least two kinds of problems. One is the connectedness of persons to a variety of other people, as well as to ancestors and spirits, with all the normative guidelines against which such relations may be evaluated. The second has to do with the partially hidden motivations of persons that infuse the relationships with intention and quality and morality. These matters are never really settled; they are constantly being reformulated in social life, and divination is a privileged arena for doing so. Even within the framework of divination, the many kinds of connectedness and the hidden nature of private selves are acknowledged. Jackson uses the term 'conditional' to describe the certainty created in divination. I think Nyole know it is conditional, even while they are creating it, because they never lose sight of the complexity of persons.

The analysis of persons is a problematic endeavour because there are qualities of personhood that constantly require further exploration and creation. They are always in the process of being brought about, because there is always a degree of uncertainty about persons. Divination not only attempts to resolve this uncertainty; it also contributes to its maintenance by providing a framework for it. Both uncertainty and its resolution are generated in divination.

Those studies which most carefully examine consultations as dramatic creations of certainty often do not follow up matters beyond the divination hut. A broader perspective includes failure and doubt. Writing of the neighbouring Gisu people, Heald emphasizes the 'pragmatic or even cynical attitude' towards divination:

> If one thinks about diviners as operating in the area between hope, the search for some certainty in the face of chronic uncertainty, and reality, the inevitable failures of any curative system in the face of disease and death, one may perhaps see the band of plausibility as relatively narrow in systems such as that of the Gisu. (Heald 1991: 310)

I do not know what happened to the Dry Tree; the diviner himself predicted that her fertility would be difficult, and suggested that they might have to try another diviner and another diagnosis. About Somebody's Wife I know more. Her husband never helped her do the ceremony for her clan spirits nor did he get earth from her ex-husband's footprints to counter his sorcery. She improved, perhaps because of the herbal medicine recommended by the diviner, perhaps because of the 'government medicine' at the health centre, which she sought despite the diviner's advice against it, or perhaps because of the natural resilience of the human body. Her co-wife left, hurt by the way the new wife had usurped their husband's attention. Soon after, Somebody's Wife left too; most people were not surprised – she was reputed to be one who 'does not stick in marriage'. The consulter remained alone, drinking heavily; although he had relationships with other women over the next twenty years, he never managed to keep a wife. It is sad to look at the text of his consultation and think of it as an effort to gain certainty and control over his life.

It is often the case that a divination establishes several proposals about the cause and treatment of the suffering. Sometimes people seek a second opinion, further increasing the options. (Diviners are very aware of this pattern of 'diviner shopping', as can be seen in the text from the case of the Dry Tree. In the records kept by Nandiriko Were, he often noted that his clients had divined the case elsewhere and were comparing results.) Thus several possibilities for action are open. As often as not, none of the 'conditional certainties' configured in divination are acted upon. When people do move to perform rituals and obtain medicines, they may justify their actions by reference to divination. But what I want to emphasize is that they take the certainty proposed and try to make it true. The relevant notion of truth is a pragmatic one: 'Truth *happens* to an idea. It *becomes* true, is *made* true by events. Its verity is in fact an event, a process' (William James cited in Jackson 1996: 4). In order to understand how people choose which idea to put into practice, we must examine the terms of action and the implications of each.

Part II

'What you cannot see': the revelations
of spirits

4   At home with the dead

Home is where you are buried. In Bunyole as elsewhere in East Africa, burial, graves, and rituals of remembrance mark the attachment of a family to a place. Dealing with misfortune by referring to shades involves considerations about home and family obligations, about the respect due to dead parents and grandparents, and about the social meaning of death itself. Acting in terms of shades has social consequences: 'wombs' of people – minimal agnatic lineages – are mobilized and acknowledged; relationships to people and resources are affirmed. In the face of uncertainty, the security and continuity of home are proposed.

Nyole say that every living person has an *omwigu* (pl. *emigu*) which is 'like a shadow'. This is the aspect of a person which lives on after death and continues to relate to the living. Perhaps it would be more correct to say that this is the aspect of the person that becomes relevant after death, for although the word can also refer to the essence of someone living, but not physically present, I have seldom heard anyone speak of the *omwigu* of a living person. Nor are people much concerned about the *emigu* of dead children or of those adults who died childless. Having left no descendants, they present no opportunity for the enactment of family relationships through generational connection. In this chapter, I describe the process by which a living person with a self is converted to a shade with a position *vis-à-vis* surviving family members.

People may be uncertain about shades in the sense of not being sure whether shades are the reason behind a misfortune; or they may be in doubt about what shades really want in order to be propitiated. Dealings with shades provide many examples of the pragmatic 'trying out' of ideas, when people make preliminary small offerings to placate agents of misfortune and see whether the adversity subsides. So there are uncertainties in connection with the shades. But people do not doubt the morality and intentions of shades, as they do those of living people. This contrast is important in relation to cursing. Living senior relatives can curse by invoking the shades; as a later chapter will show, suspicion and doubt are directed at the curser, whose feelings and motivations are opaque.

Shades, whether they are thought to act on their own, or by invitation of the living, do not have personalities and thus lack the ambiguity that is a defining characteristic of human beings. Because they are immanent in Nyole homes, shades can be taken as ideas of continuity and belonging in a world of uncertainty.

Wombs of people

In addition to kinds or clans of people, Nyole also speak of *ebida* (sing. *ehida*) of people. The term means stomach or womb, as in *ali n'ehida*, she has a womb, she's pregnant. *Ebida* are both categories and variable groups within clans. Some clans have major divisions called *ebitundu* (divisions) or *ebida*, which can be elicited by asking, 'How does your clan divide itself?' Within these categories or clan divisions exact genealogical links are not usually known, nor are they necessarily co-resident groups. Sometimes different clan spirits are even associated with these clan divisions, as we shall see; in a sense they are incipient clans.

The other usage of the word *ehida* is to refer to the agnatic descendants of a known ancestor. Such a lineage is not of fixed genealogical depth; it may be defined more or less inclusively depending on context. It can be as narrow as the descendants of a common grandfather, who would likely be neighbours living on the land their fathers inherited. An *ehida* can be a somewhat wider unit within which a widow can be inherited without having to repay the bridewealth to the heir of the deceased. (Fallers (1965: 88) calls a similar grouping among the Soga a 'succession lineage'.) Again it can be a broader group which comes together for ritual occasions and has a common sacrificer (*omusengi*).

Unlike clans, lineages are concerned with claims upon resources – wives, debts, land, and other property. These claims are discussed in terms of genealogical connections, which are brought into the limelight by death, necessitating the transfer of rights to heirs. Correspondingly, ancestral shades are the terms of the explanatory idiom that dramatize relations within the lineage.

At 'the beer of the dry banana leaf', held about two weeks after a burial, the agnates and spouse(s) of a deceased adult gather to choose a successor. In the case of a man, there might actually be several successors.[1] As heir of the estate (*omusika*), a son should be chosen; if there are several adult sons, the eldest son of the first wife would be the likely candidate. He acts as executor; his shares in the property are not greater than those of his brothers, but he has the responsibility to distribute land, livestock and money, to receive and repay bridewealth for his sisters, and to assume his father's debts and credits. If the dead man's sons are still young, one of his brothers is named as heir. He is to administer the estate on their behalf so that they receive their rightful shares upon adulthood. Conflicts often arise in such situations with men accusing their 'little fathers' of misappropriating property meant for them. This was one of the issues in the matter of Namugwere's illness; Hamala, who was later suspected of sorcery, had a running conflict with Namugwere's husband, who had administered the estate of Hamala's dead father.

If there are no sons, property goes to the brothers of the deceased unless he had clearly made arrangements otherwise. While it is possible for a daughter, or her sons, to inherit property (this is recognized in national law), it is rare in practice. The rights of widows to retain their husbands' property are now being supported by the national government. But this is not 'Nyole tradition'. A recently widowed woman in Busolwe told how her brother-in-law had tried to claim her husband's bicycle and cassette player, although he had left eight children, including sons. The local resistance council stepped in on her behalf.

Although the agnates propose an heir to the dead man's wives, the widows have the right to refuse and frequently do so. In these days of AIDS, health educators point out the dangers of widow inheritance. But even several decades ago, women often declined to be inherited; widowhood was one of the few opportunities for women to lead a more independent life. However, the pressure to accept an heir was and is keenly felt by widows. When they fall ill, they may well attribute their misfortunes to in-laws who are bitter because they refused to be inherited.

A woman's identity in relation to her own and her husband's lineages is far more complex than her clan identity. A clan is for life – in her married home, she is called by her clan name until her death. There is never any question of becoming a member of her husband's clan; that would make the marriage incestuous. But lineages, as Nyole say, come from women. At her husband's home, she is the womb that produces sons who carry on the lineage. The conflicts endemic to all lineages are her conflicts – whether she acts on her own or her children's behalf. She herself is one of the resources about which the succession lineage negotiates. If she stays, she is buried in her husband's home and her shade is honoured there with those of the lineage. Yet she is born into her father's lineage, she can always go back there if she leaves her husband, and her children have a special relationship to it as the 'place of their uncles'. She has ties to both lineages, but because she cannot inherit property, her place and her voice are less apparent.

Whereas clan is a social category, lineage is a social group. You relate to a lineage through contiguity, connections to other individuals. Interpersonal conflicts are possible, even likely, between people who touch and have to share concrete resources. Categorical clan status as a 'kind' of person is not problematic in such a personal and often bitter way (M. Whyte 1983: 145).

The homeliness of shades

For many Nyole people, the shades of the dead (*emigu j'abafu*) are part of the family; they are close in time and space. In contrast to clan spirits, shades are beings to whom you trace specific blood relationships – fathers, mothers and grandparents. Although the shades of agnatic ancestors farther removed than grandfathers might be mentioned in prayers, they are seldom relevant in practice. The grandparents of the oldest living man in a localized lineage define the genealogical limits of practical concern with shades.

The clearest evidence that the dead belong in the family is that their graves lie in or on the edge of the courtyard. Nowadays families who can afford it are cementing graves, especially of adults; a prosperous family might have a line of stepped cement oblongs along one side of the yard. A mound of earth with stones on top, and sometimes a cross, marks other graves. When I visited people for the first time, or after many years, they often showed me the graves of their parents or children who had 'gone to the other side'. Although they are gone, their place is marked and a visitor can acknowledge them, just as she can greet the living members of the family.

Among a set of brothers, one is the sacrificer (*omusengi*) who makes offerings on behalf of the other brothers and their children. Formally he is the one who speaks to the shades. But anyone can talk to the dead (*ohwenana*) at any time. A friend explained: 'You don't have to sacrifice. If you get some money, thank the dead and ask them to help you use it well.' In early 1996, I was sitting talking to the old sister of Tefiro Wamudanya, who had recently died. When I told her that I had paid school fees for some of the children in the family, she shook my hand, thanked me, and turning a bit to include the grave in our conversational space, changing her tone ever so slightly, she spoke to her dead brother as if he were right there. She reminded him how she had always included Michael as one of his children and how she had asked him to bless us, make us happy, keep bringing us back, and keep attracting more motor-cars to their home.

The home of a sacrificer should have a shrine (*omugaami*) consisting of a stone, perhaps two or three, and a barkcloth tree (*omugayire*), usually on one side of the compound. Sometimes there is no tree at all, or the tree is represented by a pole stuck into the ground with the stones on either side;

and occasionally there are wonderful huge old twisted trees with the stones lying at their roots. Sometimes too a small thatched shelter (*ehirolero*), two or three feet high, is built over the stones. Not uncommonly, such a shrine stands near one for the clan spirit. Shrines and their shelters are often ignored until a ceremony is required; then they are weeded and a shelter is built, which collapses after some time.

A senior man's courtyard may also contain a house for 'the big men' (*enyumba y'abasajja bahulu*). This is a round thatched hut, usually with a centrepole, two doorways, and no doors. Although such houses are for 'those who died long ago', living family members use them too. 'Even visitors can sit there – didn't those dead people used to have visitors too?' These houses of the big men exemplify well the intimacy and homeliness of shades. Women may sit there, peeling bananas or shelling groundnuts. People rest in the cool interior and on special occasions agnates sit crowded inside drinking beer together with the shades. Like shrines, these houses are put up when a ceremony is to be held and may later be left to fall into disrepair.

The shades of men are associated with the shrine; some say they stay there – others that they eat there in their 'dining room'. Those of women, the mothers and father's mothers, have their place on the verandah of the senior wife's house. Houses are for women in the sense that each wife has her house; women often sit working and talking on the verandah, in the shade of the overhanging thatch. When it rains, they place containers there at the eavesdrop (*ehitonyero*) to collect the water as it runs off the roof and the eavesdrop is associated with the shades of women.

When a sacrificer dies, a brother or a son should be chosen to replace him. Then the stones have to be moved to the compound of the new sacrificer; only a sister's son can do that job. In practice, shrines are sometimes neglected and the stones forgotten; new stones are initiated with the help of a sister's son. But there is an idea of continuity in the stones being moved from one custodian to another. Less continuity exists in relation to the shades of women; houses, like people, have a life cycle and when that is finished they collapse.

The location of shades in domestic space is ritually constructed; it does not just happen. When a person dies, the *omwigu* leaves the body and the home and goes wandering. 'It moves with the wind and stays in trees.' It must be collected (*ohuyoola omwigu*) by the sister's sons or daughters and brought home to the compound to be reinstalled with the family. Should the person have died far away, the shade is collected on the road leading in the direction of the place of death. This collection is part of the second funeral ceremony, which is often delayed for many years. Thus there is a period, frequently a long one, when the shades are out of place and can be imagined to be dissatisfied. For example, when Maigi's wife was possessed by the shade of her father's brother in 1970, it was said that the shade 'was quarrelling because they had left him out in the cold to sleep in trees – he wanted to be brought home to his brother's'.

In Nyole conceptualization, the dead are thought to properly belong in homes with their descendants; but the latter must make a gesture confirming that the deceased are still part of the family, albeit in a new form. At the same time, of course, they confirm that they, the living, are the children and grandchildren of those who went before and that they too belong in that place. Dealing with the dead affirms a home: their burial, their ceremonies, the collection of their shades and the way they draw descendants to a place where they can be remembered are all crucial in this process.

For Nyole who live in towns, death, burial and mourning tie them to their 'real' homes. They come home for family funerals and their bodies are brought home for burial. The famous case of the Nairobi lawyer S. M. Otieno brought this point to fervent national attention in Kenya. S. M.'s Luo clansmen established the difference between a house in town and a home, where a man should be buried with his patrikin (Cohen and Atieno Odhiambo 1992). For Nyole too, death (your own or that of a close family member) brings you home. The link between homecoming and mortality is anticipated, when fatally ill people are removed from the hospital and brought home to die. Indeed, AIDS first became evident in Bunyole not when local residents succumbed, but when Nyole working in towns fell ill and came back to their homes in Bunyole to be cared for and to die.

For many people, the shades in the courtyard have a special relevance for the family's prosperity. When they brew beer, they pour a little for the dead, at the shrine if they have one, or in the open courtyard, and at the eavesdrop for the dead women. If they slaughter an animal, they might spill some drops of blood for 'the big men' with a few words of dedication. When families make an offering of thanksgiving after the millet harvest before they begin to eat the new food, they kill a chicken (*ohudanyira*) for the shades and the clan spirit. They eat the blood spilled on the shrine stones, while the family enjoys the meat. Here too the living and the dead share a meal as families do.

The interest of the shades is not only in the 'traditional' millet, but also in other kinds of abundance. If a man buys a new bicycle or iron sheets to roof a house, he should provide a cock and ask his father to slaughter it in the compound and spill blood upon the new property, begging the ancestors to bless it and those who would enjoy it.

The slaughter of animals is an eventful way of realizing shades in the daily life of the home. Less striking but more pervasive is another way of orienting people towards their dead parents and grandparents: the pattern of naming, *enjerulwa*. Babies are named after dead family members, usually people in the generation of their grandparents or great grandparents. The senior man of the home, the paternal grandfather of the new baby, chooses the child's name. In this way the names of women from other clans pass into the agnatic group, for girls are named after 'wives of the clan' as well as after 'daughters of the clan' (father's sisters or father's father's sisters). Thus by his or her very name, a person is identified with ancestors and there is a sense in which he or she continues the existence of someone else. I do not think that this continuity is a matter of incarnating a shade,[2] or of having personality characteristics of one's namesake. Rather you fill a position *vis-à-vis* other people. Thus a girl named after her father's mother can be addressed as mama by her father, and she can call him her child. This is often done in a gentle playful way, especially between grandparents and grandchildren who refer to one another as husbands and wives. Nothing better illustrates the homeliness of shades than an old widow affectionately soothing a cranky toddler: 'I've cooked something nice for you, my husband.'

In all these ways, shades are a part of the home and the family and everyday life. But as I have suggested, they are not just there; they are constructed through a series of ceremonial activities.

Constructing and dismantling death[3]

Death sets in motion a series of rituals and activities that arrange the deceased and the bereaved in relation to one another. When a person dies, whether child or adult, word is sent to relatives and neighbours to come for the burial. People arrive with contributions of food or money to help with the expenses of the ceremony and these are carefully recorded by name and amount. The burial usually takes place on the day after death, giving time for as many as possible to come. A religious leader, a priest or mullah, is often invited to speak at the burial. The mother's brothers of the dead person must be notified of the death immediately and they have to attend in order to be sure that their child is properly buried.

The sister's children (*abeng'wa*) of the deceased have important tasks at the burial and during the first period of mourning. They should dig the grave, wash the body, wrap it in a sheet, and lay it to rest. For this work they should be paid money and a chicken in order to counteract the dangerously close contact with the dead.[4] They also have to gather firewood, cook for the assembled mourners, and run errands. They collect dry banana leaves and strew them in the compound and they keep the funeral fire burning at night to warm the mourners who sleep outside on the dry banana leaves.

The mourners 'sleep on the grave', that is in the compound, for three days if the deceased is a male and four if a female. At the end of this period, just before dawn, a sister's child of the same sex as the deceased takes some dry banana leaves to the nearest crossroads and burns them. This act (*ohwoohya ahasanja*) marks the end of the first, most intensive period of mourning; normal activities can then be resumed by all but the closest relatives, who continue to sleep on the grave and receive mourners who come to sit and converse and bring contributions to show their sympathy.

Some one or two weeks later, neighbours and relatives gather again in the dead person's compound to drink 'the beer of the dry banana leaf' (*ogw'ahasanja*) and announce the heirs to the deceased. After this, normal life resumes, the married daughters of the home can go back to their husbands, and other close relatives stop sleeping outside and take up the work of farming once again.

There are alternative ways of marking the death and the period immediately following. Today many people arrange a religious ceremony (*olumbe olw'ehisomi* – the death ceremony of reading) with no alcohol and only a simple provision of food. Muslims hold strictly to Koranic readings and of course do not prepare beer.[5] Some people say that death is becoming so common that people do not follow the 'rules of culture' anymore – a statement that is commonly made in the towns of Uganda as a comment on the AIDS pandemic. For Bunyole, at least, this is an exaggeration. No matter which specific arrangements are made, there are today, as there were twenty years ago, common features of burial and mourning.

During the first phase of the funeral ceremonies, the corpse must be disposed of and the bereaved comforted. Each of these two tasks has implications for the identity of the living. First, the corpse should be buried on the land of the 'owner of the home' – preferably the land a man has inherited from his father, his 'clan land'. A married man who has been given his share of land should be buried there in the compound, as should his wife and children. Should they die elsewhere, they should be brought to that home for burial. A woman whose marriage is intact cannot be buried at her natal home, even if she died while home for a visit. (And a woman for whom bridewealth has not been paid should not be buried at her husband's home unless he pays it before putting her in the grave.) The consequence of this principle is that the existence of family graves on a piece of land constitutes evidence of rights to the land. Thus, in the court records, land cases contain statements about burials. In 1970 there was an incident in which a man refused his half brother the right to bury a dead child on a certain piece of land, because he said the land belonged to him and he was only lending it to his half brother. So burying the corpse affirms or problematizes those social relations that give access to land in the case of a man. For a woman who dies elsewhere than at her husband's home, negotiations about her place of interment carry heavy implications about the status of her marriage.

The other principal concerns during this time of acknowledging death are the expressions of grief and sympathy and support by all those persons with whom the family and deceased have important relationships. The bereaved cannot bury the dead without the support of the mother's brothers and sisters' sons. Agnatic relatives should certainly attend; in-laws who have married women of the bereaved home cannot expect their wives to leave the funeral until they come with a contribution. Friends, neighbours, and colleagues show their concern by coming and bringing something, even a token contribution. Not to go to mourn shows that you do not value the relationship, or worse – that you have a bad heart. It might give rise to suspicion; maybe you are not sorry about the death – maybe you wanted it or caused it. People who live far away, and cannot come in the first weeks, must call to mourn at the first opportunity. Elite men working in Kampala make a quick tour when they visit Bunyole, stopping to sit, if only for a few minutes, in the homes where they have lost someone.

Thus, in the initial period people must demonstrate their concern. Even if they had not given much attention or support during the period of sickness that preceded death, they have to express it afterwards. In doing so they mark who they are in relation to the dead person; they show themselves as kin, friends, or neighbours. Time passes, and for some deceased adults and most children, there are no further opportunities for the living to manifest their relationships to the dead. Only those who leave descendants are honoured in subsequent ceremonies of remembrance.[6] Muslims and elite or very Christian families hold annual memorial services (*ehijukizo*) for their most important members. People working in town can better afford the costs of memorial services, which also provide an occasion for generous sociability with family members at home in Bunyole. Relatives assemble, religious leaders conduct a service and people eat together, affirming their relations to one another *vis-à-vis* the dead. The most spectacular remembrances, however, are the second funeral ceremonies, which alone can vie with the great celebrations for clan spirits. Like those, the second funerals demand extensive coordination and substantial outlays, so they are always talked about and always postponed. Perhaps, as a few 'modernists' prophesy, they will disappear before long. But my impression is that they were no more frequently performed a generation ago than they are today.

The second funeral ceremony is called *ohwabya olumbe*, a Luganda term that means 'to dismantle death'. It is supposed to take place about a year after death, though sometimes twenty years pass before the arrangements can be made and the sacrificial animals collected. The agency of shades in a misfortune is diagnosed in connection with the need to hold the ceremony. Often more than one person is honoured at the same ceremony; seldom is it held for a woman alone – wives and mothers are usually included in the ceremonies held for their husbands and sons.

The second funeral ceremony assembles a hundred people or more for several days and nights of drinking, music, and dancing. During this time the graves, shades, and shrine of the dead are put in order by sisters' children. The shades are collected at a crossroads by sisters' children who snatch them up in a trembling bunch of grass and run madly to the house with a crowd at their heels. The sons, daughters, and grandchildren of the deceased provide cattle and goats to be offered with prayers to the shades, thus confirming their links to the dead. These sacrifices are finished off with the giving of *ebigwasi*, the sacramental food containing bits of the liver, stomach, and heart of the animals which together with pounded sesame are inserted into clumps of cooked millet meal. Both the animals and the *ebigwasi* are offered with words of acknowledgement, naming names and asking for blessings. At the same time, relations among the living are demonstrated by the sharing of the sacramental food and the distribution of meat. Some meat is cooked and eaten at the spot; great piles of pieces are divided out to be taken home. Forelegs, rumps, backs, ribs, even the head and the tail, are given to people according to their kin relations with the dead: a thigh to the father's brother, a rump to the mother's brothers, and so on.

This truly carnivorous occasion is reminiscent of the 'right foreleg of the cow' school of ethnography with its abundance of detail on the allocation of cuts of meat. The forelegs and rumps are objects of intense discussion as people struggle for meat and argue over who should have what. Meat is used to mark relationships and the ceremony stands as a prototype of one way of expressing identity in Bunyole. The public nature of the occasion, the dramatization of social categories and relations, the acknowledgement of belonging, continuity, and reciprocity – all these characteristics contrast with the privacy and individuality of other kinds of therapeutic action.

The second funeral ceremony is the occasion for the most elaborate

4.1 Music for the ceremony of 'dismantling death'. The man on the right holds a set of gourd rattles (1991)

offerings to the shades. But offerings are also made at other times. There is a notion that the ancestors should be honoured by a sacrifice (*ohubiraga*) from time to time, say every five years. These simpler ceremonies also involve the basic elements of marking different groups of kin by sharing meat and *ebigwasi* and the obligatory participation of a sister's child.

In terms of shades

As a term for dealing with misfortune, shades carry a connotation of moral responsibility. People are obligated to shades, as they are to clan spirits; they should attend to them regularly. Most people are neglectful, however, so that shades, like clan spirits, must remind the living of their duties. Affliction is a favoured means of communication, and the most common message sent by shades is in the form of sickness.

Enosi Wabunyi's 35-year-old son, Mwangalasa Wilber, has a farm in Busoga near Jinja. As Wabunyi was preparing to sacrifice a bull to his dead father in January 1993, Wilber told me why he had come home for the ceremony.

'Is that a cow?'

In November 1992, I fell ill; I had diarrhoea and my head was confused.
It got too serious and they admitted me to hospital for a week. I couldn't
walk or see; I just sensed shapes like a picture. They gave me three
bottles of water [intravenous fluid] and injections every day and tablets.
I don't know what kind and I don't know what disease the doctors
thought this was. After leaving the hospital, I lost my ticket [treatment
form].

My father came, and took me to my house and arranged more treatment, both European and African. A 'doctor' living nearby gave me
PPF [procaine penicillin fortified] and chloroquine injections. Also a
Muslim medicine man, a Soga, gave me herbal medicines and an amulet to tie on my chest and on my arm, to protect me against the sorcerer
who was envious of my farming. My head was still confused, and
whenever they gave me any kind of treatment, they say that I asked, 'Is
that a cow?' That's how they knew – because they had promised a cow
to my grandfather, but they had never given it. When father went back
home to Bunyole, I understand he went to visit a diviner at Busolwe.
His dead father spoke to him in the divination, and said, 'I want a
meal.'

Even before this, some people at home here had been possessed.
Grandfather came on their heads and said he wanted a meal. The
gardens weren't giving good yields either, because they hadn't given him
anything to eat. They did the second funeral ceremony for him and his
wives long ago, in 1952. Later my father made an offering (*ohubiraga*) to
his dead mother, but since 1952, he had never given an animal to his
father.

Wilber's symptoms were grave and were treated extensively. Apparently
there was suspicion of sorcery too. When I asked him about this, he said
he was not sure; he thought his father went to divine in Busoga when he
was first discharged from hospital and there might have been someone
who was envious that he was successfully cultivating the land he had
bought. But as he told the story, the symptoms, even the name of the
disease, were of little import. The possible sorcerer faded into the background, as his affliction was fitted into a family history, and its treatment
became an occasion for a family celebration.

Most commonly, shades are thought to send illness. Even the deaths
of children (though not those of adults) were sometimes attributed to
them. In the diviners' records from 1971, shades were also found to have
caused failures of prosperity: crops were poor, livestock died, or children
did badly in school. Among the cases recorded were instances of barrenness and impotence and one of a man who had been deserted by five
different wives on account of the shade of an earlier wife who was
demanding her second funeral ceremony. If an infant cried constantly,

refused to suckle, or was sickly, the diviner sometimes found that a particular ancestor was annoyed because the child had not been named after him or her.

The problems sent by shades were not always serious ones; shades can also send messages in the form of signs or omens. There were instances of people going to divine because birds had entered their houses. In the diviners' records were examples of people who came to ask about disturbing occurrences which were puzzles rather than afflictions. One man complained that his plough oxen kept tangling their traces; another told how his son had been cutting a tree which fell and pinned him under a branch. Another came with his brother to ask why his cow had gone mad and tried to butt people. Why should banana beer which had been properly prepared and left covered to ferment, go sour?

Sometimes strange dreams were taken to be communications from the dead, and when shades were suspected in a case, the diviner might ask if a person had had unusual dreams. Pursuing a suspicion of shades, Yahaya asked a woman who was inquiring about her daughter's barrenness whether she dreamed of the dead or the living. Another client told him that she dreamed she was crying, and he interpreted that to mean that her dead husband wanted her to take their children back to his home where they belonged.

Shades also communicate by possessing people, causing them to feel dizzy, to faint, or to tremble and groan in the way called *ohusamira*. In several cases men's dizziness was said to be caused by the shades of their dead fathers whom they had not yet honoured with the second funeral ceremonies. Usually it was girls or women who did *ohusamira*; a schoolgirl of 14 had to be sent home on three different occasions because of falling down and making strange noises in class. Sometimes women seemed to 'fall mad', and began beating people. Because this kind of behaviour might indicate possession by various spirits as well as shades, it was necessary to confirm the agent through divination.

Except in cases having to do with the naming of a child, the motive of shades in sending suffering and portents is almost invariably the desire for a ceremony: a second funeral or a sacrifice. The treatment for problems they cause is to publicly and formally acknowledge them, to speak to them and offer an animal so that they can eat the blood while their living descendants share the meat. The response to their agency is to ritually identify kin in relation to them. We have seen how this was done in a second funeral. On a more modest scale, people do the same thing when making a sacrifice.

Paulo Mbala wrote the following account of an offering made by his father in 1970.

Sour beer

Father buried beer bananas which ripened well, and we squeezed them
. . . But when father went to check the beer – a sad affair – it was sour. He
cut more bananas and again – the same thing. He got up to go to the
diviner to ask what spoils the beer. So there the diviner told him this:
'The dead people are spoiling your beer – so they need a goat to eat.'
Father asked the diviner, 'Which dead people? I finished the second
funeral long ago.' And the diviner replied this way: 'The man whom they
call Terabana is wanting a goat – and his wives.' When these things were
finished, father returned and told us at home. Again he buried more beer
and it also got spoiled; altogether five holes of beer went sour.

The outcome was that father called the sister's son to come and do the
things concerning sacrifice. When he came, father took a goat and gave
to him to cut [the throat]. They brought the goat near the shrine and
they cut it – the blood fell on the shrine. They skinned it there in the
banana plantation, they chopped up the meat, washed and cooked it and
millet food also. Then father told the sister's son to bring the meat and
he took the liver and stomach and they cut them into small pieces. So
they took a package of millet food wrapped in banana leaves and they
carried it to the shrine. Father broke off a chunk of millet food and put
pieces of liver and stomach in it; that is what we call *ehigwasi*. He began
to pray with words like this: 'If you are the one, the dead man Terabana,
who spoils my beer, I now want it to be good. So I have given you this
huge he-goat. Eat a bit with all your wives.' When he finished speaking,
he put it under the stone in the shrine. He broke off a small bit of the
millet food which remained and put liver and stomach in it and gave it to
mama to eat. Now mama bit a little two times and she spat on each side.
That indicates this: 'Those with bad hearts, let them eat over there.'
Then she broke off pieces of millet food and gave to her daughters to eat.
Again, that which remained we boys ate with father. So these things
were finished. We left the shrine. They served the food which remained
and we ate it together with meat. So these things ended. But I forgot to
tell you this: they cooked the stomach things [viscera] and the ribs and
neck. After we finished eating food, father took a hindleg and gave to the
clan people and he took a foreleg also and gave to the clan people. Again,
he took another foreleg and gave to us, his children.

Three elements characterize responses to the shades. The first is the
killing of an animal and sharing of the sacrifice. The shades consume the
blood and the living eat the meat. Usually sacramental food (*ebigwasi*) is
also given to both the living and the dead. Meat must be shared, not only
among those present, but, if the offering is a cow or goat, portions must be
sent to other divisions within the clan. The sacrifice of an animal and
sharing of meat are necessary. Sometimes Muslims said prayers for the
dead and served tea; later misfortune might then be attributed to the fact
that no animal was killed.

4.2 Making an *ehigwasi* by inserting pounded sesame and bits of viscera from a sacrifical animal in a ball of millet food (1993)

A second characteristic is the recognition of kinship relations in respect to the deceased. In the matter of the Sour Beer, Paulo's father gathered his children, his wife, and his sister's son for the ceremony and he sent meat from the sacrifice to people of other divisions within his clan. If the person suffering was a younger man or a woman, he or she would approach the sacrificer of the lineage to make the offering. For example, Abudu Kalim Poya who lived in Busoga, went to his father's brother in Buhabeba to offer two goats and a cock near his parents' graves there. (This was in response to the problems of his children who poured tears into their schoolbooks and fainted in class.) When Eriasa Namunyu brought goats for his dead father and father's brother, after he lost his job with the Eastern Province Bus Company, his father's brother sacrificed on his behalf. In both these cases, a 'mother' of the dead men, clan people from other lineages, and sisters' children were also present.

The third element in these ceremonies for the shades is a particular kind of speech. Holding the cock or the foreleg of the goat, the sacrificer speaks (*ohusaayira*) to the dead. He mentions the names of the shades and refers to the 'huge' animal offered by their 'child'. Sometimes he refers to the reason for the offering, and he asks for blessings of wealth and fertility.

So Poya, Gamusi and Jwala, this child has brought a huge cock. Give him well-being, may he bring many wives, may he beget many children, may they all be in peace. Those who study, may they open their eyes and those who walk with Europeans, may they also continue to study and get very big work. May these homes be filled with respect. Eeeh, here is the huge cock, you drink the blood.

If the person afflicted by the shades is other than the sacrificer, he or she usually speaks over the sacrifice too, asking in a standardized way for prosperity and peace. Once I saw a woman who had provided a goat hesitate uncertainly in her address. Others prompted her with the set phrases always used on these occasions, and she repeated mechanically that she wanted many children and many wives! The act of speaking seemed more important than articulating a clear, personal message. At one ceremony, a deaf mute dedicated his own goat, even though no one could understand the noises he made.

As a strategy against misfortune, shades are relevant to two kinds of uncertainty: about the outcome of affliction and about the social identity of those involved. As a plan of action, they call for the making tangible of blood relationships to the living and the dead through the sharing of meat. Words are spoken aloud to evoke the security of fertility and prosperity. Affiliation to place is asserted through the formalized treatment of the graves and shrines that define a home.

Gendered persons living and dead

Compared to living humans, shades are simple beings. They have names, gender and genealogical placement. They belong to a home and have a right to be respected. But they do not have a life with other shades, purposes, secret motivations, enmities or temperaments. Their desires are predictable. In this sense they are not persons; death has stripped them of the complications that are essentially human. The only trace remaining of their humanity is in the recognition that some shades, like some people, have bad hearts. Yet no attempt is made to guess which particular ones are ill-disposed, for shades are positions rather than personalities. Individual characteristics are not important; only the realization of proper forms matters. The histories of shades are accounts of what steps people have taken in dealing with them: have they been collected from the bush? what offerings have they been given?

That shades are male and female is emphasized in all dealings with them. When they are brought in from the bush, they must be carried by a sister's child of the same sex as themselves. Animal offerings must be of the appropriate sex, and male and female shades are even distinguished in being located at different places in the compound. They are not of equal weight. Male shades are associated with the shrine stones; they have greater permanence. Male ancestors are remembered to a greater genealogical depth than female ones. And male shades are far more apt to be diagnosed as causes of misfortunes, to receive offerings, and to receive the most substantial sacrifices. The great second funeral ceremony is almost always for a dead man, though dead wives are usually included. This is not surprising in a patrilineal society; perhaps the significant point is that female shades *are* represented.

Sometimes dead wives are only mentioned collectively, while men are named individuals, as was the case when the offering was made to Terabana and his wives, who continually soured Paulo's father's beer. But often enough, women are remembered individually too, and not only by their biological children. When Wilber's father offered the bull, he rattled off a litany of names: 'So, the words of the big men, all of you, those of Hyesisa, of Hibulu, of Wasoko, of Wanangulu, of Wabunyi, of Wasahya, of Funa – and of the big women, of Hasahyandalo, of Nemwa, of Wamala, of Kadondi, of Namulwa, all of you – it's you who used to cook here in these homes.' It is as shades that women are finally incorporated into their husbands' lineages; they are remembered there and not in their natal homes. Their own names are mentioned in sacrifice (as opposed to the clan honorifics by which they were addressed in life), and they are spoken daily, because grandchildren are called after them.

Leaving the shades themselves, let us now consider the living actors who take shades to be agents. Shades usually 'address' men, because men have the primary obligation to arrange the second funeral and to sacrifice. The most common pattern by far is for a dead man to afflict his son, demanding the second funeral ceremony. In staging this ceremony a man confirms that he is his father's son in a manner that pleasures hundreds of people. But it is not only his identity as a son that is marked. He is a brother, and father to other members of his lineage, he is a mother's brother to the nieces and nephews who assist at the ceremony, and he is an affine to all the relatives by marriage who attend the celebration. Even simple offerings, of the kind Paulo's father made when his beer went sour, constitute men as descendants and kinsmen.

Yet women too can be afflicted by their dead parents and required to make offerings. As shades, women are mothers, members of their marital homes, but as living victims of misfortune, their identities as daughters are brought into play. In a second funeral ceremony, there is usually an animal contributed by a married daughter, who has been reminded of who she is through misfortune. This was so when Mwing'ula, the old man who offered ropes until he had the right animals for his father's second funeral, finally staged the long delayed event. His brother's daughter, Negiino, was married and lived in Busoga. She herself had been ill, and her cotton, millet, and sweet potatoes were yielding poorly. Finally she went to divine with her husband, and learned that her dead parents wanted to eat. Her husband provided two goats to be killed at the second funeral ceremony – a male for her father and a female for her mother. Negiino stood forward at the ceremony as a daughter, and the meat from her offering was distributed to all her family. Moreover, her husband materially acknowledged the power her parents still had over her by providing the goats.

There is a special ambience at the offerings to shades that has to do with the married daughters coming home together. This also happens at burials, but that is a time of grief, unlike second funeral ceremonies and subsequent sacrifices. When Wilber's father offered the bull after his hospitalization in 1993, his married sisters were there in force. Three of them had brought fowls (understood as acknowledgements from their husbands), which were also offered to their dead grandfather and grandmother. The women were drinking beer and 'white stuff', getting tipsy, laughing, singing, and dancing. At their natal homes, they could be free, informal, and relaxed, in a way that a wife cannot be around her in-laws. For women, this kind of enjoyment and sense of belonging are part of the experiential field of shades as agents. It is particularly important, and I think it is a source of considerable satisfaction to them, that their husbands contribute something on these occasions. By acknowledging their ancestral shades, their husbands indirectly recognize them for who they are. Wives return to their married homes carrying some meat from the sacrificial animal; here, too, meat marks relationships.

The final step in offering a sacrifice to shades is the sharing of the sacramental millet food, the *ehigwasi*, with its stuffing of pounded sesame and bits of viscera from the sacrificial animal. This is the occasion for separating categories of people and declaring who is who. The shades themselves are often divided; at the shrine, or in the courtyard if the ritual is not conducted at a shrine, two holes are dug, one for the shades of dead men, and one for women. Sometimes, another *ehigwasi* is thrown into the bush at the edge of the compound 'for those with bad hearts'. Then each group of kin is given its clump of sacramental food. The sacrificer takes one, bites and spits to each side 'for those with good hearts and for those with bad'; then he eats a mouthful and with both hands 'to show respect', passes the food to another, who does the same. In this way, all agnates share the dedicated food, which the dead have also been given. Sometimes, fathers and sons eat from separate clumps; usually all men of the lineage share. Women are always divided, however; the oldest 'daughter' of the lineage tastes first, and passes the food to her clanswomen. Another *ehigwasi* is provided for 'wives of the clan', in-married women of different clans. In this way, women are defined in terms of their relations to men, as daughters and wives. I have argued (Whyte 1981) that this mode of identification demonstrates the dominance of an androcentric point of view; perhaps the perspective could hardly be otherwise in the key ritual of a patrilineage. Yet I believe that as actors, many women actually welcome the affirmation of their identities as daughters/sisters and wives. Their life situations are framed by these relationships. Women who are able to maintain both have more options in a practical sense and are fuller persons in terms of Nyole meanings and values.

Trying out

When suffering requires urgent action, it may not be possible to acquire an animal and coordinate with kinsmen quickly enough. In such cases, a little ceremony of dedication (*ohusengamo*) is held as a kind of first aid response to the problem. This is a ritual promise to the shades that they will be given what they have demanded if only they will relieve the suffering now. This method of treatment is usually agreed upon during divination, as a number of Nandiriko's cases from 1971 showed.

> I divined a man from Bubinge. He has his children all suffering from sores. I divined him that the dead people, your father and grandfather, want you to perform the second funeral. He asked, 'What should I do if have not yet gotten those (things)?' The dead replied, 'If you have not yet gotten them, go and dedicate a rope in place of a cow.'

Such a 'rope' is plaited of the fibres of a banana tree and dedicated at the ancestral shrine or at the graves of the dead, with words to the effect that this rope will be used to tie the huge bull which the shades will soon eat for the second funeral ceremony. Sometimes, instead of a rope, an animal is dedicated with the promise that if the dead relieve the misfortune, the animal will soon be killed for them.

These gestures follow the Nyole principle of 'trying out' (*ohugeraga*). They provide a test of the idea: the dedication is always conditional: 'If you are the one causing this, then let the person recover and you shall have this huge animal.' The dedication is an inexpensive immediate step and a way of delaying the substantial outlays necessary for the second funeral. 'Trying out' is a hopeful, yet prudent, move that combines convenience with a realistic recognition of the uncertainties involved. The full-scale implementation of the idea is seldom undertaken until future misfortunes remind you of the promise. That is, you may use the occasion of subsequent adversity to pursue security through the affirmation of common descent.

The use of dedication as an immediate response to misfortune may be seen in this account of the events leading up to a second funeral held in early August 1970, related to us by Mwing'ula and his son Hamba, the 'owners' of the ceremony.

Ropes for procrastination

About 1964 Mwing'ula (an elderly man) began to be ill. He and Hamba went to divine a number of times in Bunyole and in neighbouring counties. All of the divinations agreed that the illness was caused by the need to do the second funeral ceremony for Mwing'ula's father and father's brother and to sacrifice for his father's father and his brother. Having no cow for the ceremony, they dedicated ropes at the shrine. Mwing'ula and his wives worked hard on their cotton and earned enough to buy a young bull in 1967. This small bull they also took to the shrine and dedicated, asking the ancestors to give them health and to be patient until the bull should grow huge when it would be killed for the second funeral. But Mwing'ula and his children continued to be ill, so he went to divine again and learned that the shades were requiring two bulls: one for his father and father's brother, and one for his father's father's father, after whom their lineage was called. In 1968 they sold the bull they had dedicated and in the following year, bought two others. In 1970, Mwingula's son, Hamba, went to divine because of sickness in his home, and he was told that the ceremony should be done as soon as possible; the dead were demanding the animals that had been promised to them. A month later, illness again sent Mwing'ula to divine and the need for an immediate second funeral was once more diagnosed. At this time too, the shades indicated the type of music they wanted for the occasion. Mwing'ula went home and again took the animals to the shrine and promised them saying, 'Let me be well, for I am starting the ceremony.' A week later they actually began cutting the beer bananas. It had taken six years, repeated illnesses, trials, and promises before Mwing'ula finally performed the ceremony he felt obligated to do before he himself died.

Second funerals are not actually treatments of misfortune in the same way that curse removals are. They have a *raison d'être* apart from therapy, but there seems to be a tendency to put them off until the shades demand them by sending troubles. (Beidelman (1993: 114) notes that Kaguru too are seldom concerned to propitiate the dead unless they are troubled.) I sometimes wondered if the 'cult of the dead' depended on misfortune, or if misfortune was simply a pretext for doing what people felt they should do. The strong moral obligation to remember your parents abides beyond the vicissitudes of misfortune. There is little doubt about that.

Compared to the other agents of misfortune, shades are more knowable. They are more personal than clan spirits, since they are your own relatives in your own home – familiar in the original sense of the word.

And being dead, they are simpler and more transparent than living relatives. They are also more predictable and more thoroughly domesticated than the clan spirits, who are associated with greater uncertainty and higher drama.

5   The fertility of clanship

Like shades, clan spirits, *ekuni*, are ideas about kinship. As a mode of dealing with adversity and uncertainty, they imply action to affirm clan and affinal obligations. Such action can take the form of sensational ceremonies in which clan spirits manifest themselves for hundreds of people. Their mediums, dressed in skins, are possessed; they go into trance, dance madly, climb trees, and race through fields and bush, pursued by crowds brandishing sticks. Other more modest and common rituals require only a few participants. In all cases, clan spirits as ideas (plans of action) are assertions about fertility, clanship, and marriage. There is no doubt about the significance of these matters. Clanship and exogamous marriage are as fundamental as homes and parents. Yet clan spirits involve more uncertainty than ancestors. They are wilder and more mysterious than shades. And although you are morally bound to them as you are to your ancestors, the nature of your obligations is less clear. There is more room for negotiation, greater latitude for exploration.

In the records kept by Nandiriko in 1970, clan spirits were identified in over 60 of the nearly 200 cases he recorded and in 1993 Luhonda divined them in 13 of the 43 consultations he entered in his journal. About two-thirds of the victims were girls and women affected by the spirits of their own clans, who demanded that they discharge ritual obligations they had as 'daughters of the clan'. In the remaining third of the cases, men were called to take on new roles as mediums or priests – roles that required the staging of great social events. I think this pattern is general; clan spirits affect women more commonly, but men more dramatically.

Clan spirits have long been an important cultural resource in Bunyole; sometimes they are described as the old religion of the time before *ediini*. Earlier written accounts of Nyole culture presented *ekuni* as the most important spirits (Higenyi unpub. MS) or cults (Wesana-Chomi unpub. MS). One scholar discussed them under the heading, 'What Christianity has failed to change', arguing that the Christian God seems abstract to Nyole, while the presence of clan spirits is directly experienced (Nyango unpub. MS: 40). In 1970, educated people suggested that clan spirits were a remnant of Nyole tradition that would disappear with time. Yet in the 1980s, there was a renewed concern with them, and many new mediums were 'caught'. Today there are more than seventy clan spirit mediums in Bunyole; it is estimated that there are thirty in Butaleja sub-county alone. Certainly there are more now than there were in 1970; many have been installed in clans where no one had worn a skin for generations. In the early 1990s clan spirit ceremonies were being announced on the radio, and the Archdeacon of Bunyole remarked that it was easier to collect money for a sacrificial bull than for the work of the church. This is not to say that people have chosen clanship over Christianity and Islam; most people consider themselves both 'readers' and clansmen. But the clan spirits clearly represent enduring themes in Nyole life and identity.

It is not simply that clanship is 'still' important. The Nyole world has been greatly transformed since 1900; clans and their spirits must have a somewhat different significance in so far as they exist in a different context. Perhaps the current interest in clan spirits should be seen as part of the movement of cultural revival appearing in many parts of Uganda. The Ganda campaign for 'their things' (*ebyaffwe*) culminating in the enthronement of the King in 1993 had a modest and egalitarian parallel in Bunyole, as one clan after another initiated mediums for clan spirits.

Kinds of people

Nyole are divided into over 200 patri-clans. Although sons and daughters take the clans of their biological fathers, clanship is categorical rather than segmentary or genealogical. The word for clan, *ehiha*, means kind, sort or species. You cannot be a Nyole without being a kind of Nyole just as a tree has to be some particular type of tree. Nyole speak of 'clans' of motorcars and 'clans' of birds as well as clans or kinds of people. Thus the Lévi-Strauss (1963) insight that clan differences are analogous to differences in nature is obvious to Nyole; the very same word is used for animal and human 'species'. The analogy is reinforced by the fact that each clan has a totem (*omusiro*), sometimes two or three, which it respects (avoids). These totems are mostly animals, but occasionally something quite different is mentioned: things burned accidentally or mud in a kraal after rain, a kind of tree or winnowing tray. The division into 'kinds' provides the conceptual structure of the social world as it does of the natural world. Therefore placing people in clans is the first step in identifying them. When you meet someone you do not know, you must first learn what kind of person he or she is. In talking of history, or neighbourhoods, or marriage, people talk in terms of clans. And in accounting for misfortune, they often speak of clan spirits.

Given the similarity of clans and species, it is paradoxical that the most important aspect of clans is the way in which they are not like species. They are exogamous – you must marry another kind of person than yourself. This is part of the fundamental view Nyole have of the nature of society and themselves as social persons. We were sometimes asked about clans in our own country and, when we said that we did not have them, people wondered how we could marry.

The rule of exogamy is extended to the clans of all four biological grandparents. Members of these clans are called by kinship terms and it is incest (*ehitalo*) to marry them. (Occasionally such marriages do occur; there is said to be a kind of pollution affliction that punishes such a transgression, but as someone remarked in explaining this, 'incest does not always catch you'. It is more common that such wrong marriages are punished by cursing.) When a person dies, payments are made to his or her father's mother's people and mother's mother's people to 'say good-bye to relationship' (*ohusebula oluganda*). Thus the children of the deceased end the relationship; they are able to marry into the clans that are great grandparents to them.

The fact that clanship is associated with marriageability is its most significant aspect for women. A wife is by definition another kind of person in the home of her husband and father-in-law. This is constantly emphasized in daily interaction: men do not usually use their wives' personal names but address and refer to them politely as woman of (*Namu-*) this or that clan: Namulubajo, Namugombe. A woman's clan identity is one of her most explicit characteristics. As if exogamy were constantly on people's tongues, a man's home resounds with the names of other clans.

Many Nyole clans have organized themselves with a president and officers representing the areas from which clansmen come. The Abagombe, for example, have officers for each of the sub-counties in Bunyole, as well as for Busoga, Buganda, Bugwere, and Bugisu, where there are also many clan members. Meetings are occasionally held at which matters of common interest are discussed, such as how much clansmen should contribute to each other's funerals and what ceremonies should be held for the clan spirit. Some clans engage in 'development' efforts: one built a social hall for its members; others have tried to collect money for scholarship funds. These attempts to organize clans along modern lines date from the 1950s and 1960s. Although there is much enthusiasm for the idea, in practice it is difficult to get people to work together for the good of their clan when they are so dispersed and have no property interests in common. In general, clans are social categories rather than social groups. Only the great ceremonies for clan spirits and their mediums mobilize clan members to act as one community. And even these often galvanize sub-divisions rather than the clan as a whole.

Spirits of clanship

Clans have spirits of two kinds. There are spirits that are ideally unique to each clan, and there are a few common spirits that are in every clan. The first are the prototype *ekuni*, which emphasize the distinctiveness of clans. But the term is sometimes also applied to the second type, the common spirits Seja, Walumbo, and Bung'ima, that are linked to clans. As a clan member, you have a permanent tie to your clan spirits; you have obligations to honour them and can be affected by them. By and large, clan spirits affect only members of their own clan; but they also establish relations to women married into the clan.

The general term for spirits (*emisambwa*) is sometimes used of clan spirits, but *ekuni* differ from other spirits in that you are born into a relationship with them, just as you are to ancestors. Thus Nyole speak of them as 'of the home' (*ya ng'ango*), as did the diviner in the case of Somebody's Wife. The unique clan spirits are also called spirits of the forest (*y'edeng'o*) in recognition of their attachment to sacred groves (*engolo*), usually stands of old growth trees or thickets at the base of granite outcroppings.[1]

Unlike ancestors, clan spirits have names that people never bear. They were never living humans ('unless in the ancient times of Olduvai Gorge', as one schoolteacher speculated) so there is no question of lines of descent. You are related to them by virtue of membership in a clan category. In principle, every one of the several hundred Nyole clans has its own specific named *ekuni*: Maliba for the Abagoye clan, Njago for the Abadeera, Hititira for the Abahewe, Hisega for the Abagombe and so on. In practice, clans may have several of these unique spirits, each associated with a sub-division. Sometimes there are two spirits said to be husband and wife. And some clans have spirits with the same names as those of other clans, though they do not celebrate them together and tend to underline their difference. For example, the Abahyuma and Abahagooli clans both claim Bugoya as their clan spirit; but they say that one clan has the female and one the male Bugoya.

A clan spirit of the forest chooses a medium (*omutuusa*) who is the focus of rituals for the spirit; he is marked out in daily activities by wearing a skin instead of clothes. The medium is a man, as are his assistant (*omuhungu*) and the priest/sacrificer (*omusengi*). A woman serves as translator (*omwogesi*), playing a prominent role in the great rituals of possession, and women are also 'wives' or 'princesses' (*abambeja*) of the spirit. In some clans there is more elaboration of 'offices' with 'policemen' (*abaserikale*) to organize people, a 'clerk' (*omutoni*) to keep the skins worn only on the greatest occasions, and a 'mother of twins' (*nabahwana*) to feed the spirit regularly.

In addition to its sacred grove, the spirit has a 'royal home' (*embuga*), a round house in the courtyard of the medium. To the centrepole of this house are tied spears, brought as offerings. Here the spirit's paraphernalia are kept – horns, gourds, clubs. A papyrus partition separates off the part where the spirit itself stays and where it is offered food on its special wooden tray (*eng'ooja*).

Besides these spirits of the forest, there are other spirits 'in clans' by which you may be afflicted and which must be propitiated by a clansman. There is Seja (sometimes known by its Lugwere name Walugono), the spirit of lameness and deformities. Seja has a priest, and in some clans also a medium, though the latter does not wear a skin. It has a shrine at the base of a tree; in the old days, it is said, deformed infants who died were placed in a pot at Seja's tree. Hunchbacks and cripples were often said to be victims of Seja, and efforts to heal them and to prevent lameness among clan members took the form of sacrificing a sheep to Seja. In 1970, lameness from polio was quite common in Bunyole and we attended a clan ceremony in which the clan priest for Seja offered a sheep, allowing its blood to run out on the stones of the shrine and dabbing it on the foreheads of crippled clansmen and young children. Although polio cases are fewer today, there are still shrines and priests for Seja in some clans.

Bung'ima (sometimes called Wima) is 'in clans' too and its shrine house is occasionally seen in courtyards next to those for the ancestors and the *ekuni* of the forest. In 1970, Nandiriko sometimes divined the agency of Bung'ima in the illness of people or cattle; a cow should be dedicated and a bell tied about its neck. This is not a common explanation of misfortune in Bunyole; I suspect that it has come to Nyole from their Luo-speaking neighbours. But it is often mentioned as one of the three spirits that are in many clans; indeed several people explained to me that Wima is the 'parent' of clan spirits.

Walumbo (also called Walumbe) is the most important of these common clan spirits today, as it was in 1970. It has a priest, or several in various sub-divisions of a clan, but no medium. Walumbo is specially associated with discolourations of the skin; it can cause other disorders too, but people often say that Walumbo has put marks on someone (even where these do not seem very evident or serious). Like the 'big clan spirits of the forest', Walumbo claims the daughters of the clan as its wives.[2]

Mediums in trees

For men, the agency of clan spirits is discovered in sicknesses of many kinds: sores, swelling of any part of the body, dizziness, weakness and weight loss, fever, headaches, and unspecified chronic illness. Certain signs such as strange behaviour are taken as specially characteristic and they are likely to be mentioned if clan spirits are considered a cause. A man of Buhabeba who was called to be a priest for Walumbe became thin, climbed trees, and hid himself in the forest. A young man of the Abang'emba clan refused to speak or eat, and he attacked people who came to see him. At Lwamboga, a man who had been sick for several weeks and was admitted to Butaleja health centre, began fainting when he returned home. But when a long drum, of the kind played for clan spirits, was brought to his bedside, he threw off his sheet, took hold of a spear and began to dance. Weird dreams, of being in water, of animals, and especially of snakes, suggest that a man has been caught by a clan spirit.

The medium of Buhyera, an *ekuni* of the Abahabambwe clan, related to us in 1970 how he was afflicted by swelling of the thighs and lameness, and later by a terrible attack of jiggers that covered his whole body. Finally, his toe was broken and had to be set painfully in hospital. It was at the hospital in Mbale that he first had a dream of a long drum being beaten and all of his relatives, together with many other people, dancing and 'running in the bush'. In another dream, his bed sheet was whirled into the air and fell across his shoulder like a skin. Two different divinations revealed that he had been caught by an *ekuni*, but months went by before steps were taken to install him as a medium. As a good Muslim, he tried to pray to Allah to fight against the spirit. But, as one commentator remarked, 'an *ekuni* is also god'; it could not be refused. He began to behave strangely, crying and moaning, 'vomiting out bad words', climbing trees; once he ran into his grandfather's house and climbed the centrepole to the place where spears are kept. Speaking through him, the spirit said that if he was not given a skin to wear, he would be lost forever.

Accepting the call to mediumship is supposed to mean a new identity and a new life. Mediums are the living evidence of clan spirits. As one university graduate, whose father's brother is a medium, remarked, 'They have to look supernatural.' With long hair and fly whisks, clad in a skin fastened over one shoulder, their appearance demonstrates their calling. Their lives also should be distinguished from those of other men by conforming to the rules of mediumship. They do not eat fish, mutton, or pork, and they should not eat 'here and there', in homes where utensils have been used for such food. Nor should they use soap, or sleep in square

5.1 A clan spirit medium in his skin, offering beer (1970)

houses, for example houses with iron roofs. They do not attend mosque or church services; in a sense they stop being 'readers' (followers of a world religion) though some are well educated (one medium with three years of secondary school begged us to bring him books to read). In addition to these general rules, particular clan spirits have their own requirements. Some forbid their mediums to drink moonshine or sodas; others disallow travelling in boats or hate the smell of petrol. To be a medium is exacting, and many find the canons too burdensome. But there are privileges as well; indeed detractors dismiss the new generation of younger mediums with the remark that 'they just want free things'.

Mediums are given generously of food, meat, and drink; occasionally they even receive wives without payment.

Although a principle of equality and equivalence of clans characterizes Bunyole, still there are mediums recognized as preeminent. Their stature is based not on the predominance of their clans, but on their talents as mediums and leaders and on the devotion and support of their clansmen. It seems to have been the case in earlier times as today that certain mediums were recognized as foremost in their areas. From the 1920s until the 1950s or 1960s, the medium of Njago of the Abadera was greatest in the area around Butaleja. Maliba of the Abagoye in north-western Bunyole, who was caught in 1950 and has danced every year since then, is still seen by many as the leader of clan spirit cults in western Bunyole. But others point to Gambisyo Nawuwere, the medium of the Ababeng'o in Budoba, installed in 1975. When a clan that has been without a medium for many years installs one, they pay a goat to the preeminent medium (in western Bunyole either Maliba or Gambisyo) to 'collect' the spirit from where it has been staying at his home. He attends the installation (as do other mediums) and his counsel is sought on matters of protocol.

The most spectacular manifestations of clan spirits are the ceremonies when they possess their mediums and people make offerings to them. These are attended by crowds of clan members, wives, children of clan daughters, and neighbours. There is banana or millet beer, and there is dancing to the long, single membrane *efumbo* drum. And there is always the tension and excitement of possible possession, for clan spirits can catch anyone, lift them up, transform them or throw them to the ground in a trance. Surprises are expected, feared, and hoped for.

The first of the large ceremonies for clan spirits are those for catching and installing new mediums. Sometimes these are arranged in response to the suffering of one individual, whose affliction has been diagnosed as a 'call'. In these cases the ceremony serves to validate the choice already made by the clan spirit and to involve clan members as a congregation. In many other instances, the ceremony is staged in order for the spirit to catch someone and reveal the identity of the true medium. A series of afflictions of various clan members are diagnosed as indicating the spirit's desire to have a medium.

The Abahing'ondo clan organized a ceremony in November 1981 to 'provoke' (*ohutuuya* – to stimulate, animate, encourage) the clan spirit to choose a medium. During the dancing, 'princesses' (*abambeja*) were possessed and the spirit spoke through them saying, 'Our visitor will arrive at 4 o'clock.' When Were Kenneth's mother saw him coming into the courtyard at the appointed hour, she began to weep. He was a secondary school student at a boarding school in Tororo – 'a clever boy and very social' according to one of his schoolmates – and his mother's ambitions for him did not include mediumship in the village. He had been suffering from headaches, which were not alleviated by biomedical treatment. So he had gone home to try other treatment, apparently without knowing that his clan was staging a ceremony at that time. As he describes what happened, he heard the long drum far away, where the crowd had gone to dance. Suddenly he found himself half-naked running towards the sound of the drum, 'just pulled by the spirit'. He danced wildly, and a medium from another clan dressed him in a skin; the crowd followed him as he moved to the homes of clansmen, and finally to the sacred grove. In the weeks that followed, he put aside the skin and tried to go back to school, but his head was confused and unclear, and he finally dropped out to accept his calling.

Sometimes, the 'provocation' of a clan spirit is a protracted affair. A friend told that in her clan they danced for three weeks before a medium was finally chosen. 'People use medicine to try to pull the spirit to their own sons and away from the natural medium.' She was convinced that many parents, unlike Were's mother, saw mediumship as a prize to be obtained for their own lineage.

Once a medium has been chosen and dressed in a skin, an animal is sacrificed, usually a bull, according to the wishes of the spirit as expressed through possession or divination. All clansmen should contribute towards this animal, just as the dancing and the construction of the spirit's house should be common endeavours. And this is only the beginning, for dancing and sacrifices are supposed to occur regularly. One of the common complaints of mediums is that their clansmen do not back them up by providing the sacrificial animals for two other ceremonies that should be done annually.

One of these is the first fruits ritual for the new millet, called *ohwesirula* (or *ohwahira obusima obunyaha*). In principle, no senior clansman should eat new millet until a sacrifice of a goat or bull has been made by the clan priest. Although this can be done even when there is no medium, all eight of the mediums interviewed systematically mentioned first fruits as one of their important rituals. Beer is prepared and there is music and dancing; sometimes the clan spirit possesses its medium or other clansmen. (In 1992, a young medium told an interviewer how his clan spirit had possessed a white man many years ago. We realized that the story referred to Michael, who had been among the dancers at a first fruits ceremony held by the Abagombe in 1971!) In practice, most clans do not stage *ohwesirula* every year. People make do with *ohudanyira*, a family affair in which the senior man offers a cock in thanks for the millet harvest. For some mediums, this is no substitute, and they do not eat millet because their clansmen have not organized a proper first fruits ritual.

The other necessary ceremony is simply called dancing (*ohuhina* or *ohwebegula*) or 'grazing on leaves' (*ohwaya ekoola*), alluding to the way the medium goes into the bush and up into trees, eating leaves like an animal. This great spectacle is the culmination of mediumship, when the spirit incorporates the man in a display that is both wild and controlled by the framework of the ritual. The performance of this event is a declaration of the seriousness with which the medium and his clan are committed to their spirit.

A medium who has been chosen in the dancing of 'provocation' and has a skin may not 'graze on leaves' until he has presented his mother's brothers with a bull 'of nephewship'. They cut his hair and give him a burial sheet. Symbolically he dies in order that he can embody the spirit. When a medium dies in fact, there is not supposed to be any mourning, but only dancing in which other mediums join.[3] No claim can be made by the dead man's maternal uncles, for they have already received their share.

The day for 'grazing on leaves' is fixed well in advance to enable the collection of money for the sacrificial animals, the preparation of large quantities of beer, and the assembly of clansmen from near and far. Nowadays, the radio is even used to announce such events. The dancing begins in the morning, at the home of the medium, where people have spent the night drinking.

'My animal in the forest'

In November 1992, we gathered at the home of Yafesi Hire, the medium of Buhyeera of the Abahabambwe clan. About fifty men and women were assembled there, many carrying sticks or spears which they brandished in the way Nyole call *ohusooma*. The medium danced briefly in his own compound and in that of his father nearby, his face expressionless, as women ululated, a couple of men blew on horns, and the *efumbo* drummer warmed up for the long day. Three mediums from other clans danced near him; later others joined us so that there were six by the time we reached the sacred grove.

Although the events of this day are called 'dancing', they might better be termed 'moving', for the medium and his crowd cover 10 to 20 miles before sundown. Each medium has points he must pass on his way to his sacred grove: a river, particular granite outcroppings, the homes of living or dead clansmen. The company hurry along behind their medium, stopping to dance in fields, at homes, at a marketplace where others join the excitement. The princesses/wives (*abambeja*) mop his face and give him water and banana beer from the gourds they carry. Others attend to the drummer, dripping with sweat from the exertion of playing and dragging his long drum over so many miles. Suddenly, the medium breaks away from the crowd and dashes madly across fields and bush (*ohubwaga amagoola*–to break the bush). People shout and chase after him, as if he were an animal (Whyte and Whyte 1987: 106–8). Sometimes the crowd tramples across planted fields; but those crops are never spoiled, I was told, for there is always a plentiful harvest where the clan spirit has passed.

When Yafesi Hire danced in 1992, he moved first to the home of the 'clerk', the clansman who kept the leopard skin used only for this occasion. The skin hung on a branch of the barkcloth tree planted at the shrine for the spirit. As people crowded close, many were possessed. Women swooned and were caught as they started to fall. All the mediums were in trance; one stared and whuffed like an animal, loudly and repeatedly. Yafesi's eyes rolled back and I thought he would fall, but another man came and put his arms around him. As he stood on the stone at the base of the tree, the crowd opened a passageway so that the 'clerk' could hand him a spear and help him into the leopard skin. He danced back and forth and then leapt up into the tree where he shook the branches, realizing the image people always mention of spirits/men who climb trees and 'dance on the leaves'.

In the midday sun, the medium and the crowd journeyed three hours to the sacred grove of the Abahabambwe clan. By the time we reached the place, the goat was practically dead of exhaustion, having been pulled, dragged, and finally carried upside down by its legs in the last mad rush into the forest. In a clearing, about 200 people pressed close together. The spirit/man lay motionless at the base of a great *omusende* tree; completely covered by his leopard skin, he looked like a fallen animal. The congregation, and by now they were indeed a congregation, sang a refrain confirming this impression:

> I have my fierce animal
> I have my animal coming
> I have my animal in the forest

Near the tree, some people danced vigorously; others stood staring, swinging their arms and twisting their torsos from side to side. They began to swoon and fall into a heap beside the tree until nine women and three men lay completely still, eyes closed, sprawled over one another.

The spirit/man rose and stood with his back in the hollow of the tree, holding his spear upright. His face was strained with exhaustion; dried saliva caked the corners of his mouth. Occasionally he staggered back against the tree, and then drew himself up straight again to address the crowd with authority. When he spoke, his voice was forced and a pitch higher than normal: 'Abahabambwe,' he addressed his clan. 'Your worship!' (*Musengwa!*) they replied. 'I'm happy to be with you. I am great and none other will be respected as I am. You must give me a goat and a cock and a hen.' The congregation sat quietly, listening, and responding when questioned. 'The Abahabambwe are one, they are united,' intoned the spirit/man, touching a sensitive point. He asked for people from different parts of Bunyole to show their hands. We all knew that there were several other mediums for Buhyeera; few people had come from Bingo, the neighbourhood of Daka, a rival medium, whom I had seen possessed by Buhyeera twenty-one years previously.

But now the spirit was embodied before us, and people waited attentively for word of the year to come and the blessings for which they might hope. 'Abahabambwe, go and give birth, deliver twins. May your children study and grow rich. Cultivate and you will get food. May you have peace.' The 'policeman' of the spirit asked if anyone wanted to put questions; one man asked why he did not have children and another wondered why his money never lasted. The spirit/man directed both to visit him at home.[4] When at last he finished speaking, the 'clerk' removed the leopard skin and dressed him in his ordinary hide again. He sat down on the root of the tree, took a long draught of banana beer and received the greetings of his fellow mediums, who shook his hand and welcomed him back.

The priest, squatting farther back among the trees, held the foreleg of the tired goat and dedicated it to the spirit, for the sake of fertility and prosperity. Its throat was cut by a Muslim and people began to prepare fires for roasting it on the spot. This sacrifice in the sacred grove was only the first step, however. The more important offering, the bull, which had been bought by clan contributions, was waiting at home, to be slaughtered there. An *ekuni* is a spirit of the home as well as of the forest.

Brides of spirits

In mediumship and in the great clan ceremonies, the wild and the fertility of the fields are important themes. Clan spirits are also weighted with another significance and that is marriage. As exogamous units, clans are marriage categories; as terms of practice, *ekuni* imply assertions about affinity. This happens during the possession ceremonies when jokes and excitement hang on the possibility that the clan spirit will 'catch' a wife for the medium among the spectators (Whyte and Whyte 1987: 111–14). But the 'marital' interest of the clan spirit is not limited to the marriage prospects of its medium. The *ekuni* are concerned with the marriages of all men and women of the clan.

If a woman left her husband, it was said, he could go to the priest of the *ekuni* who could implore the spirit to bring her back. We were present (with a tape recorder) in August 1970, when such an unwilling wife had been forced to bring an offering to the spirit of her (ex-)husband's clan. The priest for the spirit (himself the most married man we knew – with eight current wives) dwelt in his invocation to the spirit upon the power it had over wives:

> Let the women who have left this home return. May they come on their knees. Let others come walking and crying for you. Again, you follow them, spirit, follow them that they may come back, let them come back . . . lines of wives, all of them.

Later in the address, the priest spoke of how Tabora, the *ekuni*, would cause wives who left their husbands to become thin or suffer from sores. If they did not heed such warnings, the spirit might even kill them. For it is really Tabora, the source of clansmen's prosperity, that supplies the bridewealth. (At this, the listening clansmen murmured yes, yes.) In leaving their husbands, wives 'spoil the bridewealth of Tabora' and therefore he punishes them.

The priest said, in effect, that all wives of clansmen were brought by the *ekuni*, and that it would enforce its rights over them by making them suffer if they, as he said of one such woman, smear the *ekuni* with dirt by leaving the clan into which they married. Just as the spirit catches wives for itself when its medium dances, so it also provides wives for all clansmen – and takes steps to keep them. In this example, *ekuni* seem to represent the principle of clan exogamy. But they go against that principle in claiming clan daughters as well.

Evidence about this aspect of the bridal interests of *ekuni* comes from the records of consultations kept by diviners. Nandiriko, the gourd rattle diviner, wrote on 4 January 1971:

> I divined for two people, a man and a woman, from Bingo. (I said that) . . . you've come to divine because of a sick person, a girl. She's suffering in the leg, she has an ulcerating sore. They replied: true, but we want to know the reason that brought that sore. The divining spirit told them: at your home you have your *ekuni*, they call it Hititira. That's what put a sore upon this girl. It claims that (she) is its wife and it wants you to come give it a he-goat and a cock. And before this girl goes to be married, her husband must bring a cock and a spear.

Even more common were cases of married women who were declared to be the wives of their clan spirits. Again and again husbands who came to inquire were told 'your wife is the wife of Njago' or 'your wife is the wife of Malema'. Of a woman suffering from a 'sickness that makes the body thin and the head dizzy', the diviner said: 'The *ekuni* of the forest, called Namasiiro, who comes from her home, says she is its wife.'

In all these cases, the spirits require that a woman offer tribute (*ohung'onga*). She must travel to the 'royal dwelling' (*embuga*) at the home of the medium or priest, or to her father or the senior man who can offer on her behalf. Carrying a spear and a rough grass basket with a chicken or two, or pulling a goat, all according to the demands of the spirit, she enters the house and, without a word, drives the spear into the ground next to the centrepole. Her clansman takes the chicken and addresses the spirit:

> Perhaps it is you who put coldness (illness) upon this child. You leave her, let her be well. She has brought our great spear and our huge chicken – here they are. Your wife has brought us the things you have been asking for.

The spear is tied to the centrepole and when a goat is offered, its skin is dried and spread upon the floor of the spirit's house.

Cooking for Walumbe

Tom brought his new wife Aida home in February 1993 and she fell sick after only two weeks. The Panadol and Hedex tablets he bought at the shops did nothing to relieve her stomach pain and headache. It was only when her grandfather came to visit the 16-year-old bride that she felt better. But the splotch of discoloured skin on her neck remained, confirming what Tom and his father had been told at the time they 'cut' the bridewealth: that in her family all the daughters were supposed to cook for Walumbe before they married. There was no need to 'get hold of a divining fee'; the sign was clear and her grandfather reminded them what to bring – a he-goat, a cow's hoof, entrails, bananas, millet flour, and sesame – the standard ingredients for Walumbe's meal. As one of the clan spirits common to all clans, Walumbe and its culinary requirements are familiar to most people.

We were a party of five going to the in-laws: the newlyweds and their 'messenger' (*wakwenda*) and Tom's father's sister and myself, his adopted father's sister. We approached the house with a ululation and a refrain: 'We come begging [life] . . . ' (*Hwegayirire . . .*) They seated us in the two-doored house of the ancestors; as an in-law I should have stayed there with my sister and my son Tom, but I pleaded curiosity and followed Aida out to the 'royal place' in the banana plantation where they had built three small shrine houses (*ebirolero*) at the base of a majestic old fig tree.

Aida's father's father (the same grandfather who visited her) was the priest/sacrificer and he explained that although we were 'cooking for Walumbe', there were in fact three spirits involved. One shrine was for Walumbe, the main spirit in this matter, to whom the goat is offered. Another was for Hitambogwe, who 'follows' Walumbe and would be given the 'cow' (represented by a shin and hoof, bought from the butcher in Busolwe) 'since it does not eat goat'. Wagolokoka was honoured in the last shrine house; it 'follows' Hitambogwe and would be given a fowl ('which it shares with Walumbe'). The old man dedicated each offering in turn, at the relevant shrine:

> So, the words of Walumbe – I take hold of this great goat which my 'co-husband' (*musangi*) has brought to you to pay the debt for the wife who was just taken without paying the fee of a huge goat. Now he has brought the big goat and I want this girl to live long. Let her be free from cold in her owner's courtyard. Let her change appearance [get pregnant]. She went as a child; tomorrow and again, may this girl be changed to a woman. Tomorrow I wish that she may have a child on her body. Everyone should see her as an example of the happiness that comes from the courtyard of the Abayanja [their clan]. They'll say: oh, if you're without family, go and marry from the Abayanja. This is your huge goat. Be eating it slowly and peacefully. Don't feel any headache.

Tapping the hoof in the next little shrine house, the grandfather addressed the other spirit:

> Hitambogwe, your huge cow is here. Walumbe eats a great goat; you too, you eat this big cow. Give this girl child a long harmonious life. May she have good fortune. May she go on hatching male and female in her owner's courtyard where she's staying – so she won't shame us by passing about alone without a child, feeling cold in someone's home. So from today, may this girl grow calm and peaceful in that courtyard. Let her go on striking two and two [delivering twins]. Today and tomorrow, may she drag her swollen-sided belly. Let peace be there on the other side and may the poverty which you brought this boy leave him.

Hearths were prepared there in the banana plantation, and the whole family worked 'to cook for Walumbe'. Aida's little sister fried sesame, while other sisters stirred the huge pot of millet food, overseen by their mother. Brothers butchered the goat, tying up the skin to place it in Walumbe's shrine. Her father seared and split the hoof and shin, while her grandfather supervised everyone. Only Aida, who should have been a key cook, was not allowed to participate 'because she made a mistake in not cooking for Walumbe before marriage'. She sat against a banana tree, holding a child on her lap, watching, talking quietly with the family she had recently left, enjoying being home again.

When the food was ready, the in-laws were served, seated on the ground at the edge of the plantation. Aida ate with us, some of each kind of food, including pounded sesame. Then the 'newlyweds' and their 'messenger' were called to kneel at Walumbe's shrine so the grandfather could 'bid farewell' to Walumbe. His speech touched the same points as before: the great goat had been paid, they wanted peace and health, and, he added, plentiful harvests. In case there should be any doubt, he ended with plain talk to the spirits:

> Me, I'm telling you goodbye in this royal place. And never come back again. Don't complain that they made a mistake here in this chiefly place. Our friend is begging you to release his wife . . . may this girl child go well with her husband, since he has paid you the fee.

And so we took our leave, as the women of Aida's family sang and ululated.

Cooking for Walumbe acknowledges the claims of a woman's clan upon her. It provides an opportunity for her to go home and for her husband to pay a supplement to the bridewealth that is enjoyed immediately in a family feast. As a clan spirit, Walumbe is concerned with marriage and the problems of exogamy. Once a couple of women, relaxing with some glasses of banana beer, suggested to me that clan spirits affect even the intimacies of marriage. 'Walumbe and the *ekuni* of the forest – they make you not want your husband.' The younger woman cleared any possible doubt: 'You don't want your husband to come here,' she said frankly, placing her hand between my knees. This is not to say that Walumbe is necessarily associated with frigidity, but rather, I think, that it, like the other clan spirits, serves to objectify an aspect of women's personhood. As clan daughters and sisters, their sexuality/fertility is rooted in one space and realized in another, that of their married home. They have two sets of 'owners'; Aida's grandfather spoke of her in her 'owner's courtyard' referring to her husband and his family; but they in turn, by cooking for Walumbe, were recognizing that she belonged to her own clan. These double claims are reflected in women's situational assertions of one or another aspect of their identities. Their desires and their interests lie in both places and Walumbe ensures that husbands remember this.

5.2 The sister of a new bride cooking for Walumbe on
her behalf (1993)

Domestic and wild fertility

Since clans are exogamous units, and one of their basic characteristics is
the delimitation of marriage categories, it is not surprising that clan spirits
are concerned with marriage. But it is noteworthy that here marriage is
not construed as a matter of alliances, bridewealth, or claims by individual men, as it is when terms of sorcery and cursing are used. In terms of
clan spirits, marriage is about the sources, control, and acquisition of

fertility. As the ceremony for Walumbe showed, clan spirits are represented as wellsprings of fecundity. Aida's grandfather called for abundant, animal-like propagation: she should produce as a hen hatches chicks; she should drop twins like a nanny goat; her belly should swell so that she would have to drag it. A man marries wanting children; this was especially pressing in Tom's case, which was termed a matter of 'poverty' (obutahi) since his other wife was barren, and he was his father's only son. The source of wealth and happiness is the courtyard of another clan and the prayer to Walumbe suggests that the fertility of a woman is an aspect of her clanship. Her fathers and brothers and grandfathers are instrumental in the ritual work of recognizing this, but it is the spirit itself that is the source of fruitfulness.

For men the problem of fertility is solved by attracting and keeping wives, but, as we saw in chapter 2, this indirectly involves sisters and daughters. By affirming its hold on clan daughters, the clan spirit asserts rights to those who can be exchanged for wives. From this point of view it is not at all paradoxical that clan spirits claim both women from their own clans and women from others. The simple arithmetic of marriage in Bunyole requires that men have rights in daughters and sisters in order to obtain wives.

Clan spirits concern themselves directly with men's desire for wives when they catch women from other clans for the medium. More generally, they are associated with the ability of all clansmen to pull women (olubang'iso). Thus, when the Abalwa recently prepared a ceremony for their clan spirit, the consulting medium Maliba instructed the boys of the clan to pat medicine on the right sides of their chests to enable them to 'seduce girls' (ohuhobya abahaana).

In the terms of clan spirits, the reproduction of people is associated with other aspects of fertility. Agricultural abundance is celebrated in the first fruits ceremony of thanksgiving for the new millet. Even though this ritual is honoured more in its omission than in its actual performance, the fact that it is considered a clan spirit affair indicates the link between ekuni and the success of food production. When the spirit speaks through its medium in the sacred grove, it speaks of cultivation and the prospects of good harvests. Older people whom I asked about this said that the spirits sometimes talk of rain as well. As the medium of the Ababeng'o summed it up: 'These spirits are the big religion of Bunyole for through them we get food.'

Fertility is not only a matter of wombs and hoes, however. The cult of clan spirits links procreation and farming with animals and natural features of the landscape. The Nyole scholar Wesana-Chomi has written that the ekuni were gods associated with animals; and animal imagery is evident in several respects. The spirit itself takes the form of an animal when the medium is clad in a leopard skin during the ceremony of 'grazing on leaves'. Indeed, one man stated baldly that clan spirits are leopards. They climb trees like wild things and dash through the bush, with people in pursuit holding spears and sticks as if they were hunting them.[5] Finally, it lies in the sacred grove and then is transformed from a frenzied animal to a spirit concerned with its clan. Someone once told us explicitly that people sacrifice 'to cool down the wildness of the *ekuni*'. In daily life, mediums wear the skins of wild animals. Snakes are associated with clan spirits: they frequent the sacred groves and shrines, and they come around the 'royal houses'. When Maliba arranged for the Abalwa to bring their spirit back from where it had been staying at his home, he said he knew they expected to see a snake in the basket. Most of the mediums I talked to had either dreamed of or interacted with snakes in some unusual way.[6] In Nyole cosmology, only clan spirits have a characteristic affinity with wild animals. Shades of the dead and other types of spirits are interested in domestic ones.

Inanimate features of the environment figure in the cult of clan spirits as well. They have an affinity with trees and forests, rivers, and great rocks. Certain kinds of sorcery and also some of the 'little spirits' are associated with 'the bush', which is also a source of powerful medicines. But clan spirits particularize landscape; it is not just 'bush' in contrast to domestic and cultivated space. The environment is marked as containing specific meaningful features; it has places rather than being a space. Perhaps there was once a time when clan spirits had to do with claims to territory. With the multiplication and dispersion of clans, living intermixed with one another, this has certainly not been relevant for generations. Population increase is gnawing away the remaining patches of forest in Bunyole. The planting of swamps to rice has destroyed the last refuges of wild animals; hunting is virtually a thing of the past. Yet still the imagery of animals, trees, and topography remains a vivid mode of communicating notions of clanship and fertility.[7]

The *ekuni* are seen as a source of fertility in a comprehensive sense, blessing the clan as a whole with success in hunting, farming, marrying, and procreation. Prosperity today involves less hunting and more education, chasing resources in Kampala and Europe rather than waterbucks in swamps. For many people, clan spirits are relevant to that kind of fruitfulness as well.

When the Abagombe met in early 1993 to discuss their clan affairs, they spoke of the need for clan unity and development. The president of the clan displayed the rubber stamp he had had made in Kampala so that they could print the words 'Abagombe love one another' (*Bagombe Hwen-*

dane) on letters and records of clan affairs. One speaker bemoaned the fact that the clan lacked doctors, engineers, professors, and university graduates. The clan needed to work together in order to educate the children and thus achieve development. Another took up the thread: 'We have to settle the business of the medium before we can discuss development. Children studying get disturbed by the clan spirit because the ceremonies haven't been done. We should do them so that our children can study in peace.' A man sitting nearby whispered to me in English: 'Sometimes your child is sick and you try the hospital and it doesn't help, because culturally you haven't finished those things.' People were using the framework of clanship to talk about progress and prosperity. Organizing to undertake their obligations to the clan spirit was proposed as the necessary foundation for development.

Possibilities and doubts

Although clan spirits carry these shared meanings about fertility and prosperity, ambiguity and doubt often attend the working out of the idea of clan spirits in specific cases. Most Nyole know the name of their clan spirit of the forest and people who live in Bunyole are aware of the ceremonies and mediums, if only because they see men wearing skins. Many clans do not have a currently active medium, however, and in others there is debate and uncertainty about the demands of clan spirits, the commitment of mediums and the holding of rituals.

The politics of clan unity and divisions are reflected in the fact that clans often have several clan spirits of the forest or several mediums for the same spirit, associated with different sub-divisions and geographical areas. When the Abagombe met in 1993, more than a hundred strong, to consider the situation of their clan, they discussed the medium problem. There were three known clan spirits, of which Hisega was the most widely recognized. A medium of Hisega, wearing a skin, attended the meeting; but there was no consensus about his status. People knew that other mediums had been caught – among Abagombe living in Bugisu, in Budoba, and in Musitu. The medium from Doho, who was present, had apparently been installed at a ceremony in which only clansmen from his area participated. Now representatives of Abagombe from Buganda, Busoga, Bugwere, and many parts of Bunyole spoke of the need to find the 'true medium'. The majority wanted agreement on one clan spirit and one medium. They planned to hold a ceremony at which Hisega would reveal its choice by convincing possession. As one speaker put it: 'Let them all come to dance. It'll be like a job interview and we'll get one medium.' In the outpouring of support for clan unity, only one voice spoke for pluralism: 'There are many clergymen for each religion. Why shouldn't mediums be many too?'

The question of who is a true medium depends on the consensus of clansmen, but that consensus is created and the explanatory idiom frames the discussion in terms of the agency of the clan spirit. People must find out what the spirit wants. In 1992, people of the Abalwa clan gathered in Yolamu Biro's home at Lubanga to 'provoke' their clan spirit Nahiriga.[8] Many homes had been disturbed, they said; two men from Busoga had had such serious problems that they had contributed a bull so that the ceremony could be held. More than twenty clanspeople from Busoga were there and fifty to a hundred others, of several lineages. They collected their spirit from Maliba's home and danced for two days and nights to the long drum; 'princesses' were possessed but no medium. Maliba, who attended as consultant and preeminent medium, was critical of the Abalwa. They had not prepared the ceremony properly by going to divine well in advance to find out what their clan spirit really wanted. The spirit was displeased because the bull had not been provided by the clan as a whole.

Even when clan spirits possess men convincingly, they do not always keep them as mediums. Nyole say that sometimes the spirit 'does not catch well'; reasons for this can be that the clansmen do not organize the expected ceremonies or that the character and behaviour of the medium are unsatisfactory to the spirit. In 1971 one of our assistants wrote a brief report about a man of Lwamboga who had been gravely ill. They divined the clan spirit and he offered two goats in the sacred grove. He wore a skin for four months, but then the spirit left him and caught someone else who also wore the skin for a few months. The spirit left this second medium also. 'Both of those men were witches – they went out at night. They used soap too. So the spirit left because it didn't like that.'

Being a medium involves a long and demanding commitment by the man, and also, Nyole say, by the spirit. Mediumship is a process that can unfold persuasively or fade away over the years. Sickness, strange behaviour, odd dreams, and other misfortunes affecting the medium or his family are interpreted as expressions of the spirit's wishes. Or in some cases they are interpreted in other ways or ignored, thus refusing involvement with clan spirits. When we met our friend Hamba in 1969, he was wearing a skin as medium for his clan the Abasimba. He was also a trained carpenter, who got good jobs as Busolwe developed in the 1970s. His clan never managed to stage a big ceremony for him and, by the time we left Bunyole in 1971, he had moved from wearing a James Bond 007 belt over his skin to wearing a leather jacket instead. He has not dressed in his skin for more than twenty years now, though his nickname – Hyanjo, meaning skin – alludes to a possibility that he, his spirit, and his clan declined.

Mediums are an obvious and relatively public example of the uncertainty that can attend the agency of clan spirits. Every time someone refers to Hamba as Hyanjo, he reminds others of the indeterminacy of the relations between men and clan spirits. It is true as Nyango wrote that clan spirits are directly experienced; they can embody people, climb trees, and speak in the forest. But for the most part, they are potentials, not actual presences. That is, actors have to decide whether they are present and what if anything should be done about them. This is so regarding mediumship, and it is even more true when the agency of clan spirits is suspected in other connections.

Recall that in the divination for Somebody's Wife, the sick woman was said to be affected by her clan spirit, which her previous husband had ignored. Even the current husband neglected to do anything in that matter. Perhaps he would have acted differently if he had paid some bridewealth and were more fully committed to demonstrating his concern for his new wife and establishing good relations with her family. By contrast, when we went with Tom and Aida to cook for Walumbe, Tom's father had made very clear to me that he wanted everything in order with Aida's family, and her clan spirit, so that she would stay and bear children in their home. He had struggled to accumulate some bridewealth for them, and they had received it and him graciously. Thus actors' assessments of their situation and their evaluations and priorities help determine whether a clan spirit is accepted as agent and honoured as required. Here too, however, our efforts to control life were unavailing; Aida left Tom a few months later and her father returned the bridewealth.

Any misfortune is liable to multiple interpretations and there is always speculation and sometimes differences of opinion among family, neighbours and local gossips. Matters of material interest and reputation may be at stake, as when Daka's mother referred to the 'princesses' caught when he was dancing. She declared they were sickly and must come to offer an animal at the 'royal dwelling' in their courtyard. More recently I have heard clan spirits mentioned in connection with several cases of presumed AIDS. Family members stress the agents behind suffering, while others callously point to the symptoms and prognosis.

Susa had family connections to two spirit mediums. A clan spirit had caught her as a bride for one, whom she later left. At the same time, one of her brothers was a medium and she was considered a 'princess' of her own clan spirit. When she fell ill, she came home to be cared for by her family. At the time when the medium went to dance, the clansmen encouraged her to sit with the other 'princesses' on the goatskins in the 'royal dwelling'. One account had it that she became worse then and suffered a dreadful bout of diarrhoea, soiling the goatskins; the spirit was reminding her that she had neglected it in recent years when she had become very Christian. When I visited the home, I inquired of her from her sister-in-law, who was busy trying to keep the household running, while everyone else was drinking and dancing and the spirit was 'grazing on leaves'. 'Oh yes, they say it's the *ekuni*,' remarked this woman pointedly, 'but in fact she has grown slim', implying that she had AIDS. Others said that one of her ex-husbands had paid two cows which were not refunded when she left him. 'So he just kept quiet', and now they suspect that this man may have used medicine on her. Then there was the matter of the family whose enmity she had earned by reporting them to the police; they too could be agents causing her affliction. Her brother said there were 'so many things' – she could not be cured. The clan spirit was among those many things, but to say that Nyole believe clan spirits cause AIDS would be a misunderstanding. The clan spirit was a possible agent and people hoped that treating her as a 'princess' might help her. In the same way, the family of another man, who came home from town fatally ill, remembered that he had set fire to the shrine of his clan spirit. They tried to sacrifice on his behalf, even though he himself said that he knew he had 'this sickness of ours'. Others spoke of possible sorcerers and their motives. The clan spirit was there – perhaps – but in the end, people doubted that the *ekuni* was the cause of his death.

In 1996, I was back in Bunyole talking to a man whose brother, an ex-teacher, was suffering from epilepsy and generally considered dangerous and mad. I had heard that the sick man had been the victim of sorcery worked by his fellow teachers because they were envious that he was promoted to deputy headmaster. I asked whether sorcery, or perhaps a curse, had driven him mad.

> A curse can make a person leave teaching and live for 'white stuff' – like the drunkard you met last week, who used to be a teacher. He's cursed. For the case of sorcery, someone can become mad, but not wild like my brother. His case is different. Our parents think it's the *ekuni*. We're going to try a third time to find out if it's true or not. Maybe it is. But we doubt. They're going to try. It's always like this. Long ago in the 1970s they did a ceremony for the *ekuni*. Then in 1984, they did the ceremony again. They made a house and put there [the spirit's] things. There was a priest (*omusengi*) but later he got saved and burned the house and all the things. Now they want to do another ceremony and find a new priest. Of course, my brother can't be the priest because his head is spoiled. He's sick and can't do the work. It needs a healthy man. But my brother, he's an easy person (*mutu mwangu*); the *ekuni* possesses him more quickly than others. Partly it's the *ekuni* and we're preparing to do something about it to see if it's true. We're just trying – we're not sure if we'll

succeed. Some of us think it's the *ekuni* because when he sleeps after a fit, he makes a noise like an animal – a leopard.

Notice the way that doubt, hope, and reservation are combined in these plans. The concerned brother had taken evidence – the burned out spirit house, the wild behaviour, the whuffing sound made in a deep postictal sleep. The family had an idea that formed a plan of action. There was a chance – they had to try. The ceremony needed to be done anyway. Perhaps my interlocutor would have liked to believe that his brother's seizures were like possession trance. Yet he did not have illusions that his brother would be cured by becoming a priest or medium. Still . . . maybe . . . If not the clan spirit, then certainly the spirit of subjunctivity was at work.

6   Little spirits and child survival

'Mukama and Omuhyeeno are like the wind.' The word the healer used, *embeng'o*, also means cold or chill, and by extension, sickness. 'At the hospital, they can't see these spirits. So the parents have to bring their children here for treatment. To cure these troubles you have to know how to catch the air.' Clan spirits and shades are invisible too, but the wind analogy is particularly apt for the miscellaneous group of little spirits that have no fixed abode and no kinship connection. The *obusambwa*, 'little spirits' (the word is the diminutive form of the general term for spirits), are minor in relation to the clan spirits, and they have a particular affinity for children and women, minors too. There is a randomness about little spirits; unlike the spirits of kinship they have no lasting moral claims upon you; they simply strike and cause suffering – for no other reasons than simple stereotype desires. Nor are they sources of blessing and well-being like shades and clan spirits.

In this chapter, I place these small spirits in relation to the uncertainties of child health and the situations of worried mothers. High child mortality and the keen interest of parents in a wealth of children, as described in chapter 2, provide the immediate context for little spirits. I shall suggest that the idea of little spirits takes everyday experiences of women as relevant for action. In little spirit terms security is pursued through hiring a specialist rather than enacting kinship rituals as people do in connection with shades and clan spirits.

Omuhyeeno – the wrongfully murdered

Omuhyeeno is the spirit of someone killed unjustly, sometimes mistakenly, by a relative or someone who should have cared for them. In retaliation, it brings death to the descendants of the murderers, to their clansmen down through the generations, and to the children of the clan daughters, that is, the nieces and nephews of the clan. People always speak of Omuhyeeno as originating from the 'side' of the mother or of the father. Although either is possible, in the great majority of the cases in my records, Omuhyeeno was said to come from the mother's side. However, Omuhyeeno is not identified as an historical individual with a personal name; some dramatic details may emerge, as in the case of the hungry thief below, but one never knows when the murder happened, nor exactly who committed it.

Omuhyeeno is usually said to affect young children.[1] People trained in biomedicine translate the term as tetanus or fever convulsions, because clenching the body and convulsing (*ohwesinduha*) are often taken as indications of Omuhyeeno. One specialist explained that the child's body is hot, though the legs may be cold. However, Omuhyeeno can be diagnosed even in the absence of these symptoms. A nurse told of her stepchild, who developed severe diarrhoea, was admitted to the hospital and put on intravenous fluid.

> The child began to improve and spoke to me. Then suddenly it grabbed me – its eyes followed something across the ceiling, as if seeing something I couldn't see. It went unconscious and died. People in our neighborhood went to 'witchdoctors' and were told it was Omuhyeeno. My husband didn't believe it. But when we went to see the child's mother, she said yes, there was an Omuhyeeno there, of someone who had been killed and had declared that no nephew will survive. So many children have died.

The suddenness of a child's death seems to be significant in Omuhyeeno. As one healer said, 'Omuhyeeno is not like Slim – it finishes a person off in two days; it never lasts long.'

Many young children in Bunyole wear amulets (*amang'irisi* or *ebigemo*) – tied around their necks, waists, wrists, on their backs, or over one shoulder and under the opposite arm. The most common reason for these is to prevent Omuhyeeno (*ohuhingirisa Omuhyeeno*) and they are made in various designs by diviners or healers specializing in little spirits. Wasige, of Musitu, ties one around the child's neck so that it hangs in front; this one contains powdered roots. Another one is tied on the child's back; that one holds two pairs of small sticks (*ebihwi* – pieces of root). One pair is for the Omuhyeeno from the child's home (that is, from the father's side) and the other is for that from the in-laws, the side of the child's mother. Wasige says that the little one must not see the amulet on its back, for that is where the Omuhyeeno is. When the child is old enough to know that it has something on the back, the amulet should be removed and tied on the next child.

These amulets are so much a sign of spirit powers that they offend some Christian clergymen. A generation ago, when there were still Dutch priests at Mulagi Roman Catholic church, they used to exemplify their liberal attitude by pointing out that they were willing to baptize children wearing amulets. Wasige, who was a Protestant catechist before he became a healer, has stories of pastors who blindly refused to recognize the danger of Omuhyeeno. One cut off an amulet and chopped it up – and the child died. Another took an amulet and burned it; the child's mother came to Wasige to say that scald marks had appeared on the child's chest. Wasige gave her another amulet and the child survived. Wasige's own knowledge of the Bible provided the appropriate allegory on one occasion.

> I was called to the home of a certain child who was sick and they had also called a pastor. We met on the path and the pastor asked what I was going to do in that home. I explained it to him and referred him to a certain verse in the Bible. 'Someone was going to weed wheat and Jesus told them to let the weeds be. For the grain will grow up taller than the weeds and we will harvest it. So let me tie an amulet on this child and I'll go and remove it later when the child is older and healthy.'

From the Christian point of view, amulets and little spirits may well be weeds; for clergymen, perhaps the faith is the grain – in time it will grow strong and make all the weeds irrelevant. For Wasige, and for many parents, it is the survival and growth of children that is to be nourished and harvested.

When parents protect their children, it is in the knowledge of the terrible risks of the first years of life. As I pointed out in chapter 2, mothers today have lost more than a quarter of the children they brought into the world. Particularly when a previous child has died or when Omuhyeeno has been diagnosed within a kin group, people try to 'tie' the spirit. When I asked about a child who had a metal amulet on a string slung over one shoulder and under the opposite arm, the father explained:

> We lost one child and when this one got sick and trembled like the other one, we went to the diviner and learned that our first child died of Omuhyeeno which is now threatening this one. This is Omuhyeeno from both sides, but the one from the mother's side is strongest. We have not yet said goodbye to it with a sheep and a goat.

Omuhyeeno, like other agents, can be dealt with in steps; there are emergency, temporary measures and final solutions; there are cheaper and more expensive treatments. Those who cannot afford to 'bid farewell' to Omuhyeeno can at least try to save the child by means of an amulet.

The 'real' ceremony for getting rid of Omuhyeeno once and for all requires the calling forth of Omuhyeeno to tell its story and receive its offering of a sheep and a goat. Diviners officiate in an all night drama that ends with a final goodbye, where spirit goodbyes are always said, at a crossroads. The following is an account of how a family carried out such a ritual, when they feared that a 'branch' on their tree, that is a child, was about to be broken by Omuhyeeno.

The hungry thief

The baby had cried all night for three nights and the mother, Namugosa, looked worried and exhausted, when I visited their home one afternoon in July 1992. Malijani, the baby's father, is a dresser at the hospital, respected for his extensive knowledge of pharmaceuticals; he said the child had no fever and no convulsions. 'You know, there are certain problems . . . things of culture.' He had been to divine and had learned that Omuhyeeno had caught his child – Omuhyeeno from his wife's home, from someone who died long ago. There had been other troubles from her home before, from her father who had cursed her so that she miscarried five times before they tied the curse and she finally gave birth to three healthy children. The third child was a bright little girl, who fell sick when she was two; she died quickly though her father brought her the best European medicines. The divination pointed to Omuhyeeno, the same Omuhyeeno whose touch was now upon the new baby. The distress in Namugosa's face could well have mirrored her imagination of another death. The presence of her smart, carefree co-wife, still enjoying plenty of attention as a new bride, probably did not help matters. Malijani was concerned too. That very day, he rode his bicycle to the diviner's home to get 'first aid' herbal medicine to cool the infant, and they arranged for the ceremony itself to take place the following night.

By 11 p.m. the company assembled in Namugosa's house: two diviners, a man and a woman, drinking banana beer with their two assistants, both men; Malijani's mother, holding the baby; his younger brothers; his second wife; his sister; his sister's son; his two older children; and our 'team' – Michael and I and our son Zacha and our friend Veronica Namugisu, who wanted to see an Omuhyeeno ceremony. Malijani's father was outside, wanting to get his part of the ceremony over, so he could go to work – he was a nightwatchman at the nearby school. We were called out to see the old man open the way. Kneeling at the entrance to the compound, he dedicated a 'huge cock' to Were Namusigo, god of the gateway, and to Gasani Namoni Nyingi, and Nawere, the spirit of their clan, and all the shades. 'Collect together, all of you, let's eat this huge cock while we say farewell to our guest here, the one that brought a chill to our "branch" [child].' A fire was lit at the gateway, and the fowl was roasted on the spot. Then the old man prayed again, holding the liver. He broke off bits and threw them to the east and the west, saying that those with bad hearts should eat over there. The rest he distributed to his children, and we all ate the roasted chicken, standing at the entrance.

Then things got under way in the house. Namugosa herself was placed on the floor in the middle of the room, sitting with her legs straight out in front of her, facing the door. In a potsherd, some herbal medicine was burning. The woman diviner took medicine from a basin and sprinkled it on her head and feet. She gave her a sheaf of *olufubu* branches and fragrant *songasonga* leaves, into which the spirit itself would come. As the diviner team started the rhythmic shaking of gourd rattles, the female diviner addressed the Omuhyeeno: 'Perhaps you're the one eating this child. Come quickly and tell us what you want, so that we may give it to you and you leave the child.' At this she took a mouthful of banana beer and blew it onto the *olufubu* sheaf. 'Here's the beer for Omuhyeeno and its friends.'

Now Namugosa's father-in-law crowded into the small room with a sheep, a goat, and a hen. Holding the forelegs of the sheep and the goat, he addressed Omuhyeeno:

> So, maybe it's you eating this child. The animals you begged for – the huge ewe – if it's you, leave the child, let it be well. Me, I paid bridewealth for this girl, not knowing that they had killed you. Now if it's you, and as you begged for a huge ewe and a big she-goat and a large hen, here they are, all of them.

In turn, Malijani and the female diviner also took hold of the forelegs, and said words of dedication (*ohusenga*).

The diviner put two strands of cowries (*olutembe*, which diviners wear when possessed) around Namugosa's neck and they began to chant and beat their rattles in earnest. Namugosa sat staring straight ahead, motionless, until, after five or ten minutes, the sheaf she was holding began to tremble. Then her head started to bob up and down, and her shoulders took up the rhythm. Suddenly she was on her knees, her shoulders dancing furiously, 'breaking herself' (*ohwebwaaga*), as if her body were boneless. Abruptly, she fell flat, face down. The overwhelming rhythm of the gourd rattles faded to a single slow swish, as the male diviner spoke. 'We're delighted to see you, your worship. Have you reached well? Who are you? Speak to us.' Namugosa lay in silence. 'What is it? Come along slowly – don't be annoyed. Where do you come from? What is your clan?' In the silence, we heard Namugosa's heavy breathing, and then an insistent tapping on the papyrus mat where she lay. 'Are you happy with your gifts – the great sheep, the huge goat, the large chicken? Speak to us.' Namugosa began to tremble, and she, or it, spoke. 'I'm pleased – but this small chicken is a male, and I was a woman.' 'Were you a woman? Whose woman?' 'I was a mugosa woman/wife.' She fell silent again, and the diviner looked over at his colleague and told her to come and speak to her 'fellow woman'. She took up the dialogue with a question: 'What kind of girl/daughter are you?' 'I'm a mudiira girl, a mugosa wife.' 'How did you die? Where did they kill you? Why?' 'Because of the stomach [the word also means womb].' 'Did you go with other men?' 'I told you, it was because of the stomach. I was a thief because of hunger. I had slept two nights without eating, so I said to myself, let me steal.' 'What did you steal?' 'I stole millet. They speared me at the granary.' 'Where was your husband?' 'He was with his other wife.' 'Were you alone?' 'I had a child, I left my child in the house and went to steal food.' Malijani called out a question: 'Was the child a boy or a girl?' But the diviner admonished him: 'Don't you realize that's your mother-in-law? Are you questioning her?' Realizing he had overstepped the rules of modesty/shame, and that he should not be in the same room with anyone classed as a mother-in-law, even a ghostly one, Malijani stepped outside to follow developments from the verandah. Others continued the dialogue. The unfortunate woman had left a 4-month-old daughter. The diviner team started a song about her being a thief and people sang along, clapping.

The diviner challenged her: 'Maybe you're lying. Maybe you weren't a thief. Perhaps you were a witch. Or a loose woman. Maybe you were going with men.' Offended, the Omuhyeeno asked, 'Are men food? I told you, I was a thief. They killed me for stealing millet.' 'If you were really a thief, go bring what you stole. Maybe it was sweet potatoes, or bananas or cassava. Go bring it. Don't lie to us.' The rhythm became insistent again as they launched into the thief refrain. Suddenly Namugosa/Omuhyeeno leapt up, ran outside, and returned shortly, throwing a handful of millet on the floor. Malijani, standing just outside, reported that she climbed up into the granary, just as she did that night long ago. As the beating of the rattles continued, the woman herself started a song: 'We were two little birds. They killed one and one remained.' Someone called out: 'What time did you steal it?' 'It was 3 o'clock in the morning.' The diviner stopped shaking his rattle and asked me what time it was, but it was so dark in my corner of the room that I couldn't see my watch. Malijani, who had my flashlight out on the verandah, reported that it was 1.30. 'There's still time,' said the diviner.

Now another gift was brought into the crowded room, a basket containing maize, millet, groundnuts, and bananas. 'Here is food for you.' They showed the basket to Namugosa/Omuhyeeno. 'Here's a knife for peeling your bananas and here's a hoe – use it to cultivate instead of stealing food . . . But what did they kill you with?' 'A spear.' 'Is there no spear among these gifts? Quick, go and make one.' Malijani went to find a stick, which he sharpened at one end, and put in the basket with the other things. The diviner held the chicken and said: 'This is your present. We're going to cook it and eat together. Then, when the time comes, you must leave.' They cut the chicken's throat, and mixed the blood with medicine from the basin. They plucked the bird and put the feathers in the basket with the other things, and directed the woman to peel her bananas, putting the peelings in the basket, and cook them with the chicken. Namugosa became herself again and went into her kitchen to cook. The diviners' assistants fell sound asleep on the floor, and the rest of us talked quietly or dozed off for an hour.

Namugosa came in with a steaming saucepan, and gave food to all of us, including the children. As we were finishing, Malijani called out that the hour had come – it was 3 a.m. Just then the baby started to cry, and the diviner directed Namugosa to nurse the child. As we sat waiting, the diviners instructed us – how we should run, the nephew carrying the basket of food and implements, others leading the goat and the sheep. No one could remain in the house. We must return by another route, without looking behind. When we came back, Namugosa should throw a stone against the door before entering.

Handing the satisfied baby to its grandmother, Namugosa again took up her position in the middle of the room, holding her *olufubu* sheaf. The gourd rattles began their insistent measure, and soon Omuhyeeno appeared. First the bundle of branches trembled, then the woman herself began to shake and dance. Suddenly she dashed out the door, followed by the whole party, with the basket, and the animals. Outside, it was dark; by the weak light of a late crescent moon, we ran down the path to the main dirt road, and along it to a place where a major path intersected the road. There Namugosa/Omuhyeeno had fallen, very still. The diviner squatted beside her: 'Have you reached well?' 'Eeeh,' she exhaled. 'You, come and put that basket next to her head. Bring the animals here so she can take hold of their forelegs.' The diviner addressed Omuhyeeno: 'Now, here is your

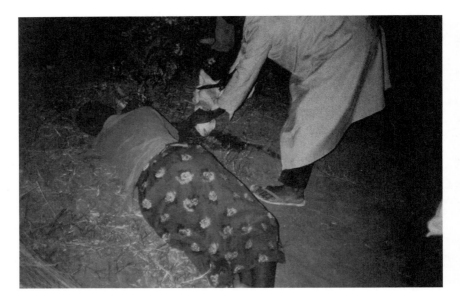

6.1 Spilling sheep's blood at the crossroads where the spirit
Omuhyeeno has thrown down its victim (1992)

huge ewe and your big goat. Maybe there's something else behind that we've forgotten?' 'No,' she replied. 'Everything is here.' 'Maybe you'll come back again to kill people?' 'No, I only want to be fed.' 'Then take your gifts and say farewell and go back to the clan and find someone else to disturb, who can also give you good things. We've given you what you wanted. Now we are tying up. Go with one heart. We want branches. Leave us. Leave the child.'

The diviners and the men and boys slit the throats of each animal in turn. They caught the blood in a large plastic cup of medicine as it gurgled out of the necks. Some of the blood and medicine was thrown on the ground in front of where Namugosa/Omuhyeeno lay. The sister's son dug a hole near the bushes at the side of the path, and they cut off the sheep's head and buried it there. One of the brothers had brought a great bundle of dry grass on a bicycle and they heaped this on top of the spot and placed the basket of food there, with the rough spear commemorating the unjust death at the millet granary. Someone set a match to the grass and flames licked up high into the darkness. The diviner spoke to Omuhyeeno one last time: 'If you're happy, leave our person, leave the *olufubu* sheaf.' 'I'm pleased,' came the reply; she dropped the sheaf and the diviner cast it into the flames. Namugosa, herself once more, sat up and looked around.

They had laid the carcasses close together and Namugosa was instructed to jump over them three times, over, back, over, after speaking the final words. 'Me, I'm a daughter; you were an in-law. Go back to the clan. I've bidden you farewell. I've given you a gift. We want branches.' She jumped and stood on the path facing homeward, her back to the scene. Then her children said their words: 'Me, I'm a sister's child. Let it go back to the clan.' They each jumped three times, the diviner helping the smallest one to make it over the dead animals. The mother-in-law jumped over, holding the baby. Next Malijani's sister took her turn: 'Me, I'm a sister-in-law . . . ' And last came Malijani himself: 'I am an in-law. I came looking for relationship – I wanted a wife. Leave my child, leave my branches. May I get something bright. I've given you what you wanted. Leave my home.' He jumped over, back, and over again. As each person finished, the diviner washed their face with herbal medicine mixed with the sacrificial blood.

They stood in a line behind Namugosa, and when Malijani finished, they moved off down the path, with us following. No one looked behind after jumping the animals. After we had gone some way, they began to talk quietly, until we approached the house. Namugosa threw a stone at the door and we all entered. Those whose faces had been anointed with blood, washed in the basin that had medicine in the water. But the diviners stayed behind at the crossroads to load the carcasses on the bicycle which Malijani's nephew, the sister's son, would help bring to their homes. That meat, plus the 7,000 shillings (c. $6) Malijani had borrowed from me, was their fee.

Next evening we happened to pass the intersection where we had taken leave of Omuhyeeno. Beside the ashes, lay the plastic cup which had held the blood and medicine, the iron hoe blade that had been among Omuhyeeno's gifts, the ropes which had pulled the animals, and even the box of matches that had ignited it all. 'No one will dare take those things,' remarked my companion.

The events began, properly, with the address to the spirit of the gateway, the high god, the clan spirit, and the dead ancestors. This was by way of a prelude, a framing of the situation; it asserted that what was to happen occurred under the auspices of these spirits. But the aspects of identity being stressed were not the patrilineal ones of the baby's clan and lineage. The real positioning of people began when they asked Omuhyeeno, 'Who are you?' and she replied with the name of her own clan, the Abadiira, and that of her husband, the Abagosa, the clan of which Malijani's wife was a 'daughter'. Like all married women, Omuhyeeno was attached to two clans. This double binding of women, with its implications for affinity and the filiation of children, was the theme of the ceremony's conclusion. Having begun with identifying the agent, the protagonists finished by declaring their own identities in relation to the murderous Abagosa. 'I am a daughter, a sister's child [niece/nephew], an in-law.'

Namugosa was certainly the star of the ceremony. Her baby, in principle the victim, spent the night in its grandmother's arms, no more nor less a part of the ritual than the other children. Namugosa was wonderfully possessed; through her Omuhyeeno told how a husband had shamefully neglected a hungry wife with a baby, spending time with his other wife. I wondered whether Namugosa, with her new co-wife, identified with that Omuhyeeno; but now Malijani had shown himself not at all neglectful, but concerned. For her and the baby, he had sacrificed animals, borrowed money, arranged the whole ceremony.

They cajoled and manipulated the spirit, first calling it 'your worship' (*omusengwa* – the one who is served, offered to), presenting it with 'huge' animals, asking it to confirm that it was perfectly satisfied, challenging it, instructing it, telling it to go bother someone else. The diviners, as masters of the ceremony, managed the spirit; in spite of Omuhyeeno's title of 'Worshipful', the diviners were the authorities that night.

In 1993, Omuhyeeno was the 'little spirit' most commonly diagnosed according to the records of Luhonda of Buwihula. Wasige, too, asserted that it was the most common little spirit attacking children and, in western Bunyole, most amulets worn by children were for Omuhyeeno. However, there are probably fashions in little spirits, depending partly on the interests of healers and diviners, who tend to diagnose problems that they are adept at treating. Nandiriko Were, who was a popular diviner and spirit practitioner in 1970, divined Omuhyeeno frequently, but even more common in his records was another 'little spirit', Mukama.

Mukama – the invisible twin

Sometimes a woman delivers a child, and wraps it in a cloth and cares for it in her house without realizing that she had in fact delivered twins. Mukama, the invisible twin, is left outside on the ground, cold and lonely, neglected and hungry. It wants to be brought into the house and cared for like a child, and to that end causes its mother, or 'twin' or a subsequent child to sicken. As a resident of the house, Mukama must be given its own tiny door, so that it can go in and out, just like other children. In time, a twinship ceremony should be held for it – as for any twin.

Nyole say that Mukama came from Busoga; the healer Wasige says it is originally from Bunyoro – and indeed the name is the title of the King of Bunyoro. The Mukama tradition in Busoga is based on a mythical royal figure (D. Cohen 1972: 124ff.); children of royal families could be born possessed by Mukama (D. Cohen 1977: 33ff.). One of Cohen's contemporary informants says that nowadays in Busoga, Mukama is not restricted to royal families: 'there are so many everywhere' (D. Cohen 1986: 283). The idea of Mukama as a twin may be related to the Ganda tradition of the Kabaka being born with a double (Ray 1991: 126), 'a small, human shaped likeness' (Ray 1972: 43). Thus the Nyole little spirit resonates with great traditions from the kingdoms to the west. But the Nyole version is homey and folksy, a caricature of the grand Soga building of enclosures for royalty and the Ganda preserving of the king's umbilical stump. The Mukama of Bunyole is cared for not as royalty, but as a child of its parents. In the egalitarian context of Bunyole, Mukama can be born into any family.

In 1971, when I was working closely with Nandiriko, who specialized in the treatment of little spirits, we went one afternoon to do the first and most common ritual treatment for Mukama, 'bringing Mukama into the house'.

Mukama's tiny doorway

An older man, Tebba, had come to consult Nandiriko about the illness of his granddaughter. The baby's parents were staying in Mbale, where the child's father, Tebba's son, was working for the railway. When the little girl fell sick, they took her to the hospital and were told that she needed two injections. But after the first one, the baby fainted. So instead of going back to the hospital, they took the next bus home. The divination showed a family history: it turned out that the baby's grandmother, Tebba's wife Namuhyama, was ill as well (the details of her symptoms were not mentioned). Nandiriko explained that the woman had de-livered Mukama with her firstborn son, who had died. They had brought Mukama into the house back then, but not properly, and it was for this reason that he had 'kicked' the little daughter of his 'brother', the second born. The image of kicking gained sharpness from the large lump-like swelling visible on the baby's back. We gathered in Namuhyama's house: herself and her husband, her visiting sister, her son home from his job in Mbale, and her daughter-in-law, holding the sick baby.

Nandiriko mixed some brown crushed herbal medicine in water and washed the baby, addressing Mukama as he did so.

> If you are in this home here, you were born in this home, and your companion went with a cloth, and you said 'Me, they never gave me a cloth. I, Nabudo [another name for Mukama], I am outside on the ground – father and mother refused to think of me and take me in.' You would have been taken in, but the one who took you brought you in badly. Now here we want you to give us peace again. Let us come for you, we bring you in, we put you in this house.

Nandiriko began to shake his gourd rattles, speaking of the huge goats Mukama would be given in later ceremonies if it let the little girl recover. At this point the spirit was supposed to catch its mother and lead her outside to the place where she had given birth to it. Namuhyama showed no signs of being possessed. She rose quietly and walked out into the banana plantation, followed by the diviner, carrying a winnowing tray on which he had placed *amabombwe*, the vines used in twin ceremonies, and a basin of medicine. He sprinkled medicine on the spot the woman indicated, and together they scooped up two small piles of earth and put them on the winnowing tray. Again he addressed Mukama in the same vein as before. Then he followed Namuhyama back into the house, behind the partition, into the sleeping section. He set the winnowing tray on the floor next to a little hole in the outer wall, at the foot of her bed. This was Mukama's doorway, which had been dug many years before at the earlier, failed, Mukama ritual. Ordinarily, the doorway would have been made at this point in the ceremony. Taking a small male chicken, Nandiriko slit its throat and sprinkled blood near the little hole, saying:

> So, this is our huge chicken, my friend Mukama. You, as you have declared yourself, you said, 'I want you to come collect me a second time because that one did not come to fix me properly.' And this is the huge chicken which is for collecting you from where you have been outside and of bringing you into the house of your mother and father. Come, be cool in the house here. Perhaps it's you who has been kicking that child of yours and your mother – you've been sitting in her chest, you prevent her from cultivating. Ah, we have wanted you to leave your mother, that one. A person digs before she gets the means of fixing up her person. And if she does not dig [what about] the goat of *ehyambi* for which you are dunning? And if she does not dig [what about] the goat you are demanding for your twin ceremony? Those things – will she just steal them? These days, if you go and touch someone's things, you have earned death! You, if you have been kicking your mother, this one, if you touched your child, that one – you said, 'Now, those are the children – since they don't like me, I want to walk on them.' Today, that child, the little body, she should sleep well on her mother's breast.

Next Nandiriko took an immature hen and dedicated it to Mukama, asking him to take care of it so that it would produce many chickens which would be traded for huge goats to be used for the next phases of the Mukama ceremony.

> We wanted you to look after this huge chicken. You leave that child, that child of yours. When tomorrow comes, it will be bouncing on its mother's breast. Let people say: 'So that's how it was; Mukama was the one who was beating this little child.' Go away from that child. When day dawns, leave that mother of yours so that tomorrow she grasps a hoe, since we are now in the millet season.

The sick woman's husband was asked to go and cut two poles from a barkcloth tree and some elephant grass. Nandiriko planted these poles and bunches of the grass outside the house on either side of Mukama's tiny doorway. With a dry banana leaf, he tied the poles together creating a rough gateway in front of the little door, and he made a final exhortation to Mukama:

> What you don't see and it sees you with one shoulder, you don't quarrel with it. You may be declaring and yet you are not Mukama. But if it is you, Mukama, soon we will return here, and we'll eat those things. We'll sleep here when we pound beer. Soon we may return again and we'll do the twin ceremony [literally, kick twinship] together with your mother's brothers, the Abahyama. They'll say, 'Ahhh, we've come from kicking the twinship of Mukama. See, this is the share we were given.'

A few days later the diviner returns to the home to give Mukama its string of cowries (*olutembe* – worn by diviners or people possessed by spirits – in this case it is a minimal representation consisting of three cowries sewn on a piece of braided cloth). I was not with Nandiriko on this occasion but he told me what the diviner must do:

> He takes that [little pile of] earth which was collected and rubs it into the cowrie string, so that the earth enters into the *olutembe*. Then he puts the cowries on a potsherd. And he takes the other [little pile of] earth and he pulls out a little thing like a bit of thread. That is folded in a cloth . . . and that too he puts on a potsherd. Then the ceremony of bringing Mukama into the house is finished.

Once in the house, Mukama should be given food regularly at its potsherds by its little door. In time, it should be seated upon a goatskin (*ohwihasa Mukama huhyambi*). The goat is killed at Mukama's doorway, and when the skin is dry, it is brought in and Mukama is removed from the potsherd and placed upon the skin. The final step is to take Mukama out for the twin ceremony. An old man told me that this used to be done long ago and that it was a great ceremony. Now it seems only to be done if the parents of Mukama later give birth to twins (or if parents of twins are found to have given birth to Mukama earlier). Mukama's twinship must be 'kicked' before the ceremony for the subsequent twins can be done.

The basic elements of Mukama are present even in simplified versions of the rituals. The winnowing tray and the potsherd, the little piles of earth and the small doorway, the food for Mukama and the hen left to reproduce chickens which will one day be traded for a goat that will provide the skin that Mukama will sit upon: these are *things* that are linked to Mukama. But Mukama is also a story theme that ties people and events in a family history. In the example above, the Mukama born with one child affected both its mother and its 'brother's' child. In 1970, when Manueri went to divine about the sickness of his child Tom, he was reminded that he himself had been born with Mukama. His parents had brought Mukama into the house and had given it a goatskin. But then they moved to another place and forgot Mukama in the old house down by the swamp. In time the roof fell in and rain beat down upon the little spirit. Manueri had to call a healer to put medicine around his house and under the four legs of the bed and to dig a hole so that the 'child' might pass in and out. The healer planted a barkcloth pole as a reminder (*ehimanyihiso*– literally, thing that makes known) and told them to be giving Mukama food at the little door.

In 1992 a teacher told how one of her children had been diagnosed as having Mukama. They made a small door in a traditional house in the village, but a later divination said that was not enough. They had to make a hole through the baseboard of the permanent house in town where they were staying. They put a goatskin there and bits of food from time to time.

Later, when their last born fell sick, they were told to do Mukama on that one too: 'Maybe the first ceremony wasn't enough. We tried so many things, but it didn't help. It's a belief.' Mukama links together parents and children, siblings living and dead, childbirth and houses, reminding the family that birth and childcare are not individual matters, through the homely signs of potsherds, bits of cloth and a hole in the wall at the foot of the bed.

Chicken toes, sheep ears, and anthills

The healers with whom I worked in 1970 treated an assortment of little spirits that followed mothers and sickened children. Often these spirits were diagnosed together and sometimes people seemed to get them confused with one another. There was Kalyawire (or Kiryawire or Nakiryawire), 'the little thing that eats at night'. Nandiriko, who diagnosed and treated this spirit regularly, also called it Nalulima and Omuhyeeno, though he explained that it was different from the big Omuhyeeno that comes from killing a relative. The animal for saying farewell to Kalyawire was a sheep; another healer, Chai, said there should be a goat as well. The animal(s) are killed at a crossroads at night – thus the name – and thus perhaps also the conflation with Omuhyeeno. But, as usual, there is a less expensive initial step – 'trapping Kalyawire'.

Trapping the little thing that eats at night
In 1971 Nandiriko was called to a family to trap Kalyawire who was affecting the first child of a young couple, a little girl of 18 months. The child had been sick for three weeks, had gotten better and then worse again. They had taken it to the dispensary at Busaba where it was injected, to no avail. So Mulumba, the baby's father's father, went to divine[2] and when Kalyawire was identified, he asked Nandiriko to come straight away. Nandiriko washed the sick baby in a basin of medicine first.

> Eee, Nalulima, when we come to the house here, we take this bit of medicine of omuhyeeno, we bathe this child. And if it is you, if you are in the house here on this little child . . . Ah, we diviners, whom you spoke of, saying, 'Go call a diviner to come in this house so he may trap my matter of omuhyeeno. If it is I who am trapped, the person should be well first before looking for the huge sheep to eat at night and then I may go.' This is our medicine of omuhyeeno. We have desired that if you are on this child, today, now, this little body, the child may sleep when it is well. And the owner of the child may say, 'Oh, today, this day, I have slept a little.' They say that what you do not see and it sees you over one shoulder, you don't quarrel with it.

Then he took two small chickens and dedicated them to the spirit, promising that in time it would eat them at night together with a huge sheep. He held the chickens' feet in the medicine and put some in their mouths. Then, laying them both in the basin, he cut off a toe from one. He let a little blood from the toe drip on some other medicine he had brought, and then sewed that medicine into two pieces of cloth, making two amulets. In one of them he included the dismembered toe. He tied these on the child's wrists and went to work on the house itself. First he sprinkled the medicine on the walls; then he dug two small holes in the floor on either side of the doorway, another in the damp hollow under the waterpot, and others behind the door and at the foot of the bed. In all of these he put medicine. Finally he poured beer on the floor, speaking to Kalyawire in the same vein as before. He took some cooked millet and formed two balls, inserting some dry pounded sesame, like *ebigwasi*. One he threw out through the space between the wall and the roof and the other he tossed on the floor 'for those with bad hearts'.

While Kalyawire can come from either the side of a child's father or its mother, another little spirit, Namatango, always comes from the side of the mother. The word itself means 'distant relative', for example someone in the clan of a parent's maternal grandmother.[3] Namatango very often goes with two other little spirits, also from the side of a child's mother: Nahitutuwusi and Nalulama, the names referring respectively to a kind of anthill and a kind of tree. Since they come together, they are usually treated together. In fact it was not uncommon for these three little spirits to be diagnosed together with Kalyawire. As Manueri said, 'One little spirit alone may not kill a child. But they are like people – they invite their friends.' When Kalyawire attacked Mulumba's 18-month-old grand-daughter, it was not alone, and the day after he trapped Kalyawire with the chicken toe amulet, Nandiriko returned to the house of the young parents to deal with the three spirit companions, Namatango, Nahitutuwusi, and Nalulama.

Distant relatives and their friends
After Nandiriko fumigated the house with burning grass, we set out in a curious procession. First came the sheep, borrowed for the occasion from a neighbour and led by a boy Nandiriko had recruited from among the children hanging around the compound. Then came Gimbo, the young mother, 18 years old or so, with a frayed banana leaf tied about her waist, representing *amayinja*, the old female attire from before the age of cloth. On her head she carried a basket containing samples of different kinds of food and in one hand she held an *olufubu* branch. Nandiriko followed, shaking his gourd rattles insistently, and I brought up the rear with my tape-recorder and Manueri who was accompanying me that day. The sick baby and its father both stayed at home.

We walked until we approached the home of a classificatory paternal grand-mother of Gimbo (who would be a *namatango* relative of the baby). The grand-mother came out to meet us at the intersection of her path and the main one. Without greeting us, she took hold of the sheep's foreleg and began to address Namatango, saying that if it was the one striking in the grandchild's house, it should go away now as they were giving it this huge sheep today. When she finished, the procession left without saying goodbye.

After a while we came into a swampy, uninhabited area and stopped at a small anthill of the kind called *ehitutuwusi*. Gimbo knelt down there and laid her branch at the base of the anthill. Nandiriko placed each kind of food – groundnuts, millet, sweet potatoes, bananas, cowpeas, cassava – on top of the anthill, and asked Nahitutuwusi to accept this 'mass of food' and to release the sick baby. He put some medicine from his banana leaf container on top of the food and patted some on Gimbo's head and the nape of her neck.

We moved on about fifty yards to a tree called *omulama* and again Gimbo knelt and laid down her branch. The basket with the remaining food was placed at the base of the tree. Nandiriko opened up his banana leaf container to make a kind of basin, mixing medicine and water. He took a little chicken, provided by Gimbo's husband, from his satchel and cut its throat, letting the blood drip into the medicine and onto the ground at the base of the tree.

> Nalulama, if it was you in the house of this daughter . . . now today we want to say goodbye to you with this huge sheep, these masses of food, this big chicken, and we beg you, don't come back again to that house. When they next go to divine, let them divine something else.

Nandiriko washed Gimbo's head and arms in the medicine. Then he took a knife and cut off the tip of the sheep's ear and placed it at the base of the tree. Gimbo rose, removed her frayed banana leaf and walked home, having been instructed to throw a stone against the door of her house before entering it.

We roasted the chicken on the spot and ate it there in the shade. Nandiriko joked a bit about a woman who had run away as we approached, fearing spirits, and about people who might find the food left in the swamp, pick it up and be caught themselves by the little spirits. The sheep was taken back to its owner, minus the tip of its ear. Nandiriko said that if the child thrives, they should buy a sheep and kill it for Namatango. But he added that in fact no one ever does this.

Some healers say that these small spirits can affect the mother alone, but in the cases I knew about, there was always a baby who was sick as well. One little spirit, however, only attacks women: Ndulundulu, which causes barrenness and miscarriages. It makes a woman sick, her stomach turns, her heart pounds, she feels dizzy, she has cramps in her womb and heavy bleeding. Biomedically trained Nyole say that some of these symptoms may indicate pelvic inflammatory disease consequent upon untreated gonorrhoea. But most people think of Ndulundulu not as a sexually transmitted disease but as 'a mixer'. They use that term to explain its action: 'it mixes and mixes in there and makes a woman bleed'. This little spirit was still being identified regularly in 1993; a woman who had been trained as a traditional birth attendant and had a successful midwifery practice explained that Ndulundulu strikes in the third or fourth month of pregnancy. 'It starts to turn in the womb and causes abortion. It's true. If you don't treat it, you'll never get children.'

There are different methods for treating Ndulundulu. Healers 'tie' it by giving medicine to the affected woman and placing a broken pot rim behind the house against the wall. There they sacrifice a cock and make sacramental balls of food (*ebigwasi*); one is tied in a banana leaf and placed in the thatch by the doorway. Another is eaten by the woman and her husband. An immature hen is dedicated to Ndulundulu with the promise that if it multiplies, a goat will be bought for saying goodbye to Ndulundulu. Another method requires a woman to tie a frayed banana leaf around her waist (again, a token of womanhood in another era). She dances to a drumbeat, after which the drumsticks are tied together with the frayed banana leaf and placed in the roof thatch over the door. Herbal medicine is given in any case.

The female centre

Like other terms in the explanatory idiom, little spirits relate suffering and uncertainty to relationships that need adjustment. Unlike the ties to clan spirits and shades, those to little spirits do not require affirmation; they should be broken politely through exchange, giving the spirit what it wants so it will relinquish its hold. Doing this involves hiring a specialist and in this respect there is a definite contrast to the kinship rituals of clan spirits and shades and cursing. There is a degree of commoditization in dealing with little spirits. You pay for the services of an expert who sells you the amulets he has manufactured or guides you through the necessary steps of a ritual. If an animal is offered, he eats it or carries it away, in contrast to the kin-based ceremonies when an animal is cooked and shared by all. The tendency toward therapy as a commodity is evident too in the use of medicines, which is typical for little spirit measures. Medicines as treatment lend themselves to commoditization. The contrast between kin-based and commoditized responses to misfortune is a fundamental one.

Little spirits are minor in relation to what I. M. Lewis (1971) calls the 'central morality cult', in this case the cults of clan spirits and ancestral shades and perhaps to some extent Islam and Christianity. They do not represent patriliny nor do they emphasize the control senior relatives, especially males, exercise over their juniors, especially females. They are not associated with prestige, influence, and modernity like the world religions. They are concerned with the most fundamental value in Nyole culture – reproduction in the sense of the conception, birth, and survival of children. But this concern is dramatized in feminine, indeed housewifely, terms in contrast to the styles of clan spirits and shades. Women, their babies, and their houses are the central focus in these rituals and representations.

While clan and lineage identities are played out in well-known terms dominated by men, little spirits suggest another kind of identity. Their domestic, familiar nature suggests a kind of feminine intimacy that contrasts with the cultural focus of clan spirits and shades. Everyone knows the latter; they are agents that imply identities fundamental to Nyole society. But married women, older women and worried fathers are the ones concerned with little spirits. Nyole friends were amused that I knew Kalyawire; it was a kind of backstage acquaintance that showed belonging in a homey way.

'Women bring little spirits'. I have heard people say, or, 'They follow birthgiving' (*bulonda olusaaye*). By this I think they are contrasting these with the spirits and shades of patrilineality. It is not that relationships to little spirits are inherited matrilineally; in fact the connections seem to be rather haphazard, if connections are made at all. In the Mukama examples, the spirit could be born with one child and affect a later sibling. Or it could be delivered by your mother-in-law and later come to kick your child. Omuhyeeno is usually, but not invariably, found to come from the side of a baby's mother. Thus the little spirits are not totally unconnected with kinship relations, but their links are not based on an enduring principle of kinship. Most important, the attachments are seen as undesireable and dangerous. The point is to break them.

Clan spirits and shades have places, permanent shrines, which serve as foci for patrilineally defined kin groups. People have lasting relationships with them – you cannot 'say farewell' to your clan spirit or your grandfather's shade. Little spirits are temporary, as one man explained: 'These little spirits don't have proper homes. They are like distant relatives (*namatango*). They have no real claim on you; they try to get what they can where they can. But they do not have any priest or shrine shelter.' Having no shrines, however, little spirits make any house their own. Clan spirits are approached in their sacred groves or in the compound of a senior male; the ghosts of the male dead are linked to their shrines in the courtyard. Only little spirits are associated with the interior of dwelling houses. Mukama is actually brought in and given its own doorway; Nandiriko says to the little spirit Nalulima, 'if it is you, if you are in the house here . . . ' Parts of the rituals are done inside the house and the house itself is treated with medicines, even in its most intimate, feminine parts – behind the door, under the waterpot, beneath the bed. When a woman returns from bidding a little spirit farewell, she throws a stone at her door to scare away whatever might have lingered there. Rules of modesty (*obuhwe*) normally prevent parents from entering the houses of their married children. For a woman, the interior of her dwelling is her space in the sense that her parents-in-law do not come there. And in general, houses are for women, each wife having her own.

These rituals are 'experience near' for women, to use Geertz's (1983) terminology. Not only are they carried out in women's space; they make use of women's things. Winnowing trays, potsherds, baskets, raw food – common items that women use in their daily activities are the ritual paraphernalia of these ceremonies. They refer to women's concerns: the place where a woman gave birth, or the sleeplessness of a mother whose baby is sick. They dramatize women's situations, as in the case of the Omuhyeeno of the hungry thief, neglected by her husband. Even Namatango, the spirit of distant relatives, represents a feminine theme in that descent through women becomes irrelevant ('distant') in two generations, whereas patrilineal descent is in principle a continuous link. Most important of all, they deal specifically with women's reproductive problems and the well-being of their infants. The children affected by little spirits are typically still breastfeeding – they are so closely linked to their mothers that they are treated as extensions of them.

Sick babies are given amulets and medicine in the preliminary treatments for little spirits and sometimes in the ceremonies themselves. But the primary figures in little spirit ceremonies are mothers, not sick babies. In the Omuhyeeno ceremony, the mother has a star role; she is the centre to which all the other actors relate. Her husband is a man who came looking for relationship; members of his family speak as in-laws; her children are identified as nieces/nephews of her clan. She is the key to their identities. Even in ceremonies that give less scope for drama, women, as mothers or potential mothers, play the central role. Their husbands stand by to assist in providing animals and other necessities, but the wives are the ones to deal with the spirits. The outlay of resources and the ritual attention serve to acknowledge a mother's anxieties, pain, hopes, and struggles.

Children and mothers at risk

The life of children in rural eastern Uganda is precarious. Infectious diseases like malaria and measles, acute respiratory infections, gastro-intestinal sicknesses, and malnutrition are widespread. A mother needs neither statistics on mortality rates nor a concept of risk to know the dangers and to feel worry, care, and uncertainty about her children's health. (Recognition of sleepless nights is institutionalized in the gift to a bride's mother, known by the Luganda term *kasuza katye* meaning 'how did the little one pass the night?') The amulets and the rituals for little spirits must be seen directly in this light; they indicate concern for the uncertain prospects of children's health. Sometimes the reason for worry is obvious; I have seen children who look chronically malnourished and sickly wearing elaborate amulets. Often the child being protected does not seem particularly ill; but inquiry reveals that the mother has previously lost a child. Tying and offering to little spirits are attempts to limit uncertainty and reassure the mother.

But these are seldom the only steps taken. In the cases I got to know about, there were always other efforts made as well. Usually it was after European medicine had failed that people took measures against little spirits. Occasionally the order was reversed as in a recent example:

The little doorway before the drip
In 1995 we heard that Grace's three-month-old baby was seriously ill with diarrhoea and vomiting. Her brother sent word that they should take the child to the hospital immediately, but when we stopped by the hospital in the evening to check on the patient, they had not come. Next morning we heard that they had gone to divine and found Mukama, the invisible twin. So instead of going to hospital, they had done the ceremony of making a little doorway in the house for Mukama. Another brother went and collected her with the baby and her brother-in-law and we took them to the hospital. The child was admitted and put on a drip; the nurse said the baby was seriously dehydrated and might have died.

Grace was newly married; she had dropped out of secondary school when she got pregnant and this was her first child. She was fortunate in being able to mobilize both of her homes when the life of her baby hung in the balance. Her in-laws attended to danger by organizing the Mukama ceremony quickly; her brothers' concern ensured that her baby received biomedical care as well.

From a practical point of view, the most important question about little spirit ceremonies is whether the sick child improved. Whenever I meet Malijani after some months and ask about his family, he always makes a point of telling me that the child whose Omuhyeeno ceremony we watched that night is doing well. With the combined treatments enabled by Grace's network of concerned in-laws and brothers, her little one recovered too. In both of those cases, the ritual attempts to push back uncertainty were enactments of solicitude. In the face of uncertainty, relatives acting in terms of little spirits extend a hand – by paying money to tie amulets and make small doorways. When the child thrives, they can remember with satisfaction that they attended to the spirits. But, unhappily, offerings and amulets do not always have the desired consequences.

The teacher who had a hole made through the baseboard of her modern house in town remembered Mukama as one measure in a litany of attempts to save a child that finally died. The case of Hassani, who was 5 years old in 1995, shows experimentation, failure, and continued uncertainty.

Continuing convulsions

When Hassani was two, he fell sick with vomiting, severe fever, and convulsions. He was admitted to the hospital for a week, where he was put on a drip and treated with chloroquine, Valium, and penicillin. The nurses told his family to buy phenobarbitone and Valium in the shops, and Hassani's mother gave him this medicine for a month. When she stopped, he had convulsions again. She returned to the hospital and saw the psychiatric nurse, who advised that she continue the same medicines. She did so for another two months, but then she ran out of money to buy the medicine. When I visited Hassani in 1995, together with Tito Wamudanya, the psychiatric nurse, Hassani was receiving no treatment and still suffering convulsions. His mother was worried about his behaviour and his eyesight too. At this time, phenobarbitone was not available in any of the local drug shops.

Hassani's father's brother phrased his sickness in the explanatory idiom as Omuhyeeno, the spirit of the vengeful dead. He was careful to distinguish this from *efuwu* (usually translated as epilepsy); Hassani did not have *efuwu* because he did not urinate or defaecate during convulsions. But Hassani's mother was doubtful about Omuhyeeno. 'We tried to say farewell to Omuhyeeno, but we failed. It didn't leave. We tied an amulet on Hassani, to protect against Omuhyeeno, but it didn't help, so we finally threw it away. We said that this might be another disease.' When I asked what disease it might be, she said that the medical people call it *omusuja gwa buwongo*, 'fever of the brain'. The nurse confirmed that Hassani had suffered 'brain fever' or cerebral malaria, and said they should struggle to get phenobarbitone for him in the city. 'Will that help his eyesight too?' asked his mother. 'What about the other medicine [Valium]?'

Hassani's mother was looking for a way forward. She did not deny Omuhyeeno; in fact, she told us that Hassani's older brother had suffered from it, but not so badly. But rituals and amulets had not helped, nor had the pills she had tried when she could get them. She was unsure about the future. They wanted to try to send him to school, but were not certain he would manage because his behaviour and his understanding were not good.

Little spirits are ideas taken up to deal with the uncertainties of child health and the precarious well-being of mothers. Like other terms in the explanatory idiom, they have no warrant of success in the sense of curative guarantees. The healer addresses them in the conditional: 'If it is you, if you are the one.' They speak in the same voice: 'If it is I . . . the person should be well first before looking for the huge sheep.' Little spirits are one kind of tactic in a continuing struggle to secure what is valuable. There is no pretence that dealing with them provides a lasting solution.

The diviner only hopes that: 'When next they go to divine, let them divine something else.'

Clan spirits, shades, and little spirits look askance at people who do not see them. Through divination and possession, people take evidence; they compare what they hear in these situations with what they know about their relations and obligations to spirits, as when Namugwere's husband reckoned he did not owe anything to the spirits who spoke through her. Through trying out, offering animals, sharing meat, and speaking words, you try to gain some security against the agency of spirits. You may be unsure as to the identity and requirements of the spirits involved; you may have difficulty in mobilizing the resources and people to carry out the necessary rituals; you may doubt the idea of spirits if ceremonies do not alleviate affliction. But you do not worry about the sensibilities of spirits, their dispositions toward you, their machinations or hidden intentions. It is in dealing with human beings that those sources of uncertainty are problematic.

Part III

'You will know me': the opacity of humans

'A Nyole is a curser', they say in eastern Uganda. Few people in Bunyole would deny the power of senior relatives to curse (*ohung'waba* or *ohulaama*) if they have been wronged. Even educated people who spoke derisively about clan spirits and said sorcery only caught those who believed in it, had examples of how curses unfolded. In fact, a common story tells how the power of elders reaches into institutions of higher learning.

DDT and failed exams

A young man went to England to do a medical course. Before he left (or in another version, when he was home on holiday) his father's brother (or mother's brother) came to visit. When the uncle left, the man (or his wife) sprayed the chair with DDT, as if to disinfect after an unhygienic episode. The uncle got to know of this (in one version he sprayed even before the older man was out of sight) and was very annoyed. Time came when the nephew sat for his exams in England and he failed. When his parents heard, they went to divine and found that he had been cursed by his uncle. They went and apologized and asked the uncle to remove the curse. He agreed and gave the millet food of removal to the unfortunate student's brother. The brother and his father went to Entebbe and sent the consecrated clump of food (*ehigwasi*) by airplane to England. After tasting this, the young man was able to pass (though weakly) on the next exams.

I heard this account in several versions in 1970. Twenty-two years later, a Makerere graduate and a boy who had just finished senior secondary school told me the same tale – as an example of the power of senior relatives to touch even the fortunate few who went abroad to study. Apparently the moral still holds: If you treat your uncle like an unsanitary bumpkin, he may teach you more respect – no matter how modern you think you are.

In this chapter I examine a tactic of dealing with misfortune that Nyole think of as specially their own: discovering a curse and reconfirming respect for their parents. As a plan of action, curse removal attempts to deal with adversity by making assertions about morality and kinship relations, rights, and identities. Of course, the recalcitrance of affliction may lead to continued uncertainty, as we also saw in the case of little spirits. But a different source of uncertainty is evident here as well: the problematics of kinship morality. Just as Jackson (1982) argued that Kuranko storytelling provides an occasion for considering ethics and ambiguity, so I suggest that people's experience with cursing as a term of explanation and action is sometimes equivocal.

'Kinship is like your buttocks . . .

. . . you can't cut it off', say Nyole laughingly. Sometimes this popular maxim is used in contrasting kinship with friendship, which might be more enjoyable but which, unlike your backside, can be severed. Sometimes it seems to express the inconveniences of kinship obligations, which, like your posterior, are ever with you. Relations to various kinds of kin are part of your identity just as your buttocks, for better or worse, are part of your self. The analogy is limited, however, for you interact with kin and in doing so, constantly recreate or transform your relationships and your identity as a person.

The most important form of relationship recognized by Nyole is that with 'parents' (abasaaye). 'Parenthood' is bilateral; it includes all senior consanguineal relatives – your own father and mother, their siblings and their fathers and mothers. To all parents you owe respect and all parents are said to have power over their children, expressed in their ability to curse. Children should acknowledge their parents by obeying them, treating them with deference and showing generosity. All parents have rights to shares from the bridewealth of their 'daughters' and this is an explicit recognition of their position. Failure to acknowledge parenthood in this way is often thought to lead to a curse upon the bride.

A father has authority over his children by virtue of his access to the ancestors, and because he controls land and livestock. Once a son has married and been allocated land by his father, the relationship is somewhat more egalitarian, but it is always marked by greater formality than that with a mother. The term for father (laata in reference and bbaabba in address) is extended to father's brothers, who may assume his authority and responsibility in case of his death. Your father's brother, sometimes called 'little father' (bbaabba muto), is often a neighbour and ideally a person concerned with your welfare. In practice there are many conflicts, especially between men and their father's brothers, in connection with property rights.

A father's sister (senge) is also a 'parent' and the term is extended to any woman of the father's generation in your own clan or lineage. She comes to visit regularly at her own home, that is, the home of your father and grandfather, and may live there for a period should she leave her husband. So you are likely to know her well. For a woman, father's sister has a special role as the female representative of her own lineage. For a man, the marriage of father's sister makes him a wife-giver as part of the lineage from which she comes. It may even bring him a wife in that her bridewealth can be used by her brother to bring a wife for his son. The children of his father's sister owe him particular respect as a 'mother's brother', a member of their mother's lineage.

Relations to parents on the side of your mother are particularly important. Because married women maintain close contact with their own families, their children know their maternal relatives and may go to stay with them for a period. The most marked relationship is that with the prototype *hoja*, the mother's real brother. This is coloured by two seemingly incongruous themes. On the one hand, the principle of the superiority of wife-givers means that *hoja* has to be greatly respected and given prestations. On the other, as a mother's brother, he is expected to share his sister's love and concern for her child. Thus the sister's children have to show the somewhat stiff formality which Nyole express by the verb *ohutya*, to fear or respect; yet they can look to their mother's brothers for support and even affection.

'If I am the one . . .'

A curse is made by a living person who feels offended and is in a position of power in relation to the victim of the curse. The typical curser is a 'parent' (senior blood relative) who has been wrongly treated and calls upon their common ancestors to punish a 'child'. Other people can curse too, especially if the situation can be modelled on that of disrespect to a parent or senior. Older siblings, senior wives, big men who look after the interests of a community, someone who has cared for you in his or her home – all of these, if wronged, can bring misfortune.

The power behind the curse is the ancestors (though some people also mentioned God, either giving a Nyole term for the high god or the Christian or Muslim ones). They make it work, but they are not seen as the ones who did it. The agent is the person on this side of the grave, who has been neglected, affronted, or angered.

Ideally a curser is morally justified. As a senior relative, a parent deserves respect. He or she stands closer to the ancestors who ensure the principle of honouring the living elders. Ancestors are by definition good and moral; by association a curser is 'on the side of the angels'. When we asked if a curse could work if there was no good reason, people sometimes said 'yes, because our parents have power over us'. In some cursing stories, the parents were represented as greedy or hard-hearted, but that did not make them evil as a sorcerer was evil. By defining the curser as a 'parent' one acknowledges the claim to respect. Stories of curses by people who were not parents emphasized clear faults against fundamental Nyole ideas of decency. The farther one moved from actual 'parent–child' relationships, the more unambiguous the fault had to be in order for the problem to be interpreted as a curse.

Cursing implies connectedness, and the power of the curse lies in the relationship between the curser and the cursed; mentioning their common ancestor affirms the connection. Someone with whom you have no relationship at all, not even one analogous to kinship, cannot curse you, no matter what terrible offence you commit. Thus to tell of cursing is to tell of ties between persons, and more specifically of who the agent is in relation to the victim.

In fact, curses are often predicated on kinship identity, sometimes expressed as biological ties: 'If I am the one who begot that child . . .' 'If I gave up our mother's breast for him . . .'; 'If this is the womb from which she came . . .'; 'If I sucked from the same breast as your mother . . .' These biological metonyms are a forceful way of concretizing kinship, but the idea does not have to be put in terms of breasts and begetting. The notion of a common connecting ancestor can be invoked: 'If I am the one keeping the shade of your grandfather in my shrine . . .' Most common of all was the simple assertion of being a senior relative.

A recurring theme in cursing stories is that the victim did not recognize someone as a relative. 'He thought that man was not his father', they did not treat her as a mother's sister, did not give the grandfather the bridewealth share to which grandfathers are entitled. By cursing, parents show who they are. You must know (acknowledge and respect) your parents and if you do not, they can teach you. Maria told us how her father had shown his granddaughters who he was and where their mother came from.

The mother's home

Namusene (Maria's sister) died leaving three daughters. Their father brought them up in Busoga, but never allowed them to visit their maternal grandparents in Bunyole. The grandfather was annoyed by this and on his deathbed, he cursed the girls that they never deliver, only abort. But he told his heir (the *omusika*) that he could remove the curse, should the girls come to be forgiven. In time, the girls married, and miscarried one after another. The heir went to their father and revealed the curse; the father accepted his mistake and gathered his daughters and told them to go with the heir to know their grandfather's home. Maria went on to tell of the goat that was sacrificed and the numbers of children that each daughter has delivered up to now.

In effect, the dying man had said, 'If I am the grandfather of those girls . . .' and the point of the narrative was that he proved it.

To curse is to have authority which is often analogous to ownership. The fathers and brothers of a girl may be referred to as her 'owners' (*abene muhana*) and there is a strong sense in which children belong to their parents. The notion that you can curse what belongs to you came out in an account someone told of an odd case of cursing. Two women were quarrelling over the ownership of a certain mango tree. Each one claimed that she had planted it and therefore owned it. Finally one of them cursed the tree that it would yield poorly and that even those few fruits it produced would rot. When this came to pass, concluded our raconteur, it demonstrated who really did own the tree.

All of this sounds like a discourse on the certainties of moral rights and relationships. But the ways that cursing as an idea were actually brought into play left plenty of room for doubt. The process was as follows: illness or other misfortune was redefined as a *consequence*; and then a relationship, an offence and feelings/motives were hypothesized as prior to the consequence. Sometimes the suspected curser joined in composing or confirming the story. Often the proposal was a product of divinatory dialogue of the kind I have described earlier. Or people in the sufferer's home put together a likely explanation. In most instances, the identification of an offence, and the attribution of feelings and motives did not come from the curser. He or she did not usually take the initiative in claiming to invoke the ghosts (as Middleton (1960) showed that Lugbara elders did). Nor did the cursed person begin with introspection to see if it was his own fault. Those who shaped the interpretation imagined the curser; the focus was on him or her and what could have prompted the desire to punish.

Words and tears

Curses are seldom uttered publicly. I never heard one made and only once did someone tell me of witnessing a curse. But there were definite notions of what cursers say and do when they are effecting a curse. The most formal method was for a man to go to his ancestral shrine early in the morning, 'half-naked' (shirtless) and there invoke the ancestors: 'Grandfathers and grandmothers, help me – if I am the one who begot that child and he despises me, let them beat him at a beer party.' He may promise the shades that they will 'eat' when the cursed comes to have the curse removed. A woman could curse at her hearthstones calling upon her own ancestors, or in some cases those of her husband. Or she could throw herself upon the graves of the ancestors of the person she wanted to punish.

Others said that a curse did not have to be uttered at a particular place. A curser can 'just speak with the mouth' anywhere or one can speak while 'hitting on the ninth finger'. You place the thumb and ring finger together and then snap your wrist so that the index finger strikes on the ring finger (which is the the ninth one according to the Nyole way of numbering them). Cursers are imagined to say 'You'll come to me' (*olinjolaho*) in anticipation of the day when the cursed will humbly come for forgiveness. Or, if the curser has been abused or mistreated, he might say, 'You'll be like me' (*oliba hyange*) foreseeing the form that misfortune will take.

All these methods of making a curse involve speaking and, in fact, one way of saying that someone has cursed is to say that he or she has 'spoken on' (*ohulomeraho*) someone. What does speech mean in this context? Although there is no living audience, the ancestors listen – perhaps in some people's views, God listens. What is said is something that can be said; it is not an evil secret. In time, if and when the curse is lifted, the words can be spoken aloud so everyone can hear who is who and what is right. Speaking has another significance too. Saying that a curser has 'spoken on' someone implies that he or she consciously intended what was to happen. It suggests agency in the sense of a person with a purpose.

If this conscious speaking were the only way of effecting a curse, things would be much simpler. But feelings tend to get mixed with intentions and notions of right and wrong. People say that when a parent feels annoyed or angry or is moved to tears because of being abused, the ancestors see those tears and register that anger and they effect a punishment, even though the curser may not explicitly have pronounced any words. The ensuing misfortune is no less a curse for not having been articulated; the important thing is that the story, the relationship, the offence, and the injured feelings are amenable to articulation.

Once a curse is suspected, someone has to ask the curser to remove it (there are ways around this, but going around it has radical implications, as I shall suggest). If the curser is a senior relative, it is often another parent who makes the request. A real mother or father might ask their own sibling, the aunt or uncle. There is a Nyole saying that, 'Where there is a child is where there is begging.' When you see your child suffering, you swallow your pride and implore the agent to alleviate the misery.

Here there was also room for uncertainty. I sometimes heard instances where a person denied having cursed and refused to undertake the ceremony of removal. Occasionally the person suspected of cursing went to divine to find out if he or she really had cursed. But the surprising thing was that the curser seemed so often to agree. I say surprising because I do not believe that most suspected cursers actually intended to cause their children to suffer so. Although the curser had never consciously 'spoken on' the sufferer, he or she might still agree to lift the curse. Maybe there had been some lack of respect that made him angry or sad. Maybe there had been a quarrel which the ancestors noticed.

'Perhaps you heard my quarrel'

Manueri asked his new wife's mother's sister to go divine about her because he had heard from her maternal uncle that she was cursed to wander from one man to another. The divination pointed to her father's brother (who was owed a cow from a bridewealth loan) and to her own brother, who was responsible for her since the death of their father. When Manueri went to tell his brother-in-law about the divination, the man denied that there could be any curse from the father's brother. He did not directly admit that he himself had cursed, but said that he had been quarrelling with his sister for marrying men who did not respect him and pay proper bridewealth. Perhaps the shades had heard his words and caused the curse. When he removed the curse a few days later, he mentioned the possibility: 'Father, Mother, I beg you – you help me. Perhaps you too were hearing my quarrel . . . I quarrelled because of her pride [stubbornness] when she was bringing men who despise me, who do not know that I too was born with this girl.'

Even if there has been no quarrel, relatives may agree to remove a curse in order to show good intentions towards the child. They are not hiding anything, not secretly nursing a grudge, but doing what they can to help, speaking out and asking the ancestors to bless the sufferer. A person has little to lose by removing a curse and in doing so, demonstrates a good heart, not only towards the unfortunate one, but to other relatives as well.

Removing words

The ideal way to 'uncurse' (*ohung'wabulula*) is to bring the 'child' to the curser who speaks aloud to the ancestors, mentioning the offence and the suffering and asking for blessings upon the child. Words are said to cancel the words that have been 'spoken on' the unfortunate person and there are three parties: 'parent', 'child', and ancestors. As one curser put it: 'Where there are three is where words are said. It is where they remove words . . .' (S. Whyte 1991b: 164). Often there are more people – siblings of the curse victim (in case the curse might have affected them too), parents, spouses, and sometimes a sister's child (*omwing'wa*) of the curser, to assist in the sacrifice to the ancestors. Although curse removals are not usually large affairs, they are open, not secret.

When the curser agrees to lift the curse, they must discuss how to do it and what is to be provided. In principle, there are two steps: 'pouring water' (*ohujuhaho amaji*), sometimes called 'blowing water' (*ohufung'aho amaji*), and 'giving millet food' (*ohung'a obusima*). The first is less elabor-

7.1 An old lady sprinkles water on her brother and his daughter as she removes her curse (1970)

ate: the cursed person kneels before the curser, in the courtyard, perhaps near the shrine if there is one. The curser speaks his piece, patting or blowing water on the head and the nape of the neck, and then the cursed person rises and walks away, without saying a word and without looking behind. For this the curser is usually paid a small amount, but in principle he can demand what he pleases. This step anticipates the next one; the curser often mentions that if the unfortunate person prospers, a large offering will be forthcoming. 'Let this baby be well, and one day the child will come with its mother, pulling a great goat of *ehigwasi*.' The ceremony of giving millet food is meant to include the gift of a 'huge goat' sacrificed so that the dead might enjoy its blood and so that bits of its internal organs can be placed in the consecrated millet food (*ehigwasi*) buried at the shrine for the dead. 'Those above', that is, the living, share the *ehigwasi* and eat meat. The cost of this ceremony can be considerable; in addition to providing the goat, the cursed person may have to pay a fine and meet other demands, such as outstanding bridewealth payments.

There is an imagery of curse removal: the righteous and authoritarian

7.2 Dedicating a goat at the ancestral shrine for the ceremony of 'giving millet'. The curser grasps the goat's foreleg as he speaks (note our microphone on the left). The sister's son is in the centre, while the victim of the curse and her children sit on the right (1971)

curser and the humble, submissive victim. 'A curser is a chief' means that you have to obey and to give what is asked. You may be humiliated by being forced to eat dry, hard millet food ('the millet will be dry' is a veiled threat of cursing). One account even told of a curser who tried to put chicken droppings in the *ehigwasi* as a final degradation. You come meekly pulling a goat. You admit a mistake, receive mercy and forgiveness. When Kyereeye removed a curse from her brother in 1970 she took the opportunity to chasten him soundly.

Speaking of a stingy brother

Kyereeye poured water on her younger brother Malijani and his daughter at the close of another ceremony, a clan sacrifice for Seja, which had assembled many people. So there was a large audience and the old woman played to it with vivid satisfaction. People kibitzed and added comments, as they sometimes did when shades and spirits were addressed. Kyereeye had a story to tell, and it was about how her brother had invited her to come stay with him in Busoga and then accused her of freeloading and begrudged her food. They had a quarrel (probably several) and he asserted that her children were turning out to be bad sorts (implying harlots) just like their mother. Finally he threw her clothes out of the house. In the logic of cursing stories, it was obvious why the brother now had little food in his garden and why his daughter was wandering from man to man.

Kyereeye started out by saying that she never had any conflict with Malijani before and that her other brother, also present, had never abused her. She situated herself on the side of the ancestors: 'I'm standing here . . . in our compound, of our father, of our grandfathers and of our grandmothers, of our mother's brothers.' She imitated (in Lusoga) how he abused her: 'You just came here to get fat on my bananas . . . you're making your children deviant just like you are.' She recounted how he tossed her clothes out of the house, and how, when her children came, he wasn't gracious enough to forget his anger and receive his sister's children generously. 'Do you deny this? Do you say that you never spoke this way? You abused me like that at your home.' Someone interrupted: 'The one who beats realizes [what he's done] and becomes humble. Now he has become humble!' Others interjected: 'To get fat on bananas!' 'Tell him out!' 'A real sister and he spoke like that!' 'That's why you got annoyed!'

She continued: 'I became annoyed and when I left, I cried tears . . . And then I also spoke – I came crying and perhaps the spirit or the dead people caught [him] for me.' She began to name her fathers, saying they had never abused her. Others too had died without abusing her: 'My grandmother, my mother Namuswa, my father's sister . . . Were, the wife of Kadokoli. And moreover they gave me respect. But you young child, really, we who are older than you – and you speak to me like that at your home.'

At this point, Kadiri, the man in charge of the ancestral shrine, reminded her that she was supposed to forgive: 'Now say that anger has left you.' She changed her tone: 'So now the anger is fading from me at this moment . . . Now I have let up on you. Now I'm removing my taint from you. And if indeed I am the one, this child [the brother's daughter] should come and settle down. After settling down, she gets a husband. Let the man marry her so she gets settled in a house. May my goat come here while I'm still alive.' (As a father's sister, the old lady would be entitled to a goat from the bridewealth.) Kadiri intervened again: 'Now turn to Malijani and say to him, you, Malijani, may your bananas ripen.' Before giving her blessing, she could not resist one more jibe, however. 'So Malijani, maybe you usually bring little women who are lazy, whose hands tremble, but . . . I, your sister, I think that I work where I work . . . you have that sort of habit of restricting people from eating. Stop it. And may your food become ripe at your home . . .' A kibitzer added: 'So that I may come and eat and get satisfied!' and she continued – 'when I get satisfied – And you Malijani, may your stomach expand and meanwhile, you just welcome me.' 'To belch loudly!' shouted an onlooker. 'So you Malijani, my annoyance is dissolving. Don't count bunches of bananas, never count bunches,' she admonished as she patted water on the back of his neck.

Kyereeye's harangue was about stinginess and insolence, and by implication the decency and generosity that should obtain between siblings. But it was also about feelings – anger and hurt. She aired her grievances in public detail with her brother kneeling before her. I sympathized with him a bit; the old lady had often come to sponge from us, as she did from everyone, and she had a sharp tongue. But in the morality drama of removing words, she was cast in the role of righteousness and he was put to shame.

In addition to the dramatic modes of curse removal where the cursed knelt and the curser spoke, there were other less stagy ways of lifting a curse. It could be done 'by mouth' (*ohugobosa omunwa*), that is, the curser could just say that 'if I was the one, then the trouble should mend'. For this, the curser did not have to be present and there were numerous examples where it was implied that this had been done. Someone approached the suspected curser with the suggestion that s/he was responsible for a child's misfortune; they might talk things over. Later things got better. A devout Muslim might read a portion of the Koran to show his good heart and invoke a blessing on the sufferer. Sometimes people said that the curser could simply touch the cursed, and that would lift the curse.

All these notions of removal acknowledge the authority of the curser and the necessity of forgiveness. The curser has to intend that the suffering be eased. The agency of the curser in assuaging the affliction is emphasized. Not so when people seek to reverse a curse by medicine. If you accept the claim of the men of medicine that the power of substances is as great as that of words, you can obviate the need for forgiveness and blessing. This is a tempting alternative for those who do not want to recognize the claims of a parent. It puts the initiative for healing in the hands of the afflicted. The medicine in question is not that of the dispensary; though people might well try that, it is only to alleviate symptoms, not to counter a curse. The medicines for curses have affinities to sorcery: 'Go to the specialist and he tells you to get sand from the footprints of the curser, grass from his roof and soil from his house and he tells you what to do with these things.' The Muslim medicine men know how to write a *duwa* (phrases in Arabic) and make an amulet that 'ties' the curser, so that his power is neutralized. To the extent that this revolutionary idea is taken up, it radically undermines the social consequences, indeed the whole rationale, of cursing. One old man, who claimed to have cursed a few children in his time, said that cursing is declining these days because now curses can be removed by medicine.

The fruits of offence

In proposing a cursing explanation, people often found analogies between the form of the suffering and the particular offence that had moved the curser. The effect was that the account provided its own evidence. Kyereeye's brother begrudged her food, and in consequence his banana plantation wasted. Or his banana plantation declined and his stinginess was recalled. Either way, the fit is convincing, as the following examples show:

> 1 There was a man named Naalo, who 'lost energy at the time of women', as a friend put it. This was attributed to the curse of his 'mama'. Once during the dry season they went together to fetch water in the evening. As they sat waiting for the water to well up in the source, his mama fell asleep. Naalo's girlfriend came along and the two of them went off together, leaving his mama to wake up frightened and walk home in the dark, alone and angry. (1970)
> 2 A boy who failed to get a wife was also found to be appropriately afflicted. His grandfather had come to visit and gone to rest in the boy's bachelor hut. On returning from school the boy said something rude about the old man sleeping on his bed. The story says that the grandfather declared that no woman would sleep there either. (1970)
> 3 A man was unable to keep any wife; he had the habit of beating them and they left him. The divination revealed that he had once attacked his own father when the latter was beating his mother. The father cursed him that he would be violent against his wives so none would stay with him. (1993)

In 1970 the most common of all cursing stories was about the barrenness of women and the sickness and death of their children. The link was made to bridewealth payments: the husband had not paid or not paid enough and his wife was cursed by a brother or father; or bridewealth was received but not distributed properly and the woman's uncle, aunt, or grandparent punished her because they were not remembered with a share. Nyole saw bridewealth problems as a major cause of child mortality and there was a fit here too. The fertility for which payment was made was cancelled.

The thirteenth child
Musa told the story of his wife, Namudiira, who lost twelve children. When the thirteenth fell ill, they went to her father's brother for removal of his curse. Namudiira's father had died and she grew up with her mother's brother, who received the bridewealth for her when she married. None was given to her father's brother and the two men had quarrelled on several occasions. In the end, Musa provided 20 shillings and a cow for the father's brother, and the child survived. But it was her lastborn.

Of the hundred or so cursing cases I counted in 1970, between a third and a half were about faults in bridewealth payment or distribution. The father or brother was supposed to give shares to various of the bride's parents according to a set of rules that seemed to invite problems. A mother's brother was supposed to get a cow 'of nieceship' from the marriage of his sister's first daughter. From this marriage, the bride's father should also pay her mother's brother anything outstanding on the bridewealth of her mother. Some said the mother's brother also had a right to a goat on each additional daughter, or perhaps only on the second daughter. From each set of sisters, a share was to be given to each of the following 'parents': the mother's father, mother's mother, mother's mother's brother, mother's sister, father's sister, and father's mother's brother. Trying to work this out over the years as a set of sisters married was difficult enough. But consider that the recipients of the shares came in sets as well: the father's sisters had to be called together to share their goat. There would almost always be possible grounds for complaint. As the divination of the Dry Tree (chapter 3) showed, interpretations dwelt not just on who had been neglected, but on where there were bad feelings as well.

By the 1990s, the amount of bridewealth actually paid had declined, although many people still considered five cows and five to seven goats to be the proper bridewealth. I wondered whether there was less cursing about bridewealth since economic hardship meant that less was paid. Since I did not systematically collect cases as I had done in 1970, my information on this point is impressionistic. People assure me that a bride's relatives still curse her over bridewealth issues and two of the eight cursing cases recorded by the diviner Luhonda over a month in 1993 turned on bridewealth.

The case of the young man who disinfected his uncle's chair was an early example of another theme in cursing accounts: the perils of success. A failure in conspicuous wealth, for example having a car and not being able to maintain it, or starting a large house and not being able to finish it, or having many cattle and losing them, may be interpreted as caused by the curse of a relative who felt neglected or offended. These stories concern men who are well known and consequently they circulate widely. In 1990 I visited a man who used to be sales manager for one of Uganda's big firms. He had had several cars, a large herd of cattle, and two wives. I found him with no wife at all; both had left him three years earlier. The cars were gone; many cows had died. Afterwards, my companions told me the story. He had inherited a wife when his father's brother's son died, that is, he became the heir of his lineage brother. Even so, he never helped his father's brother, now more than ever a father to him. The father's brother had 'spoken on' him so that he would know him. Such stories sound like simple warnings: never get too big to remember your parents. But some Nyole told them with sympathy for the victim: whenever anyone tastes a little success, greedy relatives will pull him down.

Any 'parent' can curse, and in the records kept by diviners and the accounts collected by me and our assistants in 1970 and 1993, suspected

cursers were overwhelmingly senior relatives. Curses were seldom attributed to spouses, and only slightly more often to siblings. By far the
most common cursers were uncles – mother's brothers and father's
brothers. Father's sisters were named more often than mother's sisters,
and real fathers more often than real mothers. In fact I only heard of one
case where a woman was said to have cursed her own birth child.

When asked, most Nyole said that women and men curse equally and
that both sons and daughters were made to suffer. But counting cases
showed that cursers were more than twice as likely to be men and that
curse victims were more than twice as likely to be women. In bridewealth
cases, the curse always fell on the bride; her 'parents' were the ones likely
to be annoyed, and in the logic of cursing, they were more likely to 'speak
on' her than on her husband, father-in-law or father. The first two were
not blood relatives, and the father was a sibling, not a child, to disgruntled
aunts and uncles. Women neither paid nor redistributed bridewealth,
but, in the idiom of cursing, they were the ones who were vulnerable when
the men who did so made mistakes.

This pattern of suffering for someone else's offence was not limited to
bridewealth matters. When Malijani insulted Kyereeye's children, saying
they were turning out to be harlots like their mother, she cursed his
daughter to wander from man to man. Sometimes counter-curses were
diagnosed: if your father's sister curses you, your father curses her
children in revenge.

Position and disposition

As a way of constructing persons, cursing plays on two themes. One is
about the positions of parents and children and it has to do with rights
and obligations and a kind of formal declaration of identity. The other is
about intentions and feelings; it deals with individuals and their motivations.[1]

In cursing, a person is defined in terms of position *vis-à-vis* another
person – specifically, in terms of the connection between parent and
child. Connectedness is evident in two ways. The curse itself and the
removal with its blessing emphasize that your health and welfare are in the
hands of your parents. Because of the way the relationship between curser
and cursed is put into words, this is made explicit. As an explanatory idea,
a curse is an affirmation of parental identity, and of the victim's specific
position as child.

Another kind of connectedness is implicit. It has to do with what I saw
as the 'innocent victim' pattern in cursing. Not only did 'children' suffer
because they themselves had not properly acknowledged the position of

their parents; they also suffered because their parents offended and quarrelled with one another. It seemed to me unfair that a woman should endure one miscarriage after another for a mistake her father had made. In the death of small children, there was a double innocence: they sickened and died because their ('innocent') mothers were cursed for bridewealth matters. When I commented on the injustice of this, Nyole did not see it. 'Parents suffer when their children suffer.' 'When it catches the child, it catches you.' This way of interpreting misfortune defined children as extensions of their parents. The pain of an individual infant or adult daughter was the parent's affliction and was not to be assessed in isolation. Children were dependants and not autonomous moral agents with individual human rights. And the dependence of daughters was particularly strongly stated in the stories of cursing over marriage and bridewealth.

These notions of position and connection were suffused with assumptions about morality. Parents had a right to be respected and obeyed, to be recognized through the payment and redistribution of bridewealth. As abstract tenets these were never denied and the idea of cursing helped to realize them and make them seem natural, thus reinforcing the morality of power relations between generations and genders. But to leave it there is to see people as automatons. It misses other assumptions about what persons are and it ignores the ways that cursing interpretations are actually unfolded in given situations.

Persons are identified in terms of their positions, but personal qualities and individual intentions are also part of what a human being is. In the way people spoke of both curser and cursed, it was evident that they considered disposition, motivation, and feelings – the inclinations and will to action that spring from the heart of a person. It is not just a matter of who you are and what you did, but of how and why. Relations between relatives can never be captured in a simple geometry of placement and obligation. There are histories, old grievances, interplays of emotion, and puzzling opacities. In relation to the dead, one also has a position and obligations, but the dead lack precisely the human qualities of feeling, individual style, and interactive nuance. They are translucent and one-dimensional in comparison to the living.

When analysing what moves cursers (or what dispositions in cursers move the ancestors), people spoke of annoyance, anger, and tears. Sometimes they showed feelings as immediate reactions to an event, as when Kyereeye responded to the abuse of her brother with angry indignation and tears of hurt. At other times, they seemed to assess longer term inclinations, as when the clients who came to divine about the Dry Tree spoke of the softness of a potential curser. Concerning our finding that men cursed more frequently than women, Enoch Lyadda wrote to us that in Bunyole, 'as elsewhere women are more considerate towards children than their menfolk who, on the contrary, have hard hearts'. He pointed to the dispositions of a whole category; others did likewise in confirming that real mothers would not curse their children, because they loved them. And the dispositions of particular individuals were always relevant in considering whether they had cursed. If they had seemed cool or quarrelsome, if there had been bitterness over the years, then indeed the heart might be hard.

When speaking of a cursed person, people also sometimes remarked on their inclinations and qualities. To be rude, quarrelsome, aggressive, proud, stingy or selfish showed a disposition towards a parent that might be just as weighty as the particular offence committed. In two curse removals of which I have records, the curser said of a woman who did not marry properly that she showed her 'pride' (amalala) in moving from one man to another. I think this means that she selfishly disregarded the interests of her family and behaved to suit herself. In another account, a man told how one of his wives had left him, wandered for years and returned. 'She might leave again because she is cursed to wander and to like it. That's why she won't have the curse removed. She likes the way she is.' An individual's feelings and determination were thus recognized, although in the last example the husband seemed to deny his wife's free will. She was cursed to be disposed to act as she did.

A cursed person, or someone involved in a conflict with a curser, must make a move and negotiate a situation. They are not simply passive. This holds also for women who sometimes have to convince men who do not agree with them.

Sick children and a stubborn husband
Namulwa's problems with her father went back to the first years of her marriage. Her initial failure to conceive was blamed on his curse, which he refused to remove, though Namulwa's husband Manueri quarrelled bitterly with him. When her first daughter fell gravely ill, divination revealed the father's curse. After much persuasion, he agreed to pour water on Namulwa for 10 shillings; he had wanted a goat but finally suggested that the little girl and her mother should come with a goat when the next child was born. They neglected to do so and it was after the third child arrived in 1970 that things reached a crisis point. Tom, the two-year-old, fell ill and his father Manueri went to divine and found 'little spirits' were the cause. But he did not do anything about them.

Three days later I became frightened. Tom had a high fever and seemed to be breathing with difficulty. His grandmother took me aside and asked me to try to persuade Manueri, her son (Tom's father), to go to Namulwa's father and beg for a curse removal. 'I know it's a curse because Tom gets a bit better, then worse. And I know Namulwa's father is cursing because he wants the last cow on her bridewealth. He's a bad man, but a curser is a chief – you must give him what he wants. My son says he doesn't have money to spend on his in-law, but money can't buy a child. He should pay for the removal rather than lose the child.'

Next morning I insisted on taking Tom to the hospital, and his father agreed. They diagnosed pneumonia and admitted him. When we went to fetch his mother, we found that she had gone to her father's and had been quarrelling with him. He abused Manueri as a bad son-in-law, saying Manueri had never visited him when he was in jail, that he didn't 'know' (recognize, respect) him, that he didn't give him gifts though he was earning money every month.

Namulwa stayed in the hospital six days with Tom. The new baby was with her, and as Tom improved, the baby became ill. Namulwa was convinced that her father's curse was now affecting the other child and was anxious to come home. But Manueri had refused to see his father-in-law. Finally the old man sent a message directing that Manueri should take them out of the hospital and bring them to his home. But when he brought them, the father-in-law had gone somewhere to visit.

When I went to see them, the baby was burning with fever and gasping for breath. Again I pressed for the hospital, fearing she wouldn't last the night. Manueri agreed immediately but his mother wanted the curse settled first. 'The hospital is also good, but there's no use taking her there until the curse is removed.' Namulwa was adamant. She stood cradling the feverish infant, tears rolling down her cheeks, and declared that she would not go back to the hospital until they had seen her father. Reluctantly Manueri consented, only to discover that his father-in-law had gone to mourn in another village. Trying to soothe his wife he promised to bring her father to the hospital. That time they stayed a week.

In the end, the ceremony was done in Namulwa's father's home. Manueri provided a goat and 68 shillings and he took his wife and the three children. When the father spoke his words, he seemed to refer to Manueri as much as his daughter. He said, 'This man was not bad. He saw the cold when it was in his house and he said, ah, perhaps the prayers which that big man prayed could be the reason.'

But it was Namulwa and not Manueri who blamed the cold on the big man's prayers. She was the one who pushed him, well helped by her mother-in-law, who sympathized deeply with her. There were other matters in the picture. Manueri had just brought another wife, who had given birth at the same time as Namulwa. Namulwa was unhappy and hurt by the way Manueri showered attention on the new woman. She wanted, she demanded, that he acknowledge her father, because it was also an acknowledgement of her and of his continuing commitment to their marriage. (Life goes on, after the notes about a ritual are finished. Namulwa's identity as her father's daughter was duly declared and she was blessed with eight more children and a happy marriage. But not with Manueri, whom she left for another man.)

To describe Namulwa as the 'victim' of her father's curse is insufficient; it would imply a degree of inertness and submission on her part and it does not capture the conviction with which she opposed her husband. She insisted on her definition of the situation and her plan of action even though Manueri had other 'evidence' from the diviner. In some ways this example is the contrary of the one with which this book was introduced. Namugwere's interpretation was overriden by her husband, who got confirmation from the diviner for his own views of his wife's troubles. Namulwa, with the support of her father and her mother-in-law, demanded that her husband accept what he had tried to avoid.

There were several kinds of evidence adduced to explain the positions and dispositions involved here. One relevant fact was that the last cow on Namulwa's bridewealth had not been given; her father might be wanting that. In the event this was dropped from the discussion and never paid. Another 'datum' taken up was that Namulwa had gone off to stay with her maternal grandmother after her mother died, leaving him alone. (She is his only child.) This was supposedly the reason for his first curse, and he put it that the goat and the 68 shillings were a fine for this offence. In other words, the removal was the follow-up for the pouring of water which had also dealt with the same issue. However, this old 'fault' did not in itself explain why people believed that the man had cursed. His relations with his son-in-law were strained and it was this he complained of when Namulwa went to see him in desperation over her child's sickness. His disposition was as relevant as his position: as Manueri's mother put it, he was a bad man . . . but in relation to his 'children', he was a 'chief'.

For Namulwa and her father, there was a positional relationship and there was an 'offence', perhaps several. But there was also a history and a social context which provided all the nuances of who they were. When Namulwa considered 'Who are you behind this suffering?' she weighed her father's unsympathetic response to her earlier problems, his disgruntled pouring of water when her first child was so sick, his bitter complaints about Manueri, his constant demands for money to buy alcohol, his failure to keep a wife and bear other children. He did not fit the picture of the moral, worthy and respected parent. But I think she also felt that he was her father after all, and that in deferring to him, Manueri showed esteem for her.

Uncertainty and ambivalence

The logic of cursing and uncursing is simple in principle. Senior relatives have a moral right to be respected; they can 'speak' to enforce it, with the sympathetic support of the ancestors. And they speak to 'remove words' and dissipate bad feelings, revealing themselves openly and declaring the goodness of their hearts towards the unfortunate child. They give an assertive response to the question 'who are you?', one which promises a continuing positive presence.

In practice, there was often uncertainty about the answer to the question. The possibility of doubt was incorporated in the fixed phrase, 'If I was the one . . .' which was always repeated in curse removals and often mentioned in the examples of how curses were made. 'If I was the one . . .' is a kind of oath ('As I am your father . . .'); it declares conditionality ('Let this happen if what I say is true'). But it also suggests that 'I may not be the one – there may be another.' In divination the possibility of another agent was often touched on. There was another danger too: that a curser might hide himself so effectively that he could never be known. This was the story told in 1969 by a man working as a radio operator at a police station in Kampala.

> **Barrenness and basketwork**
> At first, when my father went to the diviner, I did not want to hear of the curse that was supposedly affecting my wife. As a good Christian, I trusted in the prayers of my grandfather, who is a pastor, that she might conceive a child. After three years of marriage though, I began to believe what my father was saying. He and my father-in-law went together to another diviner; I didn't go because I was working here in Kampala. They found that my wife's maternal uncle had cursed her to be barren, because he never got his share from her bridewealth. I provided a goat and money and the uncle did everything in the proper way to remove the curse. But since then she has still not conceived. Now I don't believe in religion anymore. I think her uncle really did curse her and that he removed it truly. But I suspect there is someone else who also cursed and remains hidden. That other curser did *ohwefumiha* – if you do that no diviner can ever find out that you were the one to curse. After the curse, you either cover yourself with a basket, or you take soil somewhere and cover it with a basket, or you eat cooked bananas under a basket.
>
> Now I have two other wives, and the first one is sad and lonely because she has no child. She says I don't love her very much. But I do. She is my senior wife.

When people spoke of hidden cursers, it was with a combination of disapprobation and resignation. Their secrecy was like that of sorcerers; but in the nature of things, there was nothing to do. Or perhaps when there was nothing to do, secret cursers were at work. The idea of hidden cursers was one way of reflecting on the power and morality of senior relatives. The righteousness and basic good intentions of a curser can only be accepted if the curser steps forward to help. In a consultation by a grandfather about a little girl's illness, the client says of the curser, who has appeared in the divination, that 'I like him because he has come to catch but not to kill – if he has a kind heart, he should touch the child so they might know the difference' (S. Whyte 1991b: 164). The good curser reveals himself and heals the affliction; the evil one is never known so the suffering ends only with death.

There was another way of expressing uncertainty when affliction refused to yield to the lifting of a curse. Maybe the curser was not sincere in forgiving and blessing. While the ideal of cursing and uncursing was to disclose and mend, there was always the possibility of dissemblance and concealed malice. A curser might say that he was lifting his words 'with one heart', but later experience sometimes suggested that he had done so 'with two hearts' (*n'emioyo ebiri*) or 'half-heartedly' (*hamwoyomwoyo*). The recognition that there are bad hearts in every crowd is a fixed part of Nyole dealing with any spirits. When offerings are made, some is always poured, thrown or spat to either side so that 'those with bad hearts may eat over there', allowing the remainder to be shared by the good hearted. But with living human agents, a formulaic solution is not insurance against the secret malevolence that might lurk in the heart. Stories were told of cursers who spitefully dug up the sacramental food that had been buried at the ancestral shrine, thus nullifying the curse removal ceremony. Or, when the cursed left to go home without speaking or looking behind, the curser followed along behind, disallowing that marked separation which was important for the efficacy of the blessing. When such accounts were given, the way was open for a recasting of the curser. He or she was not behaving like a 'parent' at all, but seeking to harm secretly, as a sorcerer would. This is the theme of the following account by a man who lost so many children that he considered changing his name to 'Hurting'.

Hateful parents make life hurt

It was after my wife and I had two children and I was living at my father's home in 1959; we were all drinking millet beer with my little father and his wife Maria. There were two veterinary assistants there too and they said to me: 'Your children look good. What do you feed them?' I told them that I just give them ordinary food – sweet potatoes, millet, and bananas. But Maria started to cry: 'Praising a young child for his nice children – when my boy who is older has no children!' I said to her: 'Elder lady, don't cry because of your boy. The reason he doesn't get children is that he brings older women who don't deliver. But if he brought girls, he would also get children.' That was before her son got his two real wives – he used to just bring harlots who didn't stick in the home and wandered from one husband to another. Then Maria left. She went crying and she fell upon the graves of our grandfathers and grandmothers and she cursed this way: 'The children of Jiruma – I wish them to die. May he also be like my son.' So from that time my children go on dying – up to now. But on that day, we didn't know that she had thrown herself upon the graves; we thought she'd just left the beer party because she wanted to go home.

In 1961 we went to Buganda to rent land and grow cotton, maize and groundnuts. Both of my children got sick and died, even though we took them to hospital. The divination said: 'At home where you come from there is a woman tall and black. She's the one killing these children. She resembles your mother, but she is not the mother who delivered you.'

The next child died in 1964 when she was two years old. I brought her home to bury her in Bunyole. Soon my fourth child, the baby, fell sick. My little father came to me and he said: 'My wife is the one killing the children. Do you remember how we were drinking beer, and the vets asked what you fed your children? So then the woman ran away crying and she fell upon the dead people. So those things are killing the children.'

Very early in the morning I went to their home and I asked: 'What case makes you kill my children?' Maria questioned me: 'Who told you?' I said, 'Father himself is the one.' When he heard that, my little father left saying, 'There is your mother herself; let her finish these things. I have to go to Busaba.'

So my little mama begged 4 shillings from me and she poured water on me. Afterwards I returned home and she followed me. I met Higenyi repairing a house and I asked him to tell the woman not to come after me because she had just poured water on me. She should stay where she was. Why was she coming to my place? She just came, walked around my house and went back.

At dawn, my little father came to inquire whether the child had recovered since his wife had poured water, and I told him that the baby was a little better. Then he went back and told his wife: 'If this child gets better, they're going to say that it really was you who killed the other children. So it's necessary to kill all at once.' Next day the child died. When my mothers-in-law came to mourn, my little father came after he had been drinking and shouted something strange, trying to start a quarrel.

When my next child was born the following year, he too fell sick. Then I became so angry that I took a spear and a bush knife and went to their home. And I told them: 'If this child of mine dies, I'm going to kill all of you. I'll kill myself too because I see there's nothing to get out of life.' A week later, my little father and his wife came to me and she said: 'It's not me killing these children. If it's me who's killing them, let me die within the year. May lightning strike me down. Let's go to divine across the river. If it's me who is killing children may I fall in the water and drown.' [This kind of oath is called *ohwelaama* – to curse yourself.]

Just a week later, sickness hit Maria. She called me to bring a goat and she gave me millet, but her illness continued. My little father told me to break down the shop I had built on his land so that his wife might die when I was out of his sight. Then he called a meeting at the home of the neighbourhood clan leader and there he accused me: 'You're the one killing your mother because she killed your children. Now you better come and remove the sorcery.' I declared: 'It's not me who's killing. I am your child, I can't kill my mother. Unless it's the shades of my children, whom she killed – perhaps they are attacking her that she too should die.' He told me to take his hands. I held up my arm and said: 'God you are above and below. It's not me killing mama. But if she reached upon my children, she should die.' Then I took hold of my little father's hand. Three days later Maria died. I didn't go to mourn, I just sent burial money.

Now my last child has died too [by this time he had lost five children and two were still living]. We hadn't yet gone to divine the cause of the death when my little father met my brother at the bar and told him to take a message to me: 'Go tell Jiruma and his wife that – the child who died – I'm the one who killed it. Now you and your brother and your two wives should get together and see what you can do for me.' I got the message as I was on my way to Busolwe and I was so grieved that I turned back home and lay on my bed all day. Next morning I said that if I see my little father today, I'm going to spear him. Someone told him that and he ran to his mother's brother. They fixed a day when the mother's brothers should come and hear the case. My little father explained to them all that I wanted to kill him, even to use a gun, because he had sent a message that we should see what we could do for him. Now the people at the meeting asked him what he wanted us to do, but he failed to answer. They put more questions and in the end, he lost the case. He denied that he had killed the child and offered to drink water in which were mixed ashes from the funeral fire in order to prove it. But his maternal uncles prevented it because they knew he would die if he did so.

The man who related this long story (and I have shortened it) was a bitter and desperate 'child'. When telling me of these troubles, he remarked that it had gotten to the point that people greeted him with the word *jiruma*, an expression of sympathy meaning 'things hurt', and that the way his life was going, he could as well change his name to Jiruma. He did not mention that there were also land disputes between his father and father's brother, but that surely contributed to the bad feeling. He underlined again and again the malice of his 'parents' – the father's brother and his wife – and his own righteousness. His offence was so minor and their punishment so cruel. The little father was evil; he killed people by sorcery medicine. He and his wife might agree to do the ceremonies of lifting curses, but in their hearts, they only wanted death and suffering for their children. Here is the conundrum of cursing. Although the power is sanctioned by the ancestors, it can be misused by greedy, mean, harsh people.

Because cursing is morally acceptable and opens the way for forgiveness and blessing, it should reinforce the ties between parents and children. Unlike sorcery, cursing should lead to reconciliation. Perhaps it did sometimes. At least you were supposed to act as if all was well. After all, 'kinship is like your buttocks . . . you can't cut it off'. You have your parents for life. Yet there were cases like Jiruma's where accusations of cursing were indices of hatred, and deaths increased bitterness. No removal could truly erase what had happened. I was amazed that people were polite and ingratiating towards relatives they said had killed their children. Did they really accept moral authority so thoroughly? Even Jiruma went back to his little father to kneel and receive millet, though not with amity in his heart.

Recently a friend told me how her child, who had been sick for two years, had died. Biomedicine did not help; they tried everything. As the child began to fail, they went to divine and found the curse of her husband's mother. The grandmother removed the curse, but too late; the child died two days later. 'Now I seldom go there, unless there is a family ceremony. I can't forget what happened. Even my older children don't like to visit that grandmother – they know.' Cursing, or experiencing the effectiveness of curses – the power of parents – surely leaves many Nyole with such feelings. The idea carries with it, even for bystanders, the message that parents can kill – that things are not what they seem. These are the dispositions of the heart with which people must go on living.

Is cursing a good thing? I asked people. One woman, who was convinced she was cursed 'not to stick in marriage', told me: 'In Bunyole we really suffer with cursing and you're lucky not to have cursing in America.' I remarked that in America we have something worse: people kill each other with guns. 'We have that too', she replied. 'But anyhow it's better to kill someone at once than to make them suffer all their lives. You wander from one husband to another, you just start to cultivate somewhere and then you leave, always having to go back to your parents. And in the end, you'll die on the path.' Another person put a religious turn on his assessment of cursing: 'It's bad to curse – if someone annoys you, you should forgive and leave punishment in God's hand.' Others gave a more positive view in response to my question. 'Yes, cursing is good because it's traditional for Nyole.' 'It's good because in places like Busoga where they don't have cursing, people don't respect their parents.' 'Yes, it's good, but these days they curse for bad reasons.' The ambivalence about cursing was finely expressed by the person who explained that: 'The ancestor of the Nyole was cursed by God to be a curser – and God hates cursing.'

8 Substances and secrecy

Sorcery (*obulogo, obuloge*) is seen as the greatest danger to life in Bunyole; curses, little spirits, even shades might explain the death of children, but sorcery is nearly always the reason, in the minds of those who care most, for the demise of an adult. Not only death, but all kinds of grave illness, impotence, barrenness, snakebite, and madness were attributed to the work of sorcerers.

Sorcery is a deed carried out against another person. Where cursers 'speak on' their victims, sorcerers 'do' them or 'really work upon' them (*ohuholaholania*, to bewitch with medicines, is an intensified transitive form of *ohuhola*, to do). The words of cursers can and should be revealed openly; but the actions of sorcerers are secret works of hostility. The notion of malice hidden in the hearts of people with whom you are closely involved is central to the idea of sorcery. In exploring the last term in the explanatory idiom, this chapter examines the ways that socially produced conflict, uncertainty, and misgiving are entwined with illness and death. Acting in sorcery terms, people try to contain the perils of malevolence and suffering by the use of substances. But since suspicions are seldom openly voiced, the consequence of sorcery ideas is that uncertainty about other people is intensified.

In some respects sorcery is like other acts of personal aggression. If thieves break in, the question is: who called them? When a young woman was run over by a bus, people commented that someone must have paid the bus driver to kill her. Those picked up by soldiers during the time of the bloody regimes wondered who among their acquaintances had given their names to the military. If a house is burned down, or an animal stolen, or a person found murdered, people go to divine the perpetrator just as they do in a suspected sorcery case. They look for the agent among their enemies and they assume the same kinds of motivation that lie behind sorcery. But sorcery attacks differ from others in their use of a particular instrument – medicines.

Sorcerers work upon people through the manipulation of powerful material substances which can be acquired. Nyole do not worry much about people with an inborn capacity to harm – an evil eye, magical abilities, or psychic powers. The distinction between witchcraft and sorcery, which Evans-Pritchard (1937) identified among the Azande, and which has been analysed in other East African cultures (Middleton and Winter 1963; Harwood 1970) is not significant in Bunyole. True, there are tales of night-dancers (*abahunama*) who have weird, unnatural habits and abilities (walking on their heads, eating dead people, spurting fire from their fingertips). But these are scary stories, more than real dangers. I never heard any case of misfortune attributed to them, nor were there any in the divination records. The people English-speaking Nyole call 'witches' are those who work medicine and, potentially, that can be anyone.

Spirits, shades, and cursers have power by virtue of what or who they are in relation to you. I have called that relational power. Sorcerers use substantial power which is in principle accessible to all. The materials and the instructions on how to use them can be bought, learned, or given as one needs and seeks them. There is a kind of equity here which follows from the transactability of medicines (Parkin 1968). No one has a monopoly on them by virtue of age or sex. In consequence, no one can be totally free from suspicion.

'Medicine' (*obulesi*) is a substance that has the capacity to transform a person, animal, condition, situation or thing – for better or for worse. There is 'hospital medicine' and 'African medicine', 'sorcery medicine' and 'protective medicine', 'love medicine', 'cotton medicine' (DDT) and 'bicycle medicine' (rubber cement for patching inner tubes). Some medicine is only curative; Western pharmaceuticals are seldom seen as dangerous. 'African medicine' can both heal and harm and there is an ambiguity about it that also touches its purveyors and consumers. In 1990 when I remarked upon the many customers at a shop selling pharmaceuticals compared to the few buying African medicine at the market stall, my companion explained that people did not like to be seen buying African medicine because someone might misunderstand what it was for.

Sinister substances

The diviner's records and talk of sorcery were often more concerned with the ways in which sorcery substances were administered than with their exact content. Sorcery items can be applied directly into or onto the body of the intended victim; they can be brought into proximity so that the victim steps over or sees them; they can be removed from the body of the victim and worked upon. Finally, some kinds of remote sorcery involve no direct contact. Some educated Nyole distinguish between poison and other types, but most people assimilate all attempts to harm through substances under the term *obulogo*. You can as well die from something you 'jumped' as from something you ate.

Poison (*obutwa*) is generally introduced into 'food', 'vegetables', or beer. It is good manners to take a sip of banana or millet beer before offering it to guests in order to show that it is safe. People do not demonstratively taste food in the same way, but details of who ate what food were brought out in reconstructions of poison incidents. There are other ways of putting poison on or into people too. It can be put in bathwater, or, secreted in the palm, transferred when shaking hands. In the diviner's records was a case in which a woman was supposed to have smeared poison on a child's tongue. A woman who had gone blind explained that her co-wife had put poison in her cooking fire so that the smoke 'killed' her eyes.

Stories of poisoning were often tales of deceit, stealth, and betrayal. Someone has to get close enough to the victim to administer the poison. Who better than a neighbour, a friend, or a drinking companion? Since sorcery suspicions so often involve people you live with (agnates and spouses), plenty of opportunities can be imagined.

Battery acid in the cooking pot
In 1970 a man told how his mother was poisoned by the wife of her 'son', (that is, the son of her co-wife, his half-brother). She was cooking vegetables and went out for a while. The woman, her neighbour, sneaked into the kitchen and poured battery acid into the pot. When the cook returned and tasted the dish she was preparing, she felt pain almost immediately. She died after three days of severe vomiting and diarrhoea.

In that case, there had been bad feeling between the two women for some time, and it was the enemy herself who did the deed. But other accounts tell how an enemy pays a 'friend' to slip poison to the victim.

Money is greater than friendship
In 1970 Abudala, a book diviner, recorded a case in which a woman came to find out about her sickness. 'Her comrade is the one who gave her that medicine of asthma (*obulesi ow'olung'eera*) when their club went to mourn.' The diviner explained to me that the sick woman was leader of a club of women who go together to mourn when one of them loses a relative. Someone hated her 'because once you are a leader you have to be hated', and paid her friend to give her medicine that causes asthma. 'Her friend did it for money, since money is greater than friendship.'

The actual substances used for poison were sometimes mentioned. Rat poison (*obulesi bw'embeba*) and battery acid (*batri*) were supposed to be effective. Sometimes the name of the poison and of the sickness it causes are identical.[1] *Etumbi*, a substance given in food, is also the term for a dangerous, often fatal, condition in which the stomach swells up.[2] Leprosy was also referred to as both a substance and a disease. People spoke of 'pouring leprosy' (*ohujuha ebigenge*) whether it was put in bathwater or food, applied to someone's skin, bed, or seat.[3] Usually however, accounts of poisoning dwell on the manner of giving the medicine rather than its content or nature. The content of most medicines is secret, and poisonous medicine especially so. 'They put medicine on his beer tube; it tasted bitter when he sucked and he vomited immediately.' But few would claim to know exactly what it was they used.

Many kinds of sorcery medicine are placed close to the intended victim, rather than actually applied to the body. One of the most common 'proximity' methods is to bury medicine where the victim is likely to pass, such as the path leading to the house, causing him or her to 'jump medicine' (*ohutuuma obulesi*). Swellings of the feet and legs are likely to be traced to stepping over a hidden trap of this sort. Sorcerers also bury medicine at other familiar or intimate places: in the garden, under the bed, at the threshold, under the hearthstones, or at the eavesdrop. Usually people posit buried medicine; they do not actually find it. But occasionally, someone sees where the ground has been disturbed or a specialist actually digs something up.

When people told of seeing sorcery medicine, it was usually something left on the path, at the doorway or in the garden, as in this young man's account from 1970.

The banana leaf bowl

After my father died, my mother refused to marry Hire, the man who was appointed his heir, because she suspected he was the one who killed father by sorcery. She married another man instead and, sometime afterwards, she went one day to her garden and there she saw medicine in a container formed of a banana leaf (*edandi*). And there were footprints leading towards Hire's house. As soon as she saw it, her whole body began to ache. She called us children to come and we too saw the medicine and the footmarks. She was sick for one week. When Hire heard that his brother's wife was seriously ill, he never came to see her, so that confirmed our suspicions about him. We treated mother at home with medicine for bathing and with tablets, and she recovered.

The diviners' records include clients who did not wait for misfortune to occur, but came immediately to divine the sorcerer when they found frightening substances. Perhaps the most fearsome of all was *ehimalyo*[4] – a dead animal with medicines. The animal was generally of a kind not eaten in Bunyole: common lizards, frogs, tortoises, jackals, monitor lizards, and certain birds. Sometimes eggs were included, fertilized and ready to hatch; like the dead animals, they were not edible. In a couple of cases in the diviners' records, the *ehimalyo* was a dead sheep. One was rotting and had swollen so that it was about to burst. The other was simply dead, and was placed up against the door of the house at night so that in the morning when the door was opened, it fell inside. In 1970 Nandiriko recorded a case, which he said was incurable, in which a man suspected the neighbour with whom he had a land dispute of working upon his wife.

The murderous monitor lizard

I divined a man from Senda, a Nyole, whose wife is sick. She is ill in the arm from the palm to the shoulder. The divining spirit told him: 'This wife of yours started to plant potato vines. She had planted for two days; when she went on the third day, she found a monitor lizard in the garden. They had killed it and placed with it banana leaf containers filled with medicine. The woman touched the lizard with that arm, the right one, and there the illness caught her. The lizard was *ehimalyo* which they sent.' The client agreed, saying, 'Yes it's true, the divining spirit has known. But what shall I do?' The monitor lizard replied, 'As for me, they brought me to do work, that I may kill your wife.'

Dangerous substances and dead animals can be brought to the victim, but just as dreadful is the sorcery that removes substances from the victim and works upon them. *Ebitoolo* means the removal of something that has been part of or in contact with a person's body. Items mentioned include head or body hair, clothing, the small beads (*obunyere*) a woman wears about her waist, soil where the person has urinated, menstrual blood, sand or dirt from the footprint, a ring (*engata*) for carrying things on the head. A medicine man gave the following recipe for doing removal sorcery on your husband:

Cut a piece of cloth from the armpit of his shirt and the back of the neck and also a piece of material from the inside of the fly of his trousers. Get some hair from his beard after he shaves and, if possible, some pubic hair when he cuts it. Take some dirt from the midst of his compound and go with all these things to your own home. Find a medicine man and he will tell you what to do next. Either you put the things in ant holes or sometimes you place them in a new teapot and drop it in the river. You kill a chicken, split it open, poke a stick through it as for roasting and put that in the water also. In this way you can cause other women to dislike your husband and keep his love for yourself.

This type of sorcery, involving intimacy with the body of the victim, often occurs in sexual contexts, between partners, especially husband and wife, and between rivals, especially co-wives. It is a powerful means of driving someone mad. The man who proposed the above recipe noted that for madness, you should take some water which had collected in a depression of a large stone and put this, together with the personal items, in the hollow of a tree.

The principle of working through contact was common in the records of the medicine men. When a man's goat was stolen, he was told to bring some of its dung to be worked upon in order to affect the thief who had it. The person who wanted to 'tie' a curse might have to bring earth from the curser's footprints to be combined with medicine in order to 'soften' (*ohugondya*) the curser.

There are only a few varieties of sorcery that do not work through contact or proximity. 'Smoking a pipe' or 'reading a book' for someone are remote methods offered by some medicine men. They provide the pipe, medicine to be smoked in it, and instructions about the words to be repeated 'in one's heart' while smoking the pipe. The Islamic version is carried out by a mullah who can be hired to chant sections from the book *Ali Badiri* while burning incense. I recorded cases where boils, serious illness, motor accidents, and snakebite were attributed to this kind of sorcery.

Why you?

Sorcery medicines are in principle available to anyone, and theoretically anyone can use sorcery against you. In practice people find sorcerers amongst those they live with and to whom they attribute hatred, envy, and thwarted desire. A man is most likely to suspect his close male agnates and their wives, his colleagues, perhaps his neighbours, occasionally his wives and children. A woman mistrusts her female rivals and their children, her husband's brothers and fathers and their wives – even her husband himself. Other figures also turn up in the divination records and in sorcery stories, but the bulk of suspicions fall upon those with whom one interacts regularly.

Sorcerers, both male and female, are moved by envy. This is a theme pursued by the fortunate and those who want to explain the slow pace of 'development' in Bunyole. Educated, successful Nyole with whom I have discussed these matters, often point to the way small-minded people use sorcery because they begrudge and envy the achievements or good fortunes of others. Some have suggested that the elite avoid establishing themselves in the country because signs of wealth attract hatred. Certainly envy of success did figure in actual interpretations of misfortune. A woman thought her barren neighbour bewitched her because of her fertility. Even a man with many children divined that 'births brought him hatred'. The book diviners had several cases in which school children were given sorcery medicine because they were clever. Yet the cases in which envy alone was postulated were few. Most often, envy combined with some specific conflict, as when a woman finds that her co-wife killed her child because their husband loved that child best.

Gender patterns in sorcery tend towards a balance: men are defined as victims of sorcery as readily as women; and women are suspected of perpetrating sorcery almost as frequently as men. Nor is there gender segregation: you can as easily be bewitched by someone of the opposite sex as by someone of your own. The emotional motives imagined for men and women are similar; anger, envy, and frustration may move in the hearts of us all. But, in important respects, the specific issues which awaken these feelings differ because men and women are so differently placed in Nyole society. Men compete with one another over ownership of property, and women are rivals for the resources of the same husband.

Explanations in terms of sorcery provide evidence of the way that the organization of social relations in Bunyole produces conflict, mistrust, and uncertainty. The most fundamental goods of life, access to land, sexuality, and reproduction are arranged in ways that create as well as solve problems. The answers to the question 'why you?' that were formulated in terms of sorcery clustered around three motives: land, co-wife rivalry, and sexual agency. Tying these difficult issues to perils of health makes pragmatic sense in that the fit is convincing in terms of experience. As a plan of action, the idea of sorcery allows afflicted relatives and patients to pursue an enmity they already have in mind. Sometimes treatment provides assurance, although the very nature of sorcery suspicions encourages continuing mistrust of other people.

Land conflicts and men's misgivings

Given the population density described in chapter 2, it is not surprising that land conflicts are a major arena for sorcery suspicions. Nearly a quarter of the 38 sorcery cases collected by our assistants in 1970 were related to quarrels over land. They involved neighbours – who might be half-brothers or the children of brothers, men of the same lineage. Sometimes these disputes are taken to court; sometimes an attempt is made to settle them by a meeting of local elders. But public litigation does not diminish private suspicions of sorcery. On the contrary, misgivings are stirred as you imagine the desire of the other for the property, and the resentment he must feel at being opposed. Such conflicts often last over many years and they are continued by the sons of the men involved. These long-standing enmities may be invoked in explaining a series of misfortunes over a period of time; perhaps they are the closest Bunyole has to feuds.

Men own land and men suspect one another of sorcery in this regard. A man may well attribute the illness or death of his wife or child to the sorcery of the man with whom he is quarrelling over land.

Meningitis and the price of land

In early 1995 I met three men coming out of Busolwe Hospital looking grim. One carried a bottle of water and a saucepan. They had been visiting a patient, their relative and neighbour, Mulongo. But they were not talking to one another, and I sensed something heavy between them. Later I learned what it was.

Mulongo had fallen sick two weeks earlier. He felt feverish and chilly and sat in the sun and nursed a headache. His lineage brother, a trained nurse, saw he had 'malaria' and cough and gave him injections of chloroquine and penicillin at home. Three days later he had developed a stiff neck and a terrible fever and he could not speak; his brother the nurse said he might have meningitis and must go to hospital. Meanwhile, two other brothers and a father had gone to a Muslim book diviner and learned that sorcery had been worked on Mulongo. For this reason Mulongo's mother opposed taking him to hospital; it would be difficult to give him anti-sorcery medicines there. The nurse went to fetch the local pastor and together they convinced the others to carry him to Busolwe Hospital. But first the family called a medicine man to make cuts on his forehead and rub in medicine; they also washed him with medicine before they took him to Busolwe.

At the hospital he was put on an intravenous drip, given quinine, and injected every six hours with chloramphenicol and penicillin. He improved slowly; though he had lost his hearing, he could speak well enough to tell his friend Hasahya: 'The land I bought from Hamala is the cause of my death.' At home, his brothers were also concerned with the cause of his illness. They went to another diviner in order to check the first assessment. Then they called in a *mayembe* specialist who dug up a chicken that had been worked upon (cut in half, wrapped like a corpse, sprinkled with medicine) and buried on the boundary of the disputed land with a banana leaf container of medicine to mark the spot.

The conflict had been brewing ever since Mulongo bought a piece of land that his neighbour and clansman Hamala had to sell in order to raise cash. Hamala sold him the land at 60,000 shillings in 'Obote's money' and wanted to buy it back for the paltry sum of 600 shillings in 'Museveni's money', which he claimed was the equivalent. (In a currency adjustment, two zeros had in fact been knocked off so that 60,000 became 600 shillings, but subsequent triple digit inflation meant that 600 shillings would not even buy a kilogramme of sugar in 1995.) The immediate families of the two men had been drawn into the quarrel and the opposition between the families intensified as Mulongo's condition worsened. After he was admitted to hospital, as he wavered between life and death, one of the local clan leaders called a meeting of neighbours, clansmen, and their wives.

The meeting was attended by thirty-two people including the chairman of the local Resistance Council. Hamala was indignant; he denied having done anything to cause Mulongo's sickness. But the assembled neighbours insisted that Hamala publicly invoke the ancestors, saying that if he had quarrelled over land, he now was blessing some water and he wished that the sick man might recover. They put the water in a bottle to bring to the hospital where Hamala would give him some to drink and put some on his head. This was a way of 'pouring water' for a curse removal, suitable because the men were of the same lineage. But one term in the explanatory idiom was not enough. Hamala was also required by his clansmen to prepare porridge to take to the hospital – in case he had sickened Mulongo by sorcery.

These symbolic attempts at reconciliation were refused by Mulongo. When Hamala, two other clansmen/neighbours, and the chairman of the local Resistance Council called upon him in the hospital, Mulongo gave his hand to Hamala, saying 'I have no problem with you.' But when they made signs to him (he could not hear) showing the water and the porridge, he looked at Hamala: 'If you have brought your medicine for me, I won't drink it.' Addressing his brother, he said: 'Didn't those people send you to me three times asking me to give back the land? But when I wanted my money back, did they give it me? If I'm to die, let me die.' Later I asked Mulongo's brother whether Hamala had been angry at this rejection of the overtures he had been forced to make. 'I don't know his heart – he just left. But he's annoyed with me.'

Hamala and his family were indeed annoyed. They condemned their neighbours for having called the meeting and quarrelled loudly and bitterly when they saw them in their gardens. The brothers of Mulongo became suspicious that Hamala and his people were following them, trying to take their footprints. They declared that if anything happened to them, they would know whom to blame.

Mulongo recovered, though he still had ringing in his ears six months later. There has not yet been any healing of the breach between the two families, however, and the land issue has not been solved.

When chloroquine did not work, Mulongo's people defined the problem as grave and went to deliberate at the diviner's. In the explanatory idiom, they selected evidence from their experience (the land dispute), and treated Mulongo again in a medicinal mode, but this time within an explanatory/relational framework – they were countering sorcery, not treating symptoms. Once the association between the land quarrel and the possibly fatal illness was established, it was imperative to try a ritual treatment. I do not suppose that all who attended the meeting were convinced that Hamala was trying to kill Mulongo. But their land dispute was known, and under these circumstances it was best to take measures against this evident possibility. Making him do a version of 'pouring water' for curse removal at the same time, was tactful in the situation. Actually Hamala was a 'child' and not a 'parent' of Mulongo, but as a term of action, cursing emphasizes common descent and opens the way for reconciliation with the blessing of ancestors. Removing a curse as well as sorcery gave Hamala and his people a possible alternative version of events: perhaps the ancestors saw the bitterness in his heart and effectuated an 'automatic' curse.

The pragmatic perspective requires us to ask what has been learned from attempting to deal with a problem. Mulongo recovered, yes. But the quarrels and bitterness have continued. Whereas the conflict with Hamala was first taken as evidence in trying to deal with the problem of illness, the near fatal illness itself has now become data in the problem of the land dispute. Hamala has been cast as a mortal enemy; that is the lesson Mulongo and his supporters have drawn, and this could easily be evidence in dealing with the next misfortune in their homes.

Covert attacks by co-wives

Women as well as men need access to land – for their own cultivation and to ensure a generous portion for their sons. But the crucial concern for them in this regard is their relationship to their husband and his family, not the boundary between his land and his neighbour's. Marriage, not property rights, is the immediate focus of attention; in this arena women have their own gender-specific forms of competition.

English speaking women often translate the word for co-wife as 'rival', thus, 'I have a rival at home.' (Remember that the Lunyole word is cognate with the term for envy/jealousy between women.) Co-wives are often suspected of sorcery; they are thought to sicken and kill their rivals and their children. They try to render the co-wife barren and unattractive, to turn the husband against her and to drive her out.

The intense concern about sorcery from co-wives springs from a combination of structurally determined motivation and practical opportunity. The competition of co-wives, like that of brothers, is an aspect of the micro political economy of Bunyole. Brothers compete for land and livestock; co-wives must share material resources including their husband's cash and labour inputs, and also his attention, his support, his affection, and his nights. So there are all kinds of grounds for resentment and suspected motives. Living in such close proximity provides a wealth of opportunity for the potential sorcerer. No adult except a husband has such easy access to a woman's space, person, and children.

The diviner's records show how divination fits together motives, opportunities, and consequences to provide explanations that speak to women's experience:

> 1. I divined two women from Bingo – a mother and daughter. The daughter has her rival who is a sorcerer, who wants the husband not to like her. She gave him medicine to dislike her in groundnut sauce. Other medicine she buried under her co-wife's bed – to make her sick every day, so she fails in digging. The [client] said: 'That's true. She buried the medicine under the bed – I know where it is.' (1970)
> 2. I divined a man from Busabi – that you have a daughter who's married but she doesn't deliver . . . she delivered one child and another was

born dead. Since then, she has not made another to follow . . . This person has her rival who bewitched her, because they don't get on ['they don't speak the same words']. The client asked: 'With what did she bewitch her?' The [sorcerer] replied: 'I fed her blood from the birth of the child who came out dead.' (1970)

A woman's bed and the blood of parturition belong to her most intimate space – and her rival is always nearby.

One of the diviners, Yahaya, who was often consulted on marital and sexual problems in 1970, encouraged women with co-wife difficulties to come in person. On several occasions, he told a parent or husband who came to divine to let the woman come herself. This permitted direct interrogation and instructions about treatment.

The leaking pregnancy
A woman came from Nalugunjo, who was leaking blood from a pregnancy of four months.

> DIVINER: Had you skipped a period?
> CLIENT: I had missed four periods.
> DIVINER: How does your face feel?
> CLIENT: I feel much pain.
> DIVINER: You are badly off. In which month did you become pregnant?
> CLIENT: In the month of Ramadhan, on a Sunday. But I had been sick [before that] – I had stopped delivering.
> DIVINER: Was there any reason why you stopped delivering – either cursing or sorcery or quarrelling?
> CLIENT: That woman – we were together in one house.
> DIVINER: This comes from your fellow woman – when she was jealous she planted medicine in the hearth and at the eavesdrop.
> CLIENT: The woman has left now. My husband separated from her. So she went and married nearby. Instead of drinking water from the well near hers, she drinks the water which we drink at ours.

The woman asked the diviner to try very hard to help her and he agreed. He instructed her to go aside in private and tear off a piece of the cloth she used as a sanitary towel. He wrote Arabic words on this and told her to put it in place when she was bleeding a little, but not when she bled heavily.

The extraordinarily intimate nature of this exchange allowed the diviner and his client to relate bodily experience to an enemy's jealousy and the placement of dangerous substances in the woman's own space. She confided her worry that the rival was still seeking contact by coming to the place where she got water. Most important, it allowed her to take substantive steps that corresponded to the nature of her experience.

In records kept by the spirit diviner Luhonda of Buwihula during 1993, a woman who had been paralysed on one side came to divine about the mysterious disappearance of her underwear.

> The divination told her: you have your co-wife, a Gisu woman. She's the one who clipped a piece of your cloth and stole your underwear. She's just 'removing, removing' [doing removal sorcery] because she wants to chase you away, so you leave the husband to her.

The diviner's records showed a theme that I also heard and saw in polygynous homes: the shifting politics of co-existence. Periods of detente were broken by quarrels, sometimes culminating in the departure of one wife. Husbands tried to put a good face on things ('You just have to know how to manage women'), but in moments of honesty, they admitted the difficulties. A man who had recently brought a second wife, on the grounds that she could help when the first one fell ill and he couldn't take time off from his job, mused on the atmosphere of home life. 'These women . . . some days they talk, sometimes they refuse to speak to each other. To solve problems, I brought problems!' Because the possibility of sorcery is always in the background, these everyday tensions have a sinister dimension. The idiom of sorcery is wonderfully suited to polygyny because polygyny involves daily interaction with someone whose disposition you suspect. The combination of long-term conflicts of interest and daily interaction breeds suspicion.

Sex and agency

Adultery is a sorcery theme that illustrates both differences and similarities in men's and women's positions within marriage. Although a wife is supposed to be faithful to her husband, and I think many are, cases of a wife's suspected infidelity formed an element in sorcery stories. The husband was said to use sorcery on his wife's lover, either by medicating his wife so that her paramour fell ill or by directly giving or sending sorcery to his rival. One of the most striking examples of this type of sorcery is the medicine that causes an adulterous pair to stick together in the act of intercourse. It is assumed that a husband surreptitiously gives his wife such medicine to catch and punish his rival.

The opposite theme, of an adulterous husband, is not actually a mirror image, in that a man's extra-marital affair may be viewed as courtship rather than adultery if his lover is unmarried. He has the 'right' to find other partners whom he may marry as second or third wives. Yet to avoid quarrels men tend to conceal affairs from their wives[5] and in the secrecy that surrounds such liaisons, suspicions of sorcery can also flourish. Usually it is assumed here as well that rivals use sorcery against each other, rather than spouses 'doing' one another. For women, such rivalry is like that between co-wives and suspicions fall both ways: upon your lover's wife and your husband's lover.

It is striking that, in Bunyole, adultery is almost always seen in terms of the danger of sorcery between the rivals.[6] Within the household, the consequences of adultery could be quarrels, beating, and even the breakup of the marriage; but the unfaithful spouse was not construed as the wilful agent of misfortune. The conflict expressed in sorcery was between the rivals, not between the spouses.

Thwarted desire is imagined as a powerful motive for sorcery. A woman's affliction may be attributed to a man whose advances she has refused, just as a man's illness may be blamed upon the work of a woman who wanted him. These matters can be deadly serious, as these examples from the diviners' records in 1970 show:

> 1. A father came to divine about the death of his daughter, studying in P6. They found that she had been done on the path, when she was returning in the evening. The divination said that her teacher had 'tried to engage her' but she refused, saying that her father would surely beat her if she became a harlot while she was in school. The father arranged with the diviner/medicine man to place medicine on the girl's grave: 'I'll come to fetch you so you can trap for me the person who killed my child.'
> 2. A *mulalo* [a man from Western Uganda/Rwanda who herds cattle] who worked for some people in Buhadiwo fell ill with a swollen stomach and died in 1968. The divination revealed that he had been killed by the wife of one of his employers. 'What made her bewitch him was that she wanted him to engage her. He refused, saying that you are the wife of my master, I cannot engage you.'

In both of these cases, the alleged sorcerer's desires were illicit; they were shown as bad lots, bent on seducing virtuous people. The frustration of legitimate desire can be just as dangerous.

A woman who leaves her husband against his wishes risks that he will use sorcery to harm her. In fact women who wanted to go sometimes sought protective medicine to 'tie' their husbands, so they would neither follow them physically nor strike at them medicinally. Sometimes the diagnosis of an ex-husband's sorcery was the occasion for reconciliation; a woman went back and her husband 'undid' his sorcery. More often, the idea of his sorcery was a recognition of the anger and frustration he felt at being denied. In the divination of Somebody's Wife (chapter 4), the diviner suggested that the rejected husband was bewitching her because she had been proud and refused him. 'Even though you are proud, you will die.' Her 'pride' consisted in independence, her unwillingness to follow her husband's desire. This reference to womanly 'pride' came up in cursing stories too, as a label for women who did not stick in marriage, thus angering brothers, fathers and other 'parents'. A woman's independence as an actor is imagined to frustrate presumed agents.

The disposition of widows is another arena in which women's autonomy is problematized. She can refuse a replacement from her dead husband's clan or decide not to remarry at all. But if she denies a man who particularly wants her, she and others are aware of the pernicious resentment he may feel. In 1990 a widow entertained me one afternoon with her lively account of the thoughtless behaviour of husbands and the obvious advantages of not remarrying. But as I was leaving she confided that her chronic illness was due to the sorcery of her dead husband's agnates, who wanted to inherit her.

This is not only a widow's view of potential heirs; it can also be the potential heir's view of a widow, as a case from Nandiriko's records in 1970 illustrates. A married man had sent his brother and his maternal uncle to find out the reason for the splotches on his skin. Nandiriko wrote: 'There is a woman, a widow, the wife of his brother who died. That's the one who poured leprosy on him. They asked, "But what did she envy him?" The divining spirit replied, "The woman had wanted this person, but he refused." '

In all of these cases, there is a recognition of the wilful decision of the victim on the one hand and the frustrated desire of the sorcerer on the other. Calling the spurned admirer a sorcerer distributes virtue and iniquity comfortably, but neither men nor women have a monopoly on these qualities. Both pursue yearnings, both have a volition that is problematic for other actors.

'If they did this to me . . .'

People discover that they have been bewitched through divination, through finding sorcery material, and through circumstantial evidence.[7] Although people do sometimes find dead animals and makeshift containers of medicine, it is far more common that they 'know' a sorcerer is at work without ever seeing the medicines themselves. One kind of clue is the nature of the misfortune itself. Death of an adult, being struck by lightning or bitten by a snake are likely to be caused by sorcery. So are multiple deaths of children. When five children of an extended family died in one year, someone told us that it was the ancestors wanting the second funeral ceremony to be performed. But Manueri doubted. 'When *olumbe* is needed, children can all suffer from sores. Then they can get sick, and perhaps one or two might die. But not five.' Sudden onset of an illness is also taken as an indication of medicine at work. A diviner diagnosed a man's sickness as due to a clan spirit, but his family was convinced it was sorcery. 'In the morning he was fine and went to dig in his garden. When he came back he was sick. He must have jumped medicine.' Most of all, vomiting and diarrhoea immediately after drinking beer or eating are prima facie evidence of poison. Scenarios are proposed to explain who placed the medicine and how they did it to ensure that only the target person consumed it. To this evidence of the symptoms is added information about the behaviour and disposition of suspects. A quarrel, neglecting to visit the sick person, or failure to attend the funeral will be remarked upon. As with cursing, so with sorcery, the imputation of motives, feelings, and dispositions to an agent within the context of a relationship makes the narrative ring true.

Once a misfortune has been attributed to sorcery, there are several possibilities for treatment. One is to get the agent to remove the sorcery. This implies a confrontation and I shall discuss that presently. Another possibility is to simply treat the victim with medicines, acknowledging that the affliction was sent, but concentrating on curing the patient rather than dealing with the agent. The Muslim medicine men do this sometimes; they prescribe powerful substances to be taken in special ways without any explicit attempt to turn the affliction back upon the perpetrator. Therapy concentrates upon the symptoms of the victim, recognizing that they may be difficult because of their cause. Here there is a subsumption of aetiological in symptomatic treatment, in contrast with the usual overshadowing of symptomatic by aetiological treatment.

The most common response to sorcery, however, is reciprocity, phrased as treatment by returning the work of those who have 'done you'. The medicine man may also give medicines to be applied to the body of the afflicted person, but part of the cure involves reacting to the agent, while declaring your own conscience clear. The following account was given in 1971 by a woman whose mother had suffered puzzling symptoms of strange behaviour and odd patterns of pain for some time. The mother had been separated from her husband for many years and believed that he hated her and her children.

A shroud in return

I called Wandera to come and treat mama. When he arrived he already knew it was removal sorcery and he told us to prepare two rings (*engata* for carrying head loads), place banana leaves on them and pour water into them. Then he handed me medicine to give mama, who sprinkled it on the water and said to herself: 'Those who are against me, if God hears that I have done nothing against them, what they have prepared for me, let it return to them.' I was also given medicine to put in the water and I said to myself: 'If it's true that my mother bewitched them, let her die, but if not, let them die. ' I said these words in my heart, not out loud. Wandera told me to hold the hen I had provided by the legs and pass it around mama's head, while saying some words in my heart. Then mama was given a banana leaf and she held it on her lap with one hand underneath and one hand on top saying some words in her heart. With this and another leaf, she covered the water and medicine. Then she was given more medicine and she sprinkled it on top saying some words in her heart. Each time Wandera told us when we were to say words to ourselves. He gave mama other medicine to put on a potsherd and burn with charcoal and medicine to sniff which made tears come in her eyes. We sat awhile and Wandera's assistant went out and sprinkled the compound with water and medicine.

Wandera gave me two sticks to lift the leaves and I saw three 're-movals' in the first leaf container and two in the second. They were tied in rags and one was in a tin. When the bundles were opened I saw that some things were rotten but some could be distinguished. There were feathers, beads [of the type a woman wears around her waist next to her skin], a piece of sheepskin, the hairs of a cow and of a goat, the hair of a person from the head and from the private parts, soil from footprints and other dirt from a grave [grey soil from deep in the earth as found when digging a grave]. In the tin was an amulet and medicine with a strong smell and other things which we couldn't recognize. There were also pieces of old sheets.

They took a hen and cut it and the assistant sprinkled blood on the 'removals' and smeared some on mama's forehead and the back of her neck. Then Wandera asked: 'You have seen this – what do you want me to do?' Mama replied: 'As these people have punished me so long like this and I have done nothing, I also want to punish them.' Wandera said: 'If you want to do so, bring a sheep or a goat, but a sheep is better because these things were done by a sheep.' Mama gave Wandera 2 shillings wrapped in paper and we said some words over the coins, so he could go and ask his people [divine about] who had done this.

A few days later, Wandera returned and he told mama that there were four people: 'There are two men on your husband's side, and your husband and your co-wife. They want to kill you. Other "removals" were put in the latrine; they were rotten and I couldn't get them out. That was to make you run mad.' He told mama to sprinkle medicine on fire while saying some words in her heart.

Wandera had directed us to provide one yard of white sheet and we held it over mama's head. He gave her four amulets and on each one she mentioned the name of one of those who are against her. She folded those amulets in the sheet and sprinkled medicine on them. Wandera told her to say: 'Those people whose names I have mentioned – may they die by a snake or by water or a gun or any disease. And one day I will hear that they died and they will be buried in a sheet like this and I will be told to go and mourn.' Then mama repeated the words, naming the four names and with each name she folded the sheet until it had been folded four times. Then she sewed up the sheet still folded in four with the amulets inside and she was told to keep it in her trunk at home.

Wandera gave mama so many different types of medicine: three kinds for drinking in tea, one to bathe in at the crossroads, one for smoking in a pipe, another for drinking with water when she feels stomach ache. There was one which she is to cook and whip up to get foam with which to wash; another is for burning on a potsherd – you cover your head and the medicine with a sheet and inhale the smoke. There were three types of medicine to mix with sand from their footprints; you say words over the mixture and throw it in an old anthill. There was also medicine to rub in cuts on her arms and legs, chest, and the back of the neck. Wandera gets some of that medicine from the Arabs in Mbale and he uses Nyole medicine too.

We dug a hole in an anthill, put the 'removals' in it, killed the sheep and sprinkled some blood on them. Wandera added more medicine and we buried it all. They smeared blood on mama's forehead and the back of her neck. Then they brought a cock and cut off the longest toe, which they put with medicine into an amulet to tie around mama's waist. Wandera wanted me to keep that cock, but my husband doesn't know about this, and he might decide to kill that cock for visitors. So Wandera agreed to take it home. If those people die, mama will bring the sewn sheet and perhaps they will kill that cock. He told us to take the ash from the fire upon which mama had sprinkled medicine and go at night and put it in the river. That night I sent my boy to take it to the swamp. Next day mama went back home feeling a bit alright.

Wandera's treatment began with an oath of innocence declared silently in the hearts of the two women. Such pledges figured significantly in responses to sorcery, affirming that the victim was a good person, forced to take drastic steps. The same pattern of justifying what you are doing appears in planting 'traps' for thieves, adulterers, and other wrongdoers. As a medicine man explained, you should do *ohulaamirisa*, fixing a condition on the medicine: 'If someone did so and so, let this happen.' He added that it only works if it is true and you are honest. Although you are using medicine to harm, even to kill, you cast yourself like a curser, as a righteous person who has been wronged.

Next Wandera revealed to his clients the full horror of what they were up against. There was mama's own hair, and her beads, and the very earth where she had stepped, mixed with rotten things and worked upon with animals and medicines and things of death – grave dirt and burial sheets. Thus confronted, she declared that she wanted to respond in kind and that is what they did – with a sheep and a winding sheet, medicine and instructions to collect footprints, medicate them and put them in an anthill.

Most revelations of sorcery are not this dramatic nor are most responses this elaborate and expensive. Yet the principle of secret vengeful reciprocity runs through one sorcery story after another. It is reflected in the words whispered as the chief mourners throw the first earth into the open grave: 'Let he who caused you to eat this fresh earth follow you hither before you rot' (Wesana-Chomi unpub. MS). It is implied when people bury medicine to harm their attackers. We met it ourselves when we went to divine the sudden death of our dog. We learned that thieves had poisoned the dog because they wanted to rob us. The diviner/medicine man offered to put medicine where the dog was buried to get the thieves.

The reciprocity of sorcery contrasts with the attitude towards shades and spirits. You should not quarrel when seeing is asymmetrical (what you don't see although it sees you); even cursers, insofar as they are identified with the shades, must be placated. With sorcerers, the relationship is symmetrical and the identification of someone as a sorcerer justifies hatred and revenge. Justifies? Perhaps that is too strong a word, for there is seldom an open acknowledgement of sorcery and responses to it. Privately, in your heart, within the confidence of those closest to you, you intend that if they made you suffer, they should suffer in return.

Secrecy and civility

As a way of talking about human relations, sorcery emphasizes the possibility of evil. The aura of secrecy surrounding sorcery has the effect not of keeping it secret, but of reminding people that there are unspoken intentions and concealed actions behind the surface of social life. People speak of them, but in confidence, thus reminding the listener that these are hidden things. When I asked to attend the tying of 'removals' described above, Wandera told his clients that I should not come, but that they could tell me privately what happened.

Silence is used to frame and underline the existence of the hidden. The mother and her daughter are told what to say, but they are to repeat the words in their hearts, not aloud. When you smoke a pipe against your enemy, you speak your intentions to yourself, silently. But the fact that you speak silently is always mentioned. The image of cursing is of speaking words and removing them aloud in the presence of witnesses: 'Where there are three is where words are spoken.' The image of sorcery is silence and secrecy. This does not mean that life always approximates the images. As I have shown, suspicions about what is concealed may permeate cursing tales; but the point about cursing is that revelations should be made. Acts of sorcery may be witnessed and confided to others. Suspicions and intentions are revealed to those you trust – in fact such confidences are a mark of solidarity. But the point about sorcery is that malice is hidden.

Kidneys and secrets

A young woman who was worried about someone she thought was against her consulted a medicine man for protection in 1971. As part of his treatment he gave her a powdered medicine to cook with kidneys. He instructed her to take the kidneys out of their membranes and separate each section with care. Pulling apart the sections was to make her know the secrets and bad things people were saying about her.

In this way the treatment objectified and perhaps magnified her original concern – that people were concealing animosity and bad intentions.

Occasionally hidden evil comes to light in a way that reveals and confirms the truth in your worst fears. Revelation allows confrontation and resolution of a sort. There are procedures in Bunyole by which a sorcerer publicly removes sorcery from the victim – as cursers do. They are the exception; they were used as treatment in only four of the thirty-eight sorcery cases recorded by our assistants in 1970. Still they are instructive because they show so clearly the malicious and secretive nature of sorcery. Since people do not willingly admit that they have used sorcery against someone, they cannot be approached in a friendly way to remove it, as cursers can. They must be pressured to do so either by a family head or by a group of neighbours and clan leaders, as happened in the meningitis/land case of Mulongo.

When the suspect is a woman, her husband or another authoritative male figure can insist that she undo her work. 'Undoing sorcery' (*ohulogolola* or *ohutambulula*) brings things out into the open under the control of a senior man. A standard scenario is that there is strong evidence that one wife has used medicine against the other or her children. The husband may force her to remove the medicine if it has been found, or to give *eng'aaso*, a counter medicine. Another 'traditional' possibility is 'to give porridge' (*ohunywesa obusera*), a parallel to the giving of millet food for uncursing, but with a significant difference. If sorcery is suspected within an extended family, the head may direct that each woman prepare millet porridge to give to the victim (or alternatively that each person give from a single pot of porridge), as in this case related in 1969.

Porridge for Mutono

Mutono was ten years old when she fell ill with a swollen stomach in 1968. Her father divined that someone on her mother's side had given her *etumbi* medicine and they took her to her maternal grandfather's home to undo sorcery. They stirred porridge and called everyone in the home. Each one made her drink porridge, saying, 'If I am the one who bewitched you, may you get well when I make you drink this porridge.' The girl died anyway. It was her uncle's wife who killed her because she was envious of the child. That sorcerer is still married to her uncle, but she and Mutono's mother don't visit each other. They just greet, but, in the heart, they hate each other.

When everyone gives porridge, no sorcerer is identified. No one has to admit ill will and all show their good intentions towards the sick girl. Neither is there any airing of grievances. Afterwards life goes on with civility on the surface and hatred in the heart.

The literature on witchcraft and sorcery in African societies often describes open accusations of and confrontations with malefactors. Witch-cleansing movements identify evildoers in the community and attempt to purify or disarm them. Suzette Heald (1989) has described violent patterns of dealing with witches among the neighbouring Gisu people. She shows how marginal men, squeezed by a shortage of resources, may be identified as thieves or witches, and murdered, or confronted and threatened by vigilante groups. Such action requires a consensus that a person is habitually bad, and Heald demonstrates how demographic, political, and economic patterns fit together with Gisu vernacular psychology to create such verdicts. In Bunyole this is far less common though not unknown. There were occasional incidents when people identified as thieves were murdered. There were those of whom it was said that they had killed many people by sorcery. In a few cases neighbourhood meetings were held and they were told to leave; and it seems that this was possible where their claim on the land was tenuous or contested.

Viewing sorcery as one of several explanations of misfortune, however, I do not see witches or sorcerers as 'public enemies'. Bunyole is full of occasional, circumstantial sorcerers, in the sense that some people 'know' who has 'done someone' in a particular situation. But there are few habitual sorcerers, in the sense of individuals widely recognized as repeatedly harming others, because that is their character. Everyone has their own sorcerers. I know who hates me and you know who is out to get you. Perhaps that is why witch-cleansing or anti-sorcery movements have not been important here. They would require a public consensus that seldom exists.

Life in Bunyole is made smooth by courtesy and civility, often warmed by friendliness and hospitality. The cordiality of interaction contrasts with the existence of malice, not only in general ('Nyole are good people but they make each other suffer') but also in specific cases, where people continue to speak amicably to individuals they think have killed a loved one. Granted there might be signs of coolness noted by those most closely involved. But since there is seldom a confrontation and accusation, hostility is only surmised. If you think someone suspects you, you may be extra careful to show sympathy and a good heart.

Burial as usual

When Musa finally died in 1992, after wasting and weakening for many months, his mother and stepfather were convinced that he had been killed because of land. His father's land was in Mwihyalo, but his father had gone mad and died, and his mother married Saawe, a clan brother of her husband, from another lineage in another place. After he married, Musa put up a house on his land in Mwihyalo, and he lived there until he became very ill and his wife left him. Saawe, his mother and her other children brought him to their home to look after him, together with his 12-year-old son. Musa confided to them that his brothers and fathers in Mwihyalo had set *ebitega* medicine for him because they wanted his land. It was a big portion and he was the only son of his father; they were eager to get rid of him, so they could take it over. In his last weeks, we took Musa to the hospital hoping to save him. But he had given up hope and begged to be brought home. By home he meant the place where his mother was, with Saawe – and that is where he died.

Immediately people gathered, women crying and men sitting in solemn groups. As the time came to prepare the grave, Musa's mother came dancing with the restless step of mourning towards the house where his body lay, chanting: 'You wanted to be buried here, but you should go in peace to where they wanted to kill you.' Soon the old man Saawe went into the house with a group of men. Weeping, he placed a chicken on Musa's breast and said: 'Now my son, go in peace to your own house.' A vehicle was brought up to the house, but before they lifted the corpse, Musa's mother's brother spoke angrily, standing with his back to the pickup, as if to block the way. It is the duty of a maternal uncle to ensure that his nephew is buried well, and he demanded to know why Musa could not be buried here where he preferred to be. Saawe replied that he did not refuse to give Musa a grave. Then his voice became more strident: 'Those people wanted to kill him and eat him there. Now they have murdered him. Let him be brought to those who did it. May they be satisfied with their work!' In more even tones, he continued: 'Musa must be buried on his father's land in Mwihyalo for the sake of his son. Otherwise the boy will have no voice for that land. He should have the land, even if we later decide to sell it and buy land for him somewhere else.' At this, the uncle agreed and stepped aside to make way for the body to be placed in the vehicle.

When the mourning party arrived at Mwihyalo with the corpse, some of his relatives from there collected. One of them wept and wiped his eyes as he spoke to Saawe. A son of Saawe with whom I was talking motioned discreetly with his lips in their direction: 'That's the one who did it.'

Next day, after the burial, when members of Musa's mother's clan and of the various sections of his own sat talking in groups, Saawe chatted amiably with his clansmen of Mwihyalo, the very ones whom he had identified as murderers the day before.

Saawe was a 'big man' (*omuhulu*), elderly and respected, and he mastered the calm dignity and courtly speech that are honoured in southern Uganda. He aired his anger at those who sent death to Musa, but then he coolly did the correct thing, asserting that Musa belonged with his father's people, hiding his antipathy in order to complete the burial properly and keep options open for the future.

Sometimes long-standing hostility seemed to reach a breaking point in connection with suspicions of sorcery.[8] A man might migrate to Busoga or go to live with his maternal uncles when he decided that sorcery had become too much. The breakup of a marriage might be explained by one of the parties as due to the sorcery of the other. To say someone was a sorcerer was to discredit him or her and to credit your own actions. However, there were many instances where people continued to live near individuals who, they whispered, had used sorcery against them. When suspected sorcerers are kinsmen or affines, it may not be possible to break off relations with them. Or the price of doing so may be too great, as Saawe reckoned it would be if an open confrontation with his clansmen at Mwihyalo weakened the land claims of Musa's son. Moreover, maintaining a minimum of civility keeps open the option of resuming more cordial relationships after the grief and pain have passed. Nyole recognize that, in desperation, a person blames others for suffering and loss. 'The bereaved just cries like that' implies that in grief a person may make accusations that should not be taken seriously (see note 8). In time you may be less certain of the cause of an affliction; perhaps there are other agents. So it is better not to make an open declaration. Finally, if someone really is a sorcerer, the last thing you want to do is anger them further; they may intensify their sinister efforts.

Evil, agency, and substances

Of all the imagined agents of misfortune, sorcerers are the most dangerous and the most evil. Like cursers, sorcerers are people with whom you are bound in strained or disturbed relationships. But a diagnosis of cursing entails recognition of some kind of morality; it puts problems in the frame of parents and children, respect and blessing; and it allows bitterness to be expressed and mutual identities to be reconfirmed. Sorcery seldom allows reconciliation. On the contrary, suspicion of sorcery justifies hatred and secrecy. It casts problems as matters of individual resentment, rather than as a lapse in normative relations between moral positions. In cases of sorcery, you are not reconciled as good co-wives or supportive neighbours.

In cursing, the instrument of the curse is the ancestors, who cast an aura of morality and legitimacy over the human agent. In sorcery, the instrument is a substance and a technique for administering it. The thing itself is powerful, but what makes it deadly is the agent who uses it. A medicine man compared sorcery medicine to a gun; it is neither the weapon nor the arms purveyor that kills – it's the gunman. The instrument itself has no moral sense or control, as ancestors are assumed to have. This puts all the onus upon the sorcerer – the source of aggression is in the intentions and disposition of the person.

Sorcerers are not supernatural inversions of ordinary people – they are not inhuman or non-persons as witches have been characterized in some other African societies (Middleton 1973). They are people who are intent on your property or person, who are yearning, selfish, envious, competitive, vengeful, and hateful. That could be anyone. Parkin, writing of the Giriama people of eastern Kenya, says that they see evil as located in people, not outside of them: 'they . . . see witches as reflections of themselves as ordinary human beings, and as a regrettable but inevitable part of the moral community' (Parkin 1986: 218–19). Even protective or reciprocal magic may be seen as witchcraft: 'As I was often told, "nearly everyone is a witch, for does not a man feel bitterness when his son (or whoever) dies?"' (ibid: 216).

In Bunyole too, sorcery is the underside of communal life, an unavoidable part of the human condition. The 'natural' tendency towards reciprocity is a justification for good people who have been wronged to engage in aggressive acts. Moreover, the broad-spectrum powers of medicines facilitate the transition from protection to aggression, from enablement to disablement. The exact purpose of a substance is seldom pronounced aloud as is done when prayers and blessings are uttered. Many different kinds of consequences may be attributed to concealed intentions.

The hidden nature of sorcery is a constant reminder of the difficulty in fathoming the agency of other persons. Opacity gives rise to suspicion and uncertainty, particularly where you must continue to interact with those you mistrust. Sorcery discourse seems to paint a dark picture of community life and of Nyole views of personhood. People are malicious, treacherous and concerned only with their own ends; your fellow man is evil, unknowable, and untrustworthy. Yet I think the Nyole image of sorcery can be understood in another way. When people are evil, we suffer. When money is greater than friendship, we die. Individual desire, anger, and hatred are normal but dangerous. When you divine them in the hearts of your comrades, you see a reason for your suffering and for the movement of similar feelings in your own breast.

Part IV

The pragmatics of uncertainty

9   More questions

The explanatory idiom, with its implications about the relations of agents to victims, has persisted in Bunyole. 'Who are you?' is a question of the 1990s as it was of the 1970s, and I have mixed recent with earlier examples in all of the foregoing chapters where I have shown how people try to circumscribe uncertainty by dealing with relationships. In this one, however, I describe other questions that are particular to the present time. I examine changes in the medicinal means of dealing with the uncertainty of illness; and I discuss AIDS, a new source of unpredictable peril. I shall argue that the pragmatic approach to uncertainty helps us to understand these newer phenomena as well.

Institutionalized biomedicine has paradoxically both expanded and deteriorated since 1970. Biomedicine has contributed new terms to the symptomatic idiom, and the medicinal means for dealing with symptoms have increased. Awareness and expectations of biomedicine are greater, and so are suspicion and mistrust of it. Use of 'hospital' medicine is riddled with uncertainty: will we get attention from the health workers? are they cheating us? how much will we have to pay? will we get medicine? will it be 'good' medicine? In this climate, people have welcomed the commercialization of medicines that has occurred in Bunyole as in the rest of the country. The easy availability of medicines, both pharmaceutical and herbal, gives people a sense of greater control.

The experience of AIDS is a phenomenon of the 1990s, when it has become visible in Bunyole. Health information campaigns have made people aware of AIDS, and awareness itself is a source of uncertainty, given the impossibility of accurate diagnosis. The advent of AIDS in a family raises with excruciating clarity the issues of hope, problem definition, and action that are central to all dealings with misfortune. It also adds another twist: in dealing with the possibility of AIDS, uncertainty may be preferable to identification of the problem.

Contemporary uncertainty

In considering these current questions, we may begin by asking in what sense historical changes have affected the precariousness of existence in Bunyole. Should Nyole experience of uncertainty be explained in terms of a changing national or global political economy? I hope I have made it clear that doubt is not a monopoly of modernity or post-modernity, but a human disposition that is particularly relevant to dealing with affliction. In a discussion of 'the decolonization of consciousness' in African anthropology, Eric Gable describes the 'pragmatic and disenchanted skepticism' towards spirits and custom he met among Manjaco people in Guinea-Bissau. But to explain pragmatic skepticism as a product of increasing exposure to a world system would be to assume fundamental differences in mentality. Gable warns against inscribing African lifeworlds in a master narrative that makes sense to Europeans and assumes a boundary between us and them, modern and traditional. 'Because the world-system perspective is so persuasive to writer and audience alike, this ready-made construct in not put to any test by the ethnography it ostensibly explains. The frame becomes too big for the picture' (Gable 1995: 255, n4). I have tried to frame the picture of everyday life in Bunyole in terms of people's own purposes and the means they have at hand for realizing them.

New experiences are also part of the picture, however. In addressing the question of change, it is useful to distinguish between sources of uncertainty and means of dealing with it (although we have to recognize that the means themselves may give rise to doubt). Jean and John Comaroff have made this distinction in a discussion of spirit and witchcraft rituals as means of responding to the ambiguities of modernity in post-colonial Africa: 'It may be phrased as follows: ritual, as an experimental technology intended to affect the flow of power in the universe, is an especially likely response to contradictions created and (literally) engendered by processes of social, material, and cultural transformation . . .' (J. and J. Comaroff 1993: xxx). Thus the Comaroffs direct us to look at ritual as a means of dealing with uncertainty arising from the contradictions and opacities of (often oppressive) expanding national and world systems.

This view may serve to clarify, partly by contrast, the interpretation I am suggesting about uncertainty in Bunyole. I have emphasized the sources of uncertainty in sickness, failure, and human relationships rather than in expanding national and world systems. Indeed there has been little expansion during this period of chaos and weakness at the national level; what people in Bunyole are complaining about is rather a lack of opportunity to participate in the larger world. The fundamental issue is whether uncertainty – about adversity, about prospects for improvement, and about your place in the social world – is an innate aspect of experience or a product of modernity. Attention to the details of the ethnographic picture convinces me that doubt and questioning were widespread in 1970 as they are in 1996. While AIDS is indeed a new source of uncertainty that was at first seen as coming from 'outside', it is now referred to as 'this sickness of ours' – one among others. AIDS creates doubt and worry, but so do other afflictions which have been putting questions to people in Bunyole all along.

John Dewey had a grand vision of the development of mankind. He believed that uncertainty is ever with us: 'when all is said and done the fundamentally hazardous character of the world is not seriously modified, much less eliminated'. Development consists of better means of making existence more secure; it lies in 'the methods of insurance, regulation and acknowledgment' provided by science, technology, and social institutions (Dewey 1981: 44–5).

From a pragmatic perspective, what is important is the means of dealing with uncertainty. The Comaroffs' view of ritual as an 'experimental technology intended to affect the flow of power in the world' fits with this view because it makes us see people *trying* ritual. In Bunyole too people attempt to control (relational) power through ritual. But the uncertainties and inconveniences of relational power also make non-ritual means of dealing with misfortune attractive – to many people, for much of the time. They frequently use powerful substances such as medicines of foreign provenance to circumvent ritual and to avoid the explanatory idiom of which those rituals are a part. It is here that transformations in national and world systems seem most relevant; the commoditization of medicines and services has made these other 'experimental technologies' more readily available.

Untrustworthy health services

Biomedicine with its medicinal mode of intervention seems to planners and modernists to provide a promise of better health; Nyole too are attracted by that promise. But the reality of institutionalized biomedicine in Uganda today is problematic. The deterioration of government medical services in the 1970s and 1980s was grave all over the country (Dodge and Wiebe 1985). In Tororo District, the situation had become acute by the beginning of the 1980s. Salaries to health workers and supplies of medicines to health units were so poor that many health facilities were barely functioning. Efforts to rehabilitate the health sector were undertaken, but proved burdensome (Macrae et al. 1996). With the initiation of the Uganda Essential Drugs Management Programme in 1986, drug supplies began to flow, although salaries were still low and irregularly paid. Under these conditions drugs took on added value as a resource for health workers, and the attention of patients became even more sharply focused on the medicinal means of symptomatic treatment. In the 1990s few people rely upon government medicine with confidence. They mistrust health workers, find the services inconvenient and insufficient, and object to demands for money.

Health workers themselves talk about being 'demoralized'. Their conditions of service are poor; career prospects are dismal. Being posted in a backwater like Bunyole is particularly unattractive and staff continually move away to more urban locations. After years of poor pay, health workers are not fully committed to their jobs. Since most are generating income on the side in order to survive, they do not spend many hours a day at the unit. As a patient, you may have to wait long hours to be seen or you may have to go looking for the staff member who is supposed to be on duty. The consultation is likely to be very brief. People complain that the health workers do not care about them; sometimes they are brusque; usually they seem uninterested. When I wanted to bring a man with a wound to the hospital in 1996, he begged to be taken to a drug shop instead: 'At the hospital they take a lot of money for no work.'

The unofficial practice of paying something to the health worker for 'tea' or 'soap' was well established by the end of the 1980s. The amount is negotiable and if you know the health worker you might be treated for free. One afternoon in 1989 I brought a patient for treatment at a government unit. There were other sick people waiting, but no medical assistant was to be seen. Finally, our companion went and found one–a friend of his–who commented ironically: 'Our unit has modernized nowadays; I can relax somewhere all afternoon, waiting for people to come looking for me.' The implication was that he had to be paid to come–unless, as in this case, he was helping a friend.

For those who did not have friends or relatives working at a facility, there was uncertainty about whether they would have to pay, how much, and whether they would be given the medicine they needed if they did not pay. In the early 1990s, all of the government units in Bunyole, except the largest one, Busolwe Hospital, introduced fixed user fees. The idea was to enable individual institutions to top up staff salaries and supplement equipment and supplies, especially medicines. The income realized has been small, however–not enough to boost staff motivation and ensure a constant and adequate supply of medicines. A study in several districts of Uganda including Tororo concluded that user fees had not improved quality of care in government facilities (Mwesigye 1995).

The debate about user fees was heated at Busolwe where the Resistance Council chairman said that people would not mind paying set fees if they could be sure of getting what they paid for. But they feared that they would be required to pay for consultation and still be told that they had to buy the necessary drugs from local shops because they were not available at the hospital. Busolwe Hospital initiated a schedule of fees, dropped them, and then re-established them, which caused confusion about the policy. In general people were wary not only of fees, but of unexpected expenses and demands that they might not be able to meet. When I asked people why they had not taken their sick children to hospital, they said they had no money.

In 1996, paying the user fees does not ensure receiving the medicine that is supposed to be supplied. Shortages of drugs are often reported and patients frequently have to purchase their drugs at local shops. Patients admitted to the ward pay a steep fee by local standards, which is supposed to include medicine. But medicine (and often equipment) still has to be purchased in many cases. Parents of desperately ill babies are told that they have to buy intravenous solution. Or patients may be told that the storekeeper has disappeared with the keys to the medicine cupboard, so they will have to purchase the medicines they need from private sources.

The institutions that deliver government biomedicine are mistrusted because it is believed that health workers not only neglect their work, but misuse their positions as part of their survival strategies – demanding under the table payments and diverting drugs (Van der Heijden and Jitta 1993). Such views are supported by the facts that health workers treat people and sell drugs from their homes and that the shops to which patients are referred are mostly owned and operated by government health staff.

These suspicions are not converted to confrontations with health workers since people are dependent upon them. An open accusation might mean that you or your relatives will not receive help when you need it. The pragmatic civility that is such a valued part of Nyole social life, as we saw in the chapters on cursing and sorcery, reigns here as well. In fact, one disaffected staff member, who was extremely critical of the practices of his colleagues, said that health workers were 'like small gods'. People courted them with special favours as insurance against future illness.

Pre-existing connections are the best insurance. Friends, neighbours, and relatives rely on their relationships to health unit employees to obtain treatment inside or outside a health unit. When Maria's mother fell ill, she got her friend who worked in the hospital dispensary to give her some 'good drugs' (antibiotics) to take to the patient at home. When we asked about the last illness of our old friend Samwiri, we heard how his son, who worked as a groundskeeper at the hospital, had done his best – bringing medicines home to inject his father. This personalization of what in theory are supposed to be impersonal institutions is one way forward in the medicinal mode.[1] People use existing patterns of sociality to mobilize resources – and the resources are medicine and advice about how to obtain and use it. Yet access to medicines in this way can be difficult, and for some people it is almost impossible. In general, the inconveniences and failures of access to medicine through government facilities encourage interest in other sources.

Substantial business

The commercialization of medicines has greatly facilitated the medicinal mode of dealing with misfortune in the 1990s. All over Uganda, curative substances have become profitable; the combination of poorly functioning public health service and high morbidity makes materia medica a solid source of income. The biggest business is that of retailing pharmaceuticals; the commercialization of African medicine has proceeded more slowly. The sale of medicines allows families and individuals to deal with symptoms experimentally without dependence on institutions that have failed them or rituals that link suffering to relations and identities.

In 1970 there were no drug shops in Bunyole. By January 1995 there were nine in Busolwe alone, a remarkable number for a small town of 1,750 people. Shops and storefront clinics have appeared in other small trading centres too. And these are only the obvious retail facilities. Provision shops carry pharmaceuticals alongside tea and soap; a study done in three districts including Tororo showed that they are in fact the major suppliers of drugs (Odoi Adome et al. 1996). Medicines are sold by individuals from their homes as well.

For those dealing with sickness, there are many practical advantages to the new terms of treatment. It is convenient to have access to drugs at any time, rather than being limited to the few hours a day that health units are open. You avoid waiting. There is plenty of room for choice. If you know what you want, you can shop around and get it. If you don't, you can examine different drugs, and discuss them with the provider. You can purchase one or two capsules or tablets if you cannot afford more. Privacy and discretion are offered if you wish, as well as friendly conversation if you have time. A significant advantage is treatment by proxy; someone can fetch the drugs for the sick person; there is no need to go in person. Poor transportation facilities (it is hard to carry a gravely ill patient on a bicycle) and the uncertainties of actually obtaining care on the terms you want at a health unit make home treatment appealing.

9.1 Drug shops in a trading centre make medicines easily accessible (1990)

The ease of buying pharmaceuticals permits experimentation – indeed it encourages it.[2] There is little notion that such drugs could be dangerous, or that they might interact wrongly with one another. Using several different medicines at once appears to enhance the chances of success. Some customers ask for a sampling of different capsules and tablets, and they mix them together (S. Whyte 1991a: 141). People are open to suggestion and optimistic about medicines. Not knowing about medicines can even contribute to their attractiveness; the allure of powerful exotic substances is great (Last 1981).

Such experimentation may be wasteful and ineffective. One thoughtful medical assistant, selling medicine in his private clinic, remarked that a customer was buying drugs for his wife to show her that he cared about her. But if he really was concerned about her illness, he should bring her for a proper examination: 'Now this man may go and buy drugs at a drug shop, and give his wife different medicines without ever getting to the root of the problem' (S. Whyte 1991a: 139). As a trained health worker, he was aware of the need for establishing a disease diagnosis and treating a pathological process. But as a retailer, he was acting like so many others I interviewed – pleasing his customers in order to make sure they would return. 'If I don't sell them the medicine, they'll just buy it somewhere

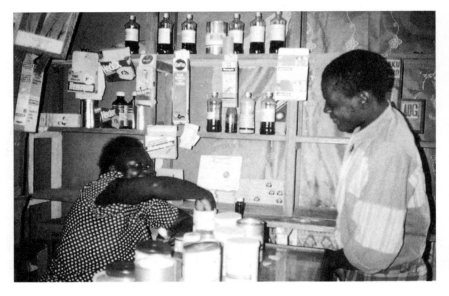

9.2 A drug seller serving a customer (1990)

else', was a common remark. The tokens of hope and healing with which people are experimenting are a business.

'African medicines' have also become substantial businesses in the 1990s. In general, the current discourse on 'traditional medicine' by the World Health Organization, donors, health development planners, and national governments tends to focus on medicinal rather than cosmological elements, in terms compatible with Western conceptions (S. Whyte 1988). The professionalization of African medicine (Last and Chavunduka 1986) is proceeding slowly in eastern Uganda, where competing organizations of traditional healers are recruiting on an ethnic basis. Nyole practitioners are mostly joining 'Uganda n'Eddagala Lyayo', which has a strong Ganda element and appeals to Bantu speakers. Membership is relatively expensive, and few can afford the fee. But for those who can, the certificate allows better business opportunities in that it permits them to practise and sell medicines in other districts.

One of the currently most successful herbal entrepreneurs in Bunyole has his main 'clinic' in Busoga, but comes to his branch in Bunyole once a week. His advertisements on the Lunyole radio broadcasts were described by one English speaking listener as using 'very commercial language'; the sales pitch promised treatment of madness, 'pressure' (hypertension), curses, impotence, and other problems beyond the capacity of biomedicine. He consults with patients at length, and prescribes herbal medicines that he dispenses as powder wrapped in paper or liquid poured into double plastic sacks.

The commercialization of medicines, whether pharmaceutical or herbal, is part of a pattern that has been called 'the commodification of health', that is, 'the tendency to treat health as a state which one can obtain through the consumption of commodities' (Nichter 1989: 236). What is commoditized is not exactly health, however. It is the idea of power substantiated, a possibility of intervention and control that generates hope of health. Commercialization always depends on appeals to the desires and needs of customers. But the commoditization of medicine is a special case because of the urgency of illness and anxiety about what may happen. The exigency of sickness, the care (in the senses of both affection and worry) of those affected, the intention and hope in the attempts to modify uncertainty, the desire to keep trying – all of these make the acquisition of medicines attractive. Anne Reeler (1996) argues that the commoditization of health care is empowering in that it permits the purchaser a sense of personal control over the situation. In the pragmatic spirit we can say that commercialized medicine allows people to acquire what they hope will secure them against sickness and death.

This means that we cannot regard people as simple dupes – nor are purveyors of medicines merely cynical smart operators. I believe that in many cases both parties are well aware of the experimental grounds on which they are interacting. When I visited Maganda's clinic in 1995, he was treating a patient with a 'private' disease, *kabotongo*, sometimes translated as syphilis. The man told how he had been seeking treatment on and off since 1992. They had even taken a blood test; he had tried so many injections. He would recover, and then relapse. The healer advised him to stop all other treatment and try this one alone. 'Then if that fails, you should go and try somewhere else.' Another patient, a middle-aged woman, had received her plastic sack of brown liquid medicine for 'pain in the tubes', but hung back until other patients had finished so that she could ask the healer one more question. 'How shall I say goodbye to the spirits that are troubling me?' Maganda answered that she should go and try the medicine first, and after that, if the spirits were still following her, she should come back. He knows that his customers know that uncertainty can only be hedged, not ruled out. He also recognizes that the patient and family have responsibility for the task of dealing with the problem. As consumers they are purchasing the substantial power of medicines to try to control their prospects. They are the ones to judge the effects; they will not take his word as truth.

Money and commodities give people a sense of control and possibility of action, but they are not necessarily empowering in respect of achieving a cure. They are often ineffective without knowledge, which is why people ask others for advice about what medicines to use, and where to go to buy good treatment. Knowledge of how to use medicines depends in part on knowing what you are treating, and this is a problem for practitioners as well as patients.

Treating what?

The idiom of biomedicine in rural Uganda in the 1990s is a symptomatic one. From the patient's point of view, biomedicine is symptomatic in that it does not address the relational causes of affliction. Even from the point of view of medical professionals, rural biomedicine tends to be symptom oriented. In principle, biomedicine should identify and intervene in pathological processes, but this cannot be done without adequate examinations. Failing these, accurate diagnoses are difficult to make, and the tendency is to treat complaints (symptoms) rather than signs of disease. The underlying disease is not identified with precision, and its aetiology cannot be addressed either.

Most rural units do not have any laboratory facilities. Even those that have do not use them systematically, in part because of lack of equipment and supplies. Patients may be asked to pay extra 'for reagents that the technician himself supplies privately'. When lab results are obtained, they may still be doubted by both patients and health staff. In one situation, a doctor wondered about the high rates of positive VDRL results (for syphilis) on lab tests; he suspected that the technician, who was earning extra money doing tests for men who approached him directly, tended to give his customers positive answers so that they would feel the payment had been worthwhile.

In practice, patients tell the health worker what symptoms they or their children have, and a medicine is suggested for each symptom. This 'pill for every ill' approach is a recipe for polypharmacy (Kafuko et al. 1994). It is also a prime example of the focus on symptoms that is characteristic of one approach to misfortune. In the symptomatic method of prescribing, the patient says cough, and the health worker writes Septrin (co-trimoxazole); 'swollen abdomen' indicates mebendazole. Fever is automatically treated with chloroquine.[3] When Manueri fell sick with what looked like pneumonia (fever, difficult breathing, chest pain), the medical assistant prescribed antibiotic injections and capsules, Ventolin, Panadol, and a chloroquine injection. We objected that he had already taken chloroquine and the health worker countered, 'but there's fever . . .' Every fever needs chloroquine, no matter what larger picture it forms part of.

Thoughtful health workers are trying to cover every eventuality, when they do not know for sure what disease they are treating. The medical superintendent once remarked to me that he often felt he was treating in the dark. The best medical assistants and the doctor are concerned about not being able to make adequate diagnoses. Many other health workers seem unworried; they have simply adopted the symptomatic idiom of their patients to the extent that they take the patient's brief statement of complaint as the basis for medicating. They do not ask further questions to elicit an illness history or exclude possibilities.

It is striking that health workers seldom inform patients and families about the diagnosis (Kafuko et al. 1994; Mwesigye 1995). There seems to be an understanding that this is not the patient's concern. This may partly reflect an assumption on the part of health workers that patients are not interested in or able to understand biomedical diagnoses.[4] It is true that many patients do not ask; they have learned through experience not to expect an explanation at hospitals and health centres. What they expect is medicine (cf. Sachs 1989). But the lack of communication about diagnosis may also be associated with the fact that the health workers themselves are unsure of what they are treating. Now that AIDS (Slim or Silimu) has begun to appear in Bunyole, this issue has become more complex.

Slimming?

There is no place in the county where an AIDS test can be obtained; such tests and the counselling that goes with them belong to city life. At the hospital, some staff members have attended seminars about dealing with AIDS patients, but as Sister Nambafu, the nursing sister-in-charge explained:

> You can't counsel someone when you're not sure they have it – and there is no screening here. The only people who admit they have AIDS are those who have been living in towns. Local people with signs of AIDS [slimming, the 'belt' of herpes zoster] don't come to the hospital because people will talk badly about them.

On another occasion, she remarked:

> People here will not accept they have AIDS. In Kampala it's okay – they are referred to TASO [The AIDS Support Organization] and they go. Here they get angry and hate you – even the family hates you if you say it's AIDS or suggest TASO. They go somewhere else.

Not only do health workers not know for sure whether those they are treating have AIDS; they avoid raising the possibility with patients and families because the suggestion cannot easily be voiced. It is too brutal to say to someone that he or she is going to die, and that there is no way to help. In fact it is cruel to the point of being seen as malicious and causing anger.

Biomedical authority is based on objective examinations and signs; this contrasts sharply with the kind of authority we saw in diviner consultations where life threatening dangers are also examined. In divination, clients negotiate the 'truth' with the expert; it has to be acceptable in terms of their own experience. If it is not, they will go to another diviner. As Sister Nambafu recognized, many people are unwilling to acquiesce in a biomedical monopoly on certainty – especially when the consequences are so overwhelming.

All of the health workers with whom I have discussed this say that they do not tell people when they see signs of AIDS. 'We just treat them psychologically,' said one medical assistant, explaining why he gives plenty of capsules and injections to patients suffering from herpes zoster. 'You don't tell them what they're suffering from. You just know.' Words spoken in the framework of ritual are a primary means of delimiting uncertainty. But in the case of AIDS, silence and uncertainty are preferable. No assertions are articulated during the ceremony of consultation.

In 1995, many people spoke of the need to have AIDS testing in Bunyole. I suspect that this idea is attractive as a way of resolving the uncertainty about others. However, it is not clear that worried people would choose to resolve the uncertainty about themselves by seeking a test – at least not without persuasion and counselling. It is better not to know for sure that you are doomed.

In a recent analysis of letters to a Ugandan health advice column, Rose Asera and colleagues discuss the letter writers' frequent preference for not knowing their HIV status. They feared the test and dreaded getting the results. As one man wrote:

> I fear to go for the test lest the machine give me bad news. Recently I got kissippi (herpes zoster) and the doctor said that it is associated with AIDS. I have a wife and 2 children and have been with my wife for five years with no other woman. Words from the doctor haunt me; some words just break our souls. (Asera et al. 1997: 7–8)

People from Bunyole could go to town to be tested. But they are afraid. It is very difficult for family and friends to push them to do so, as I know from sad personal experience.

Avoiding the question

In 1992, worried about a friend, a widower who was planning to marry, I screwed up my courage and suggested he go for a test. He countered that he had no money to travel to town. So I gave him some cash and tried awkwardly to explain why it was important. Next time I came back to Bunyole, he was happily married; his whole family was pleased for him and approved of the new bride. Before long he became a father. Neither then nor in the following years could I bring myself to ask him if he ever went for the AIDS test. Finally in 1996, when he was very sick, I tried to bring up the topic with his brother. 'Yes, he told me you asked him to go for a test. But he feared and he's never gone. And we don't want to make him go because we're afraid of what he might do to himself if he's positive.' By not putting the question, my friend did not have to get an answer. Not knowing, he could go ahead and remarry and finally have a child. When he started to become sick, there seemed no point in going for a test. He could live in doubt and hope. A positive test would have undermined that subjunctive condition. His family worried that he might take his life in despair.

Uncertainty is sometimes preferable to a certainty that is too painful. But uncertainty can also prove deadly for others.

Conviction or tactics?

AIDS is not dealt with in the explanatory idiom in the sense that when the term of action is spirits or sorcery, then the affliction is not named as AIDS. To say that someone has AIDS is to discard the explanatory idiom as I have defined it here. Whereas spirits and sorcery involve meaningful plans of action for dealing with uncertainty, the idea of AIDS does not for most people in Bunyole. The programme of 'living positively' or of sharing your suffering with other Christians provides such a plan for some Ugandans, but this is uncommon in rural areas like Bunyole.

Most of the people I have known who probably had AIDS (and I cannot be sure either) looked for agents, procured anti-sorcery medicine, and undertook rituals. Their families went to divine and struggled for money and animals so they could bring medicinal and relational powers to bear upon the problem. Different relatives had different ideas about the affliction. Sometimes the same person expressed different ideas on different occasions. When I asked one man about the death of his daughter, he told me that they had sacrificed to the spirit of their clan. The spirit of her husband's clan was also there, he said; it had been sent by her in-laws because she had tried to leave her husband. Later however, he insinuated that her mother-in-law had used sorcery against her. Another man who was ill spoke of enemies in a land dispute; he wondered whether his neighbour was in league with them – it would be so easy for him to place medicine near the house. To his most trusted relatives and friends, he confided suspicions and they helped him to visit medicine men who could sell him the powerful anti-sorcery substances he thought he needed. But he also sacrificed to his clan spirit who was protecting him – he hoped.

Few people are willing to say that they themselves, or one of their close relatives, have AIDS. Only those who are 'saved' Christians, or who are urbanized or educated enough to have been in touch with the national 'enlightened' discourse of 'living positively with AIDS', are likely to announce AIDS openly. For them, declaration may bring respect, comfort, companionship, and a sense of helping others. They speak in charity and hope for charity in return. Archdeacon Zebulon Mung'esi, who has been a leader in speaking out about AIDS in Bunyole, tells others about AIDS in his own family. He wants to show that it can be said, and by doing so to make it possible for other people to put their worries into words. But he also remarked that it was difficult in Bunyole: 'People don't want to talk to a family or individual directly about their having AIDS. The family doesn't want it said that their person is going to die. So they talk of spirits and waste money.' AIDS means death, as information campaigns have stressed; there is no negotiation. People prefer the idea of an agent of misfortune that can be placated.[5]

Father Benedict Muduku, the Roman Catholic priest serving in Bunyole in 1995, spoke of the preference Nyole seem to have for explaining the suffering of people with AIDS in terms of cursing and sorcery: 'I'm not sure whether it is their conviction, or whether they simply want to avoid saying that the person has AIDS.' To say that you have AIDS is not just stigmatizing because of how you might have contracted it. It is hopeless because there is nothing to do about it – except perhaps, as a few men have chosen, to take your life rather than endure a lingering misery. Loys Migamba, who had attended a short training in AIDS education and counselling, was equally sensitive to the *consequences* of the terms adopted. She knew of people with AIDS for whom the family had offered to their clan spirit of the forest, or to Walugono (Seja), or to the shades of their dead. Divinations *never* point to AIDS as the cause of suffering or death, she said. Even though the sick person, or those who care about him or her, might suspect AIDS especially near the end, it is very unusual that they pronounce their suspicions. The explanations in terms of disturbed relationships invite action and support and hope. Carrying out rituals for spirits, or counteracting sorcery medicine, has consequences at least for relationships, if not for the course of the bodily sickness. It allows people to remain in the subjunctive mode of possibility and hope. But there is no benefit to declaring that you have AIDS. Loys Migamba pointed out that in some places, The AIDS Support Organization (TASO) provides medicines and bedding and gifts of food for people with AIDS. It constitutes a social framework for the resolution to 'live positively'. However there is no organization in Bunyole offering such support.

What Father Benedict and Loys Migamba seem to imply is that it may be more illuminating to consider the tactics of practice and consequences than convictions about truth. In confronting the terrible peril of AIDS, Nyole are not engaged in a philosophical quest for certainty, but a search for whatever measure of security they may be able to grasp. They are concerned with the consequences more than the verities of the ideas (plans of action) that are available to them in the 'continuing conversation' that is the social texture of their situated lives.

Careful talk

How you talk about and deal with the uncertainty of AIDS depends on your position in a situation. A family with AIDS speaks carefully and acts hopefully, while more distant acquaintances of the sick person may engage in straight talk. Depending on where you stand, saying that someone has AIDS may be interpreted as 'backbiting' or hostility. The pragmatics of what you say to whom require considering such social implications.

Within the circle of sympathetic family and friends, talk about grave illness that might be AIDS is careful and subtle. Sickness should not be hidden, so people inquire solicitously: 'How are the bones? How is it hurting you?' The reply is direct: 'The bones pain me sharply. The sickness is hurting me.' When others meet family members, they make a point of asking: 'How is the sick one at home?' An individual's ill health is widely known and tactfully discussed. But there are ways of phrasing that are heavy with meaning: 'His diarrhoea (or fever) is on and off.' 'He has become thin.' Or, 'We treat one thing, and then she gets something else.' Many are aware of what this might mean but no cruel truth is announced.

Thus those who are closest to the sick person do not name the sickness they fear. Even trained health workers are careful, as I came to understand when I asked a medical assistant about his sick brother. Since I had often discussed diagnoses of patients with this man, I asked directly – in retrospect I can see how clumsily.

> SUSAN: Is it a serious illness?
> GABRIEL: Yes. He might die.
> SUSAN: What disease is he suffering from?
> GABRIEL: [long pause] We don't know for sure.
> SUSAN: This sickness of ours?
> GABRIEL: Yes, it might be.

If I had been sensitive, I would have heard what Gabriel meant when he said his brother might die.

On another occasion I heard a conversation between two health workers concerning the illness of their relative. One, Samwiri, had been away for some months, and he began by asking Taamiti about the health of Hiisa.

> TAAMITI: His health isn't good.
> SAMWIRI: How do you mean, not good?
> TAAMITI: I doubt his life.
> SAMWIRI: It was a bad attack. [referring to an attack Hiisa had suffered a year earlier]
> TAAMITI: [looking down] Maybe it was the attack.
> SAMWIRI: Has he been examined at the hospital? What did they say? I wish they took a blood slide.
> TAAMITI: He refuses to go to hospital. He wants me to treat him at home. He says he can buy medicine from the drug shops.
> SAMWIRI: That's useless when they haven't examined him. They just sell anything to make money. Why does he refuse to go to hospital? Money?
> TAAMITI: But when he came back from Kampala he had money. He got very sick then and refused the hospital. I treated him with chloroquine and chloramphenicol injections. His brother came with some tabs too – I don't know what. He got some vitamins. Now he complains he has no appetite. Yesterday he had diarrhoea. The diarrhoea is off and on. Even his wife has diarrhoea. I treat them with Flagyl and oral rehydration salts.
> SAMWIRI: Who can talk to him and make him go to hospital?

During this conversation I had a strong impression not only that Taamiti was holding something back, but that he was making it obvious to Samwiri that he suspected something else. When Samwiri diplomatically mentioned the attack a year earlier in which Hiisa almost died, Taamiti looked down and sounded doubtful. Going to hospital might have entailed insinuations or a confrontation with a diagnosis Hiisa did not want; his relatives realized this, even though, as health workers, they confirmed a mutually held principle that gravely ill people should go to hospital. Later I asked Taamiti whether Hiisa knew his sickness. 'Yes,' he said, 'but he's just dodging.'

When people inquire 'how is the sickness hurting you?' in the concerned way that Nyole etiquette prescribes, a patient with a mild case of malaria or a bad cold might answer, 'I'll recover.' But when the illness becomes grave, no such reassurance is forthcoming. 'It's in God's hands', is a fatalistic reply that suggests resignation. Relatives of Hiisa said: 'He's really very sick – we don't know what will happen.' 'Ah, his sickness – we don't know . . .' 'A young man suffering like that – I have many thoughts.' They say they do not know, but in this situation the declaration of uncertainty suggested that they were rather sure of what they did not wish to put into words.

Demanding my grave

The same Hiisa, whose family repeated that they did not know what would happen, told of a visitor who came quarrelling. Hiisa had borrowed a cow from him, and the visitor wanted the debt repaid.

> 'You're dying and you haven't repaid. That cow belonged to someone else and now he wants it. If you don't repay in a week, I'm going to the Local [Resistance] Council. Sell all those goats of yours and give me a cow. Even if you die without paying the cow, I'll get the money from those who come to mourn you.'

The sick man explained: 'He's demanding my grave.' That is, the money collected for burial and for cementing the grave would be taken for the debt.

Later that day, when people were talking of planting millet, Hiisa remarked softly: 'Anyone can die at anytime – whether sick or well. I know I can die and I'm already old.' At first I thought he had wandered off the topic, but then I realized he was thinking of the millet harvest he might not see. As it happened, he did not even see the sowing. He died two weeks later – 34 years old.

The man who demanded his grave put into blunt words what he and his family gently phrased in the subjunctive – as possible or unknown. Only wrath or malice could call forth such harshness. Those who care are care-ful in their talk.

Who is a 'victim'?

The Uganda AIDS education campaign has stressed the impossibility of *seeing* who is infected (and thus the necessity of being ever careful). The logic is that people who recognize uncertainty (anyone might be a victim) will always guard against infection. However the increased consciousness of invisible danger also promotes suspicion and a special combination of rumour, gossip, insinuation, and worry.

People wonder who is a 'victim' (the English word commonly used for a person with AIDS). Did so and so 'fall into the net' by 'playing sex' with a victim? Using a football term for those who have played with a victim, they speculate about who is 'in the line-up'. When someone dies, others might joke that his or her sexual partners have been 'screened'. The implication here is that the death of someone you played with is the equivalent of a positive AIDS test. There are many euphemistic and ironic terms for AIDS used in gossip: 'this sickness of ours' (*obulwaye bwefwe*); 'the persistent one' (*oluhoodi*); 'get thin and I pass' (*pwerera mbite* – a kind of grass that closes when you touch it); 'the nice little thing' (*ahatu*).

As a hidden evil transmitted by other people through contact, AIDS resembles sorcery. Like sorcery it invites speculation about the nature of malice. There are all kinds of rumours and remarks about 'victims' who do not want to die alone and entice unsuspecting men and women into playing sex. Musiho Muluga, a university student, assisted us in 1992 by recording his discussions on AIDS with secondary school students in Bunyole. Here are some of the answers they gave to the question 'What do people do when they think they have AIDS?'

> 'They try to spread it.'
> 'Both men and women decide to start raping others.'
> 'They try to look very smart [attractive, seductive].'
> 'They donate a lot of money [spend, give gifts] in order to find a market for themselves.'
> 'They spread the idea that Slim appreciates the human body; if you are positive, you can't stop having intercourse because AIDS comes through bodies and it likes bodies.'

Archdeacon Mung'esi told of the efforts he and his colleagues were making to fight the anti-TASO rumours current in early 1996. It was said that: 'TASO distributes pig pills to victims so they get fat. Then they can befriend people who don't realize they're victims.'

Such rumours of bad-heartedness were almost always anonymous; unnamed 'victims' were posited. Rarely did I hear of specific individuals who intentionally tried to kill people and were publicly confronted about it. (An exception was a case from Doho in 1992 in which a man was evicted from the area by the local Resistance Council, allegedly because he was a 'victim' and was giving girls money to sleep with him.) Such rumours could be interpreted as evidence of Nyole antipathy towards people with AIDS, a kind of smear campaign that reinforces stigma. But they can also be understood as commentaries on the danger of hidden malice. Like general talk about sorcery, they are imaginations of what the world would be like if our worst fears about others were true.

When it comes to actual suspicions about specific individuals or categories of people, the parallels with sorcery conjectures are less pronounced. The main difference is that particular people are seldom suspected of transmitting AIDS intentionally in order to hurt a targeted person whom they hate. Ignorance, carelessness, and the selfish pursuit of private pleasure or gain are more often the worries people have in relation to specific agents. The positions from which people speak of sorcery agents and AIDS transmitters differ as well. Sorcery becomes a relevant idea once someone is afflicted. Speculations about routes of AIDS transmission are preventive, not treatment oriented. Prophylactic worrying about risky behaviour may lead to divorce, separation, or avoidance of certain contacts; but identification of agents is of no help whatsoever in alleviating suffering.

The usual suspects in sorcery cases are competitors (brothers, neighbours, colleagues, co-wives, a spouse's lovers) and spurned partners. The
suspects in prospective AIDS transmission are categories (health
workers, traders, prostitutes) and individuals (spouses, lovers, and their
partners) with whom there is a sexual link.

The mistrust of government health workers is over-determined. When
AIDS education programmes stressed the dangers of unsterilized
needles, anxiety about AIDS transmission through 'public' injections
reinforced existing suspicion of government health facilities. People
reckoned that government workers did not care about their work and
were not conscientious unless motivated by special payment or personal
relationship to the patient (Birungi 1994a, 1994b). In a sense, institutional health workers are 'usual suspects' for other reasons and mistrust of
their injections fell on fertile ground.[6]

Rice traders come to Bunyole from Buganda and they often stay for
short periods while buying up rice from local growers. Particularly in the
first years, when AIDS was new and perceived as brought from outside,
people in Bunyole blamed rice traders. The fact that some of these traders
were women probably made them more likely suspects. In 1989 a story
circulated about a man who befriended a visiting Ganda rice trader. One
morning she was gone, leaving him 15,000 shillings and a letter saying he
should enjoy the money because her husband had died of AIDS and she
was infected too. Whether or not this story was true, it fits with one image
of danger. Smart, prosperous Ganda women easily transmit to poor local
men that which made them widows.

People have long been disposed to censure Nyole women who were
'loose', who did not stick in marriage, or who went to town to live
independently as, it was imagined, barmaids and prostitutes. As I mentioned in chapters 1 and 7, marriage failures were considered a misfortune in themselves and parents and brothers were thought sometimes to
curse when their rights in women were neglected or denied. Warnings
about the perils of casual sex, bars, and discos fit well with male biased
views on the need to control women. Such assumptions were evident in
the remarks a man made about a young woman who had died: 'That one
was a life-ist [that is she enjoyed 'the life' of bars and discos]; I used to see
her moving with different men in Busolwe.' Independent women are also
'usual suspects'. Just as 'foreign spirits' can be seen as representing the
dangers of uncontrolled movement of women and the attraction of commodities (S. Whyte 1981), so analyses can be made of the meaningful
connections between movement, money, women, and AIDS (Weiss
1993). But to leave it there would be a misleading oversimplification. For
men are also a danger – and not just sugar daddies, but also husbands.

Women feel that they are at risk because of their husbands who think it is their right to 'play sex' on their own terms. In 1992, a woman who is a schoolteacher explained it to me as follows:

> Men don't want condoms – they want body to body. If you ask for a condom, they'll go outside saying: 'You don't love me enough. You want me to die alone. Another woman will give me body to body.' So you're encouraging him to go outside. He'll say you don't trust him, and he won't trust you. So we're very worried. And the men think it's their right to go outside.

Because men have other partners, either wives or lovers, the existing suspicions of rivals, already described in the previous chapter on sorcery, have become mortal fears. Another woman, also well educated, spoke about her husband, working in town, who had taken another wife:

> These men are not satisfied – although he has ten children here. But maybe it's my fault for leaving him alone in town . . . She's a harlot but he won't believe it . . . Now I am worried. And you can't tell your husband to wear a condom. We don't know – we're all going to die.

Thus the 'usual suspects' – co-wives and outside lovers – are no longer the only problem. Now husbands themselves are dangerous.

One man with whom I discussed this reminded me that men suspect their wives too. He told of a local trader who used to stay with prostitutes when he was in Kampala on business. Because of the AIDS danger, he now stays alone in a hotel room. 'But he's afraid when he comes home because he doesn't know what his four wives do while he's gone.' However, it seems to me that women feel the threat most intensely, since they cannot deny their husbands' demands and men's rights to multiple partners are accepted.

In one sense the AIDS epidemic reinforces the 'usual suspicions' that danger comes from other people. Some of those other people are the same suspects you might have in mind in a sorcery case. In another sense, however, the uncertainties about AIDS transmission are not merely a matter of the usual apprehension. This is because specific AIDS worries do not generally posit intent, as sorcery suspicions do. It is not that your husband means to kill you; he was thoughtless or selfish, not moved by hatred of you personally. There is a difference between malice and irresponsibility.

AIDS casts light on the contrast between preventive and remedial measures in relation to misfortune. Conjectures about transmission of AIDS in specific cases tend to be prospective to a far greater degree than is the case in the explanatory idiom. Unless you are actually afflicted, you are not much concerned about who might curse you or which spirit might catch you. People are prospectively and prophylactically worried and uncertain about possible AIDS agents, whereas in the explanatory idiom, they are uncertain in retrospect and for purposes of selecting a plan of remedial action. (They are also worried in retropect when a partner or a partner of a partner dies, but these speculations do not form responses to an affliction.) Thinking that a sexual partner may have AIDS, you can try to take action in the hope of protecting yourself. But if you develop symptoms, the identification of the source of infection has no therapeutic value.

On the basis of this reading of the situation, we may suggest that AIDS is contributing to the emergence of a new idiom of action in relation to the uncertainty of misfortune: an idiom of individual responsibility for avoiding affliction. The notion that individuals must take care to prevent suffering is explicit in AIDS education. You can choose, you must change your behaviour, you must be alert to danger. Get on board the boat of abstinence, of faithfulness, or of condoms. The same assumption – that misfortune can be avoided by proper action – underlies other forms of health promotion, such as immunization programmes and lessons on child nutrition. But AIDS is a special case. For you have not only to worry about your own behaviour, but also that of others with whom you are or have been involved. Are they acting responsibly – loving carefully or faithfully? Danger and uncertainty inhere in others; it is not just a question of your individual responsibility but also of theirs. Thus the new idiom falls short as a means of providing security, despite the implication that you can take charge of your life by self-discipline.

10 Consequences

For acting subjects, dealing with misfortune is a process of apprehending uncertainty, questioning experience, considering terms of action, implementing ideas, and looking to the results. This is not to say that everything actors undertake is instrumental, that they are coldly rational or even that they are able to appreciate the complexities of their problems and the tangle of results that ensue from their actions. It is to say that afflicted people are situated and intentional. From a position in a given moral world, you are familiar with various ideas, their significance and implications. When misfortune befalls, you mean to do something about it. You face it with purposes that are more or less explicit in your mind. You try, consider consequences, doubt, reconsider, revise your purpose perhaps, hope, and try again. In the process, you may never achieve certainty, though you may gain some degree of security. Sometimes you simply have to accept uncertainty and live with it or try to ignore it.

Anthropology requires that we integrate such a view of people as individual subjects with an analysis of cultural phenomena and social conditions, as well as reflections on our own scholarly assumptions. In closing my account of misfortune in Bunyole, I will briefly touch on uncertainty in ethnography and summarize in terms of three questions. From whence does uncertainty arise? What means are at hand for managing it? What are the consequences of dealing with misfortune and uncertainty in these ways?

Uncertain ethnography

There is a good deal more space for uncertainty in the anthropology of the 1990s than there was in the 1970s when we finished our first two years of fieldwork of Bunyole. Some of the most interesting new ethnographies of experience highlight the indeterminate nature of life and show the problems of capturing what they are trying to study in analytical concepts and systematic representations. Michael Jackson sums up this position. 'An anthropology of experience shares with phenomenology a skepticism toward determinate systems of knowledge. It plays up the indeterminate, ambiguous, and manifold character of lived experience' (Jackson 1995: 160).

Unni Wikan's ethnography of Balinese management of turbulent hearts sets up an opposition between cultural analysis and lived experience, emphasizing the seductive order of the former and the uncertainties of the latter. 'Ambiguities, inconsistencies, and confusion plague the lives of people . . . I hope to retrieve the ambiguity and imprecision that adhere to cultural symbols in use: not to ponder their elegance and form, but to convey the practical life implications . . . I would argue for the need to stand back and let uncertainties speak . . .' (Wikan 1990: 33–4).

Recent ethnographies of narrative and discourse also acknowledge uncertainty and ambiguity. Mary Steedly tells how Karo people in Sumatra mistrust spirits.

> about the spirit world: Who knows? Who ever knows? . . . Questions of belief in the existential sense are hardly at issue here; or at least they are hardly of interest. What is interesting to Karo, and came to interest me very much as well, was the question of plausibility, of how one goes about making sense of something you can never get to the bottom of. (Steedly 1993: 35)

Michael Lambek's long, rich ethnography of knowledge and misfortune and the discourses of Islam, sorcery, and spirit possession in Mayotte provides a recent example in the Africanist tradition: 'explanations of misfortune are not particular manifestations of closed, self-affirming systems of thought, and . . . they do not serve to close off further questions, but . . . they are rather provisional and contestable readings of events, moments in the life of narrative . . .' (Lambek 1993: 385). He ends his 400-page monograph succinctly: 'In conclusion, inconclusion' (ibid.: 406).

Other examples could be adduced, but these may serve to set the pragmatic approach I have followed in the foregoing chapters in perspective. Anthropologists like those cited above have been concerned with two related issues. One is that uncertainty should be included in our studies. In highlighting uncertainty as an aspect of social experience, they remind us that the discourses and narratives we human actors use are partial, incommensurate with one another, and often incapable of convincing us fully. There are always areas of uncertainty – more salient in some historical circumstances – about which social scientists must theorize. As an aspect of cultural phenomena and social life, ambiguity and doubt are to be studied in relation to knowledge claims and the promotion of new certainties (Wendy James 1995). The second issue is about the challenge that uncertainty presents to ethnographic representation. If real life, practice, is not as clear cut as anthropological analysis makes it out to be, then we may need to find other ways of writing and analysing. This is a salutary reminder of the need for humility, humanity, and verisimilitude in ethnography. The uncertainty with which I have been concerned is relevant to these larger issues, but it is a more concrete and practical one.

By starting with misfortune I wanted to found this study on Nyole definitions and existential positions. The uncertainty with which I began was their uncertainty about what was going to happen: to sick children, impotent men, or Somebody's Wife. This is a desperately interested and specific uncertainty. From an ethnographic point of view, the task is not only to describe how people experience this position of worry. It is to examine the ways they go ahead. How does undergoing (an affliction) become undertaking (a response)? What can you do to hedge uncertainty, to try to ensure the good outcome? The pragmatic perspective on uncertainty is a grounded one: persons engage problems with purposes and they judge the consequences of their efforts accordingly. This approach is not necessarily suitable to every kind of ethnography. But for the study of misfortune it seems fitting.

The pragmatic philosophy of John Dewey helped to set this much of the framework. But if the real analytical concern is not uncertainty itself, but ways of dealing with it and consequences of doing so, then it becomes necessary to move from individuals-in-situations to a more general level of cultural and social analysis. For the ways of undertaking a response are adopted from a common 'conversation' within a shared historical condition. That is why I organized the discussion around the ideas (plans of action) that Nyole usually use when they question misfortune. I have tried to show individuals implementing these ideas and I have stressed that this process itself gives rise to uncertainty – because of the nature of social relations and because of the recalcitrant quality of many misfortunes. I have suggested as well that there are consequences on a social level – effects on the shared social experience of many individuals.

Sources of uncertainty

Anthony Giddens recognizes that ontological security is problematic in all societies and proposes a table of terms for analysing the environments of trust and risk in pre-modern and modern societies (Giddens 1990: 92–111). He suggests that pre-modern societies root a sense of security in kinship relations, locality, religion, and tradition. But while trust and security are culturally well founded, dangers from nature (such as infectious diseases) are extreme. In modern conditions, natural risks are fewer; the sense of risk is socially created and dangers are socially mediated. At the same time, trust is more problematic since it is not localized, but vested in abstract systems of institutions that span time and space.

This kind of dichotomy creates the pre-modern as a mirror of the modern and requires a digital categorization that is misleading for the analysis of societies like Bunyole. There is no simple contrast between natural and social security, let alone progression from one to the other. The dangers of disease, as we have seen, are associated with the uncertainties of personal relationships in Bunyole. Relations to kin, neighbours, and spirits are at once the source of security and uncertainty. A 'natural' infectious disease like AIDS is socially mediated and socially constructed as a risk. And that socially created sense of risk is reinforced by the daily experience of illness and death.

In Bunyole uncertainty arises when the values of children, marriage, health, prosperity, and harmony are imperilled. Life is precarious because of disease, shortage of resources, and the difficulties of getting on with those with whom you are deeply and daily involved. While some sources of peril have been reduced (smallpox, warfare with the Adhola, starvation), others have appeared (AIDS, traffic accidents, employment difficulties). All of these have in common that they are experienced as concrete problems of ordinary existence which people act to solve.

As people move to control misfortune, new uncertainties arise. Anthropologists, and to some extent the people with whom we work, emphasize the way that divination and ritual practices give purpose and assurance in the face of ambiguity and uncertainty. But as anyone who has followed these matters through knows, they do not necessarily resolve doubt and they are not always satisfying. In the explanatory mode of dealing with misfortune there are three sources of uncertainty and a good possibility of inconvenience. You may doubt the divination, you may be unsure about the desires and motives of the agent, and you may be dissatisfied with the results of your attempts to deal with the agent.

You go to divine and you get an answer to the question 'Who are you?' You may well get more than one answer. A divination usually involves the consideration of the variety of possible agents who might be the cause of the misfortune. While the diviner often concludes with a suggestion that a certain agent should be dealt with first, other suspects are hanging about in the background. Moreover, given the uncertainty about whether diviners tell the truth, or whether agents appearing in the divination 'are deceiving', you may well decide to consult another diviner. Nyole people recognize that diagnoses of the same case may vary.

Having identified an agent and embarked on a course of remedial action, there are still sources of uncertainty. In Bunyole misfortune may be caused by spirit agents, whom you cannot see, and human ones, whose hearts you cannot know. Concerning spirits and shades that look askance at you, while you do not see them, the problem is to find out what they want, and, while appearing submissive ('don't quarrel with them'), to negotiate an exchange which is possible for you and satisfactory to them. Attention is focused on what is to be offered and on procedure and whether these are acceptable to the invisible agent. The human actors involved may be in disagreement on some of these points, and sometimes consensus is only achieved when the spirit in question possesses someone and speaks its wishes. With human agents, I have argued, the problem of uncertainty is greater, even though you can see them and talk to them. Because cursers or sorcerers are people with whom there is a conflict, they are by definition people with anger, malice, or resentment in their hearts. Like many African people, Nyole use the metaphor of the heart to speak of volition and emotion, the self that is often opaque to other people. Although the identification of a curse aims to make public and to assuage resentment, there is still the possibility that the curser may not lift the curse 'with one heart'. Cursers, like sorcerers, may hide so well that they are never found. Or they may continue their secret malevolence about which you can only guess through details of behaviour, disposition, and your own sense of the other person's heart.

These in-built sources of uncertainty are brought into relief by the course of the affliction itself. When misfortune continues and worsens, when another family member falls ill too, when a man fails to keep a wife, when the patient dies anyway, people reflect again about whether the diviner spoke truly, whether other causes were at work simultaneously, whether rituals were done properly, or whether the agent identified had desires and purposes that had not been fully understood. Thus uncertainty about the problem, the means of dealing with it, and the outcome are interrelated.

Strategies for security

The first response to a problem is usually a restricted one. The difficulty is seen as limited in scope and amenable to a simple solution. In the case of illness, the symptomatic perspective almost always entails a medicinal mode of action. As substances, medicines substantiate the affliction in the body of an individual (Van der Geest and Whyte 1989). They disregard conflicts and obligations and relations to agents, bringing to bear an impersonal reified power. Conveniently available as commodities, medicines are an attractive strategy in many ways. Pharmaceutical medicines are especially promising in that they incorporate powers of modernity, distant centres of advanced technology, and professional expertise. As I suggested in chapter 9, however, there are questions about how to gain access to medicines, and about how to use them properly.

Unlike the symptomatic perspective, the aetiological one formalizes uncertainty by implicitly or explicitly questioning misfortune. Why? Who? Acknowledging indeterminacy is strategically significant because recognizing the chanciness of a particular condition is the first step toward hedging insecurity. 'Barely to note and register that contingency is a trait of natural events has nothing to do with wisdom. To note, however, contingency in connection with a concrete situation of life is that fear of the Lord which is at least the beginning of wisdom' (Dewey cited in Hook 1981: xv). The beginning of wisdom is not certainty but a questioning posture toward uncertainty. In Bunyole, this orientation is evident in divination where uncertainty is formally constructed as a prelude to the systematic review of the possibilities in a risky matter.

In the explanatory idiom, uncertainty is extended from the affliction itself to spirits and persons. The unpredictable course of misfortune is tied to disturbances in and uncertainties about relationships; two sources of unsureness are linked and must be dealt with together. With the exception of sorcery, the ideas (terms of action) that people bring to bear on such uncertainty involve a set of common methods. The first method of reducing uncertainty is mobilizing kin. Whether a crowd of clansmen for an *ekuni* ceremony, household members for a matter of little spirits, or a sister's son for curse removal, someone else will stand by to help instil confidence. The second means of promoting clarification is ritual speaking. The agent and those who importune the agent put their names, relationships, dissatisfactions, and intentions into words. They make assertions about how things are and how they should be. The question 'who are you?' is explicitly answered; both the agent and the victim are identified. Sometimes a spirit agent is embodied – it catches a person and speaks directly through him or her. At other times, it is only addressed. Speaking is accompanied by a third means of dealing with what is intangible: offering, always with a proposal about exchange and change. 'You take this huge goat, and let her go back and be a woman.' Control of uncertainty is attempted by making relationships and intentions sensible in words and gestures of giving.

Only on rare occasions is sorcery removed in a public ritual. Usually its means are medicinal and the idea is that the agent (and thus the affliction) can be controlled through the manipulation of substances. The terms of this kind of action against uncertainty are businesslike; you buy the medicine, knowledge, and services of a specialist. Insurance against hazard is available for cash.

Idioms and consequences

From a pragmatic point of view, we must attend to consequences rather than convictions. This is not as simple as it might seem. For consequences may be more or less amenable to awareness and reflection, and they will be evaluated differently according to the positions of those involved. Moreover, consequences, like intentions, seldom occur in the singular. In the explanatory idiom, since terms of action are relational, there are social consequences as well as 'therapeutic effects' affecting survival, recovery, and fertility. A grand ceremony for a clan spirit, or a second funeral for the shades of grandfathers can be a social, aesthetic, ritual success, even when the therapeutic effect on one individual is negligible. 'The operation was a success but the patient died' is an aphorism that captures contrasting perspectives and criteria for judging strategies and consequences.

Within the explanatory idiom, each term of action has social consequences because it involves assertions of identity, support of other people, and offerings of resources. In choosing terms of action, people are aware of some of the probable social effects, as when Manueri opted for the hospital because he did not want to acknowledge his father-in-law's curse upon his children. But there are also more extended social effects, not usually noticed by those involved, to which an ethnographic analysis may attend.

The explanatory idiom as a whole frames uncertainty in terms of agents and thus continually problematizes relationships and identities. Rather than simply reinforcing social structure, the ideas provide a whole set of plans for exploring, negotiating, asserting, and considering who you are. The consequence is not so much a sense of secure identity as a preoccupation with others – upon whom you depend and with whom you are involved for better or worse. The explanatory idiom produces an extreme relational consciousness in the sense that it links suffering people to agents.

Long ago, Evans-Pritchard taught us to see this area of experience as the domain of secondary explanations. He claimed that Zande did not doubt the premises of their thought, just as later scholars have emphasized the persistence of theoretical constructs in the face of evidence to the contrary (Horton 1967) and the way that falsification of knowledge is blocked in 'core areas' of culture (Prins 1992). In Bunyole too the explanatory idiom is strikingly persistent; the discourse on cause is sometimes maintained even when it is unable to bring about the results that aetiological therapy is meant to achieve. However, people do not blindly cling to an idea no matter what. Recalcitrant experience, non-compliant afflictions, and all the uncertainty and concern that they engender, also dispose some people to other modes of acting. It is not so much a matter of falsifying knowledge or doubting the premises of one's thought. Those are intellectualist formulations of the issue. Rather people simply try other things in the hope that they might help.

Add to the doubts about diagnosis, and dissatisfaction with the effectiveness of therapeutic measures, the fact that in some situations the suggested measures seem expensive, inconvenient, or downright disagreeable. A man may not have the bull his dead grandfather demands; he may not wish to show the deference to his father's brother which a curse removal entails. A woman may not want to take up the call to be a diviner; she may hope that her son will continue his education instead of becoming a medium for the clan spirit.

One of the consequences of all this is the extreme interest in medicinal solutions evident in Bunyole. The symptomatic idiom is welcome because the explanatory one often does not work, is inconvenient, expensive, and stifles individual control. Yet the strategy of substances has no warrant of success either. The symptomatic use of Western pharmaceuticals, so full of promise, is so often disappointing. Thus the uncertainties and difficulties of each idiom promote interest in the other. Michael Lambek, writing of Islam and spirit possession in the Comoro island of Mayotte, suggests that each of these discourses produces its own form of certainty and that 'the certainty of each is compromised or at least contextualized by the presence of the other' (Lambek 1995: 266). One can turn this around and say that each idiom of dealing with affliction produces its own forms of uncertainty, misgivings, and dissatisfaction making the other more attractive.

Bunyole is not specially conservative. It has experienced a quarter century of 'decentralization' in which state institutions were weak, and security of work and travel outside was poor. People have had to rely, economically, socially, and medically, on their own efforts. The explanatory idiom, with its problematizing of relationships, provided relevant terms of action in this long dry season of enforced 'self-reliance'. Pressure on land, impoverishment, lack of opportunity for education and off-farm work, the heavy dependence on relatives and neighbours all contributed to the continued meaningfulness of sorcery, home spirits, and fertility rituals. At the same time, biomedicine has been eagerly embraced since it became more available in the 1980s – not just because it was effective or because it was promoted by the rehabilitated state or because, in recent times, it was spread by commercial interests. It was also welcome because of people's experience with the consequences of terms in the explanatory idiom.

The same pragmatic attitude of experimentation informs people's use of government health facilities, drug shops, and private practitioners of biomedicine. They try out different kinds of medicine and use contacts to get care they think they can rely upon. If they do not use biomedicine in the way the donors and the Ministry of Health would like it to be used, it is as much because of their experience with the quality of biomedical care as because they are attached to another idiom of affliction. To put it bluntly, the consequences of insufficient immunization programmes, poorly functioning health centres, and uninformed use of pharmaceuticals are continuing interest in amulets against little spirits and visits to the vendors of 'protection' against sorcery.

The most important evaluation of consequences should be an assessment of the amelioration of suffering. Through these pages I have tried to show how people in Bunyole look to that goal. From the point of view of those involved, both medicinal and relational measures sometimes help. Too often, however, problems are not resolved. The sick one dies, the condition becomes chronic, the marriage breaks down. The insufficiency of the means people in Bunyole have for dealing with misfortune seems clear to me, as it is to them on many occasions. Yet the conclusions I draw from my years in Bunyole are not pessimistic. What I admire, and what I hope to have conveyed to the readers of this book, is the spirit not of optimism but of meliorism. William James (1974: 84) defined meliorism as the doctrine that 'improvement is at least possible'. John Dewey spoke of 'the belief that the specific conditions which exist at any moment, be they comparatively bad or comparatively good, in any event may be bettered' (Dewey cited in Campbell 1995: 261). Belief in the possibility of improvement is what people bring to diviners' huts, rituals, and drug shops.

Hope, faith in a better future, and active engagement in the situation inform their efforts, and so does intelligence.

> Memory of past and foresight of future convert ['dumb pluck'] to some degree of articulateness. They illumine curiosity and steady courage. Thus when the future arrives with its inevitable disappointments as well as fulfillments, and with new sources of trouble, failure loses something of its fatality, and suffering yields fruit of instruction not of bitterness. (Dewey 1922: 289)

Questioners of misfortune in Bunyole are aware of uncertainty and of the chanciness of their endeavours to circumscribe it. It is that realistic appreciation, and the willingness to learn from consequences, that provide the human basis for the improvement of life in eastern Uganda.

Notes

1 MISFORTUNE AND UNCERTAINTY

1 This passage was recorded by Florence Nang'endo of the Child Health and Development Centre, as part of the research on the Tororo Community Health Project in which I am participating.

2 They were particularly sought after for the treatment of venereal disease, which was common. Unlike the staff at government health facilities, the needle men did not ask indelicate questions or demand that one bring a partner for treatment (S. Whyte 1982). Nowadays, so many people know how to give injections that the term 'needle man' has gone out of use.

3 For any type of misfortune, there are always several possible agents; indeterminacy necessitates divination. In the records I assembled, I can see that alternative explanations were in fact used; barrenness was not always attributed to cursers, splotches on the skin were not always blamed on sorcerers. Yet the connection between the type of affliction and the type of disturbed relation is not an arbitrary one either. There are tendencies to associate certain kinds of misfortune with certain kinds of agent: the death of livestock with ancestral shades, swelling of the body with sorcery, a bride's barrenness with cursing, impotence with the divining spirits. Nyole often see or create a kind of fit in such things. A parent who was not given a bridewealth share can by cursing cancel the fertility for which bridewealth was paid. Ancestors who were not offered animals in sacrifice kill them themselves. And a girl who 'ate' a suitor's money was made to eat other suitors' letters. Part of the process of finding meaning is the discovery of such resonances, and once found, the appropriateness makes the interpretation more convincing.

4 Thus suede shoes were jokingly called Maliki shoes in Buganda, because, like the followers of the Maliki sect who refused all European and African medicine, suede shoes did not need 'medicine' (Welbourn 1961: 53).

5 The literature on personhood, individual and self in Africa is large, as Paul Riesman's review article (1986) richly demonstrates. These terms are defined differently by each scholar; see for example Beattie 1980, La Fontaine 1985, and the contributions of Fortes (1973), Middleton (1973), and others to *La Notion de Personne en Afrique Noire*. For the sake of simplicity, I restrict discussion to Harris' basic distinction in order to clarify some aspects of the Nyole process of dealing with misfortune.

2   THE PURSUIT OF HEALTH AND PROSPERITY

1   The conceptual problems regarding the notion of 'tribes' as bounded units are particularly difficult in eastern Uganda and western Kenya, an ancient migration corridor now inhabited by a mosaic of Bantu and Nilotic speaking groups. It may be the case that the present sense of ethnic identity is largely a twentieth-century creation (Twaddle 1969; Southall 1970); but this does not correspond with Nyole views that they have existed as a separate people for hundreds of years.

2   In 1959, the last census year in which ethnic affiliation was recorded, there were in Uganda 92,642 people who reported themselves as Nyole. Of these, 42,202 were living in Bunyole County (together with 6,783 non-Nyole). Over 27,000 were living in Busoga District and most of the rest were elsewhere in Eastern Province, mostly in Bugwere, Busamia, and Bugisu.

3   Twenty to thirty years ago, the hiring of labour in Bunyole was usually on a daily basis of people working for others in their own community, sometimes for beer rather than money. As the Uganda Census of Agriculture (1965: 58–60) indicated, the pattern of monthly contracts for cash, common in Buganda and parts of Busoga, was infrequent in Bukedi. Both men and women could work as 'porters' (*abapakasi*), but men seemed to take such jobs more often. Unmarried men might even be paid to work for their own brothers. Today there is a much livelier labour market, especially in connection with rice production. Hired labour is still mostly male.

4   The Annual Report for 1956 noted the difficulty in getting the people of Bukedi to work in the cement factory at Tororo. 'In fact the local people did not fully avail themselves of the opportunities of employment which could provide people with insufficient land with a steady income and thereby do away with the need to emigrate to Busoga and Buganda.' (Annual Report for Eastern Province 1956: 15).

5   The first years are the most dangerous. Our figures show that in 1970, 14 per cent of children died before age 1, and 24 per cent before age 2. The corresponding figures for Bubaali 1993 were 13 per cent and 19 per cent.

6   Health workers claim that the number of syphilis and gonorrhoea cases has declined in recent years, as the AIDS message has reached more people. Hospital records in Busolwe seem to confirm this: the average number of cases seen per month fell from 164 in 1990, to 127 in 1991, to 100 in 1992. Private and informal providers of antibiotics, who are often sought for treatment of these diseases, also say that there has been some decrease.

7   From 1970 to 1992 there was a slight increase in the figure for completed fertility. The figures are based on relatively small numbers of women over 45: n=44 in 1970 and n=42 in 1992.

8   The single exception, found in 1970, was one woman in Buhabeba who had been given land by her father. Significantly, she had spent many years in Buganda where there is a much stronger tradition for independent women, both in towns and in the rural areas (Southwold 1973: 168; Obbo 1980).

9   In the court records there were a few cases of women who brought cases against their husbands for sending them away without reason and making them lose their property. In 1969, for instance, a woman sued her husband in the

Budumba court for 'chasing' her from his home, leaving her property in his house. She claimed four cocks, five plates, two baskets, four gowns, one granary of millet, two sacks of groundnuts, one tin of cassava flour, and the money for her cotton, which he had sold. In the event, she did not appear in court and was reported to be back with her husband. Out of 348 civil cases examined for the years 1964, 1965, and 1969, there were only 7 in which a woman sued her husband over property, mostly crops. None were successful; most of the cases were dismissed. There were also a few cases in which men sued their wives for having taken their blankets, sheets, etc., for example while the husband was serving a jail sentence.

10 The frequency of polygyny is higher in the predominantly Muslim community of Buhabeba, but probably only partly because Islam accepted plural marriage while Christianity did not. The greater prosperity of men in Buhabeba allows them to realize a Nyole ideal also shared by many Christian men.

3 GOING TO ASK

1 Portions of this chapter appeared in S. Whyte 1990a.

2 Diviners worked with sets of four to eight foreign spirits, of which the majority were said to be Ganda. No two diviners had exactly the same team of spirits, although Mukasa, a Ganda spirit, was mentioned by all six of the diviners who gave me the names of their spirit colleagues. Other Ganda spirits mentioned were: Nabubi, Kintu, Kirongo, Kitambogwe, Kiwanuka, Jiraya, Katema Muti, Musoke, Omulalo Omulagusi (meaning Hima diviner!), Kidali, Luwanuka, and Musisi. Those named as Soga spirits were Musoke, Walumbe, and Giraya. Jiraya was also mentioned as a Gwere spirit. Masaaba and Lugingo were named as Gisu spirits and Mukambi as a Swahili spirit.

Foreign spirits, including jinns (*amajini*), fit a widely documented pattern of exotic spirits that objectify the nature of foreignness in eastern, northeastern, and southern Africa (e.g. Beattie 1969; Boddy 1989; Ngubane 1977). This is the type of spirit which Lewis (1971) described as peripheral in terms of both the geographical provenance of the spirit and the social status of the victim. In Bunyole, both men and women are said to be 'caught' by these spirits. The response can be either to 'settle them' by taking up divination or to 'say farewell' to them with an offering left at the crossroads. In 1970, the divination records suggested that the latter option was often adopted when foreign spirits were divined as the cause of illness or strange behaviour in women (S. Whyte 1981).

3 John Taylor (1958: 198–9) describes the 'fraudulent' techniques Ganda owners of such 'fetishes' used.

4 Many Nyole Muslims can read or recite Arabic, without understanding or being able to speak it. This gives *lamuli* plenty of leeway in tailoring the Arabic passages to Nyole realities. One popular book diviner presently working in Budumba is blind. He says that when he holds his books, God helps him to see the letters.

5 The mode of communication is thus fundamentally different from that used in Zande oracle divination. The Zande oracle was a digital device that answered

yes or no. Creativity and flexibility lay with the consulter: 'a man can...define the terms of the answer by stating them in the question' (Evans-Pritchard 1937: 351). Nyole divination is more open-ended, able to carry more information and to propose questions that the consulter has not considered. Correspondingly, the number of possibilities and the amount of uncertainty expressed is much greater.

4   AT HOME WITH THE DEAD

1 In addition to the heir (*omusika*), a 'successor of the belt' (*omusika w'ekoba'*) was appointed from among agnates of the dead man's own generation. The belt referred to was the one used to tie the loincloth worn in the old days. In 1970, it was the clothes and spear of the dead man which were passed on, signifying the assumption of his positions, as sacrificer to the dead, for example, or as the one able to remove any curse he might have made before he died. Such a person had to be of the same generation (or of the generation of grandparents or grandchildren which were equivalent) because Nyole conceptions of modesty would prohibit 'a woman washing the shorts of her father-in-law'. As a sexually active adult, a son could not take the clothes of his father. This successor of the belt was very close to the Soga concept (see Fallers 1965: 86); it does not seem to have been used in all lineages. A third kind of successor, the 'caretaker' (*omuhusa*) is chosen to care for children and wives. He or she should protect the interests of young children and ensure that the problems of daughters and wives are attended to.

   In practice the terms for the various kinds of heirs and successors were not always used in the same way. Sometimes only a caretaker and heir were appointed. Sometimes people differentiated between the 'heir of the lineage', who was the senior man and assumed ritual authority, and the 'heir of the deceased', who was the executor of the property. The common feature in all these arrangements was the separation of functions; property always went to the sons, but the fact that wives and position could go to others gave substance to lineage relationships. This also provided a kind of check on the heir to the property. The caretaker and/or successor of the belt should see that distributions were made equitably.

2 John Taylor (1958: 143–4) considered the question of reincarnation in connection with Ganda customs of naming children after their grandparents. He too concluded that most Ganda did not conceive of the spirits of the dead as reincarnated in their namesakes.

3 The cycle of death ceremonies and their significance in terms of social relations are more thoroughly discussed in M. A. Whyte 1974.

4 Contact with a corpse is dangerous, partly because of the pollution of death, but mainly because of the danger that the *omwigu* of the dead may follow what has touched the corpse. Thus the driver of a car that has transported a corpse is always given a chicken, which should be struck against the tyres and killed, in order to keep the dead soul from following the vehicle. I have never heard of a case of misfortune being attributed to contact with a corpse.

5 Shrines may be taken as a sign of paganism, as we found during our household survey of the predominantly Muslim, mixed clan neighbourhood of
   Buhabeba. When we asked, 'Where is your *omugaami*?', we often got answers
   like 'My shrine is the mosque' or 'the Koran' or 'my prayer mat' or 'We are
   Muslims, we don't have one.' (By contrast, nearly every household head in
   the nearby community of Bubaali identified his ancestral shrine, either in his
   own compound or in that of his father, or father's brother.) Muslims made a
   point of saying that they did not sacrifice to the dead and that they did not
   hold the second funeral ceremony of *olumbe*. But they did hold commemor-
   ative cere-monies, at which animals were killed and eaten by kinsmen, neighbours and fellow Muslims, great quantities of tea were consumed, and
   prayers were recited for the dead. (In one of Nandiriko's divinations, a dead
   man complained that his son, a Muslim, had only provided tea at his funeral
   ceremony, though in his life he had been a drinker of beer.)
6 In the old days, we were told, when a childless person was buried, the compound was swept and the broom laid in the grave with the corpse to show
   that the existence of that person was finished – nothing remained behind,
   everything was swept away. Suicides were not given a normal burial, nor
   were they entitled to be honoured in later funeral ceremonies.

5   THE FERTILITY OF CLANSHIP

1 The sacred grove is where the spirit addresses and blesses the assembled
   clanspeople, speaking through the medium at the great rituals. Many clans
   have their groves in the western part of Bunyole, near the Mpologoma River.
   This part is more wooded and less densely populated, but for Nyole what is
   important is that many clans passed this way when they migrated into present
   Bunyole from Busoga. Historians of eastern Uganda have taken the location of
   clan shrines as evidence of the chronology of clan migrations (D. Cohen
   1972: 44; Ogot 1967: 88) and there may be something to this. But in Bunyole,
   sacred groves are revealed to new mediums; I knew some who were waiting to
   be shown a place. So the history of clan migrations and the evidence of sacred
   groves should not be taken too literally.
2 The exact relationships between the kinds of clan spirits and the nature of the
   claims they had on women were explained differently by different people. I
   often heard that Seja, Walumbe, and Bung'ima were the 'policemen' of the
   ekuni of the forest. Some say that clan daughters are wives of Walumbe and also
   of the spirits of the forest. In one family, they said that Walumbe was the child
   of the *ekuni* of the forest, and thus also of the *ekuni*'s wives. So when the clan
   daughters went to marry, they should cook a fine farewell meal for their child
   Walumbe. I do not think that people were very concerned about the precise
   nature of the relationships among clan spirits; they used different metaphors
   when pushed by my questions. The important thing is that they all are 'in clans'
   and that they can lay claim to clan daughters.
3 When the medium of the Abalubajo died a few years ago, the family mourned
   for him in the normal way. For this they were made to pay a fine to the mediums
   of other clans.

4 As servants and representatives of the spirits, mediums may assist other members of their clans who are afflicted. In 1970, the healing functions of mediums mainly consisted of receiving offerings brought by daughters of the clan. Today more mediums do paid work as healers. Many have a range of herbal medicines, and treat spirits of various kinds as well as the effects of sorcery. Usually they say that the clan spirit has instructed them in these skills. Although they do not divine through spirit possession, some mediums explained that their spirits helped them to know the causes of misfortune and appropriate treatment. Practice is not restricted to their own clan members.

At a meeting a few years ago, the clan spirit mediums decided not to join the organizations of traditional healers that were campaigning for members in Bunyole. They did not want to associate themselves with ordinary healers who are doing a business rather than submitting themselves to the service of a spirit. If you belong to a spirit, you do not need a certificate to show your calling. Nevertheless, there is talk of forming an organization only for clan spirit mediums, 'so we can develop', as Gambisyo, the medium for the Ababeng'o, put it.

5 Perhaps this drama reenacts a myth of arrival. The medium of the Abagoye clan told us that his ancestors came from Masaba on a hunting expedition into what is now Bunyole. They shot a waterbuck which ran into a grove of trees. There it died and they skinned it, and just then Maliba, the *ekuni*, revealed itself for the first time, directing them to go and fetch their wives and settle in that place.

6 In southern Uganda, there is an old pattern of spirits manifesting themselves as snakes (Kenny 1977: 727) and a python god was honoured in Buganda (Roscoe 1909). The snake theme may well be seen as a variation on a wider regional one.

7 If the culture history of Nyole clan spirits could be written, it would probably relate them to the old 'nature spirits' reported in historical accounts of eastern Uganda (e.g. D. Cohen 1972: 21; Roscoe 1924: 8–9) or the protective spirits said to be 'semi-tame' animals such as leopards or snakes (Mwamula-Lubanda 1978: 111). See Whyte and Whyte 1987 for some speculations about a connection to Bunyoro, and Ogot 1972 for a discussion of the political history of clan spirit cults in Padhola.

8 The Abalwa's 'big' clan spirit is Mwerusi, which already has two mediums, one at Mulandu, in another sub-division of the clan and one at Kachong'a; 'But we need a medium on this end – it's difficult to travel so far.' The sacred grove of Nahiriga is here as is the paraphernalia of the last medium, who died in 1936. The medium Maliba says that Nahiriga was originally a clan spirit of the Adhola and that it left them and ran here because it was badly treated. Ogot (1972: 127) notes that the great cult of buru which united the Adhola at the beginning of the century came from Bugwere where it was called Nyakiriga, another form of the same name. This suggests, as we have argued elsewhere (Whyte and Whyte 1987: 117–19), that spirits or cults which come into Bunyole from neighbouring areas may be assimilated to the framework of clan spirits.

6   LITTLE SPIRITS AND CHILD SURVIVAL

1 I have heard examples of women being caught by Omuhyeeno, and specialists in its treatment insist that, though it affects children most, it can catch anyone. If a woman dies in childbirth because the people of her home fail to help her, Omuhyeeno can punish their descendants by causing other women to die in childbirth. It can cause a woman to be barren if she marries into a clan where someone once killed a member of her clan.

2 Extracts from this divination are presented in S. Whyte 1991b: 162–4.

3 Namatango comes through grandmothers: fathers and their fathers are always your own clansmen, and mother's fathers and their fathers are always of the clan of your 'mother's brothers' (*bahoja*).

7   SPEAKING OF MORALITY

1 In her analysis of anger-removal rites among the Taita people of Kenya, Grace Harris makes a similar distinction between what she calls jural and familial (or consociational) aspects of relationship (Harris 1978: 101).

8   SUBSTANCES AND SECRECY

1 The notion of sickness as something substantial that can be passed along is reflected in popular remedies for certain ills, which involve leaving a thing at a crossroads to be picked up by someone else (*ohumalya*). For certain kinds of sores called *ehisumuli*, you press coins against the sores and leave them at the crossroads. For persistent severe headache, you can wash your hair in medicine and leave it in a banana leaf container where two paths join. The person who steps over or touches the container picks up the headaches, which then leave you. In this way illness is dispersed but never eliminated (Parkin 1995).

2 In 1996 I took to hospital a woman whose body was swollen and who was said by her family and neighbours to be suffering from *etumbi*. The doctor examined her and diagnosed congestive heart failure.

3 By 1970 the leprosy camp in Bunyole had been closed, but the image of the disease was vivid, so that any skin condition was cause for concern. The clan spirit Walumbe was associated with changes in the skin, but if the condition was identified as leprosy (*ebigenge*), then it was a matter of sorcery. Nandiriko recorded that he divined about a man who had spots: 'Don't think he has a clan spirit. Rather there is a woman, a widow, the wife of his dead brother. That is the one who poured leprosy on him . . . She gave it to him in steamed bananas.'

4 The word *ehimalyo* seems to derive from the verb *ohumalya*, to cure, especially by giving the misfortune to someone else. There used to be 'good' *ehimalyo* too. Periodically 'in the old days', a sheep was escorted from one community to another and was given presents of money and food. The custom had not entirely died out by 1970. The purpose of this sheep was to cleanse or restore the country (*ohuhosiira ehyalo*) and it was escorted particularly when there was flood or drought. The sheep brought blessings if properly treated, and disaster if it was mistreated. It was a kind of scapesheep which carried off the evil of the community as it passed through. In a sense the sorcery animal is the opposite. It

is a dead animal that is deposited with a load of evil for an individual, rather than a living one that passes and removes evil from a community.

5 A medicine man told of a man who brought his wife for treatment. He admitted privately that he had a lover who might be bewitching his wife, but asked the medicine man not to tell her.

6 I heard of no cases where the illness or death of a child was attributed to the adultery of a parent, or where adultery caused pollution states that required purification, as is common in some other East African societies (Whyte and Whyte 1981; S. Whyte 1990b).

7 In the cases recorded by our assistants in their neighbourhoods, a little over half (twenty-one of thirty-eight) were diagnosed by divination.

8 The splitting of descent groups on the pretext of sorcery, as Middleton (1960) described for the Lugbara, has parallels in Bunyole. The story of the division of the Ababeng'o clan tells of two brothers, Wakoli and Mudenya. Wakoli moved away to Busoga after a disagreement about a precious stone belonging to Mudenya, which he had borrowed and lost. There Wakoli's child died. Not wanting to bury it in exile, he preserved the body by smoking it above the hearth. Mudenya sent word to his brother that he should come home and bury his child. Wakoli set out with his people, but as he approached Mudenya's home, he sent a drumbeat message: 'You brought me sorcery; let our relationship die' (*Wundetera amalogo, oluganda lufwe*). Mudenya drummed a generous reply: 'The bereaved just cries like that' (*Owomufu wuwe alira atio atio*) implying that he knew his brother spoke out of grief. Wakoli buried his child and settled again in Bunyole, but he took another totem (the giraffe, *ekooli*) to emphasize his break with his brother, who he still believed had killed his child. Here I am not concerned with these uses of sorcery accusations by senior men, but rather with the everyday experiences and suspicions that ordinary Nyole live with.

9   MORE QUESTIONS

1 Birungi Harriet, in her study of injection practices in neighbouring Busoga, has richly described processes of personalization as a way of meeting health care needs (Birungi 1995).

2 Health workers also experiment with drugs to find out which one relieves the symptom best, when they do not have the drugs of their choice. In a recent outbreak of bloody diarrhoea, a doctor explained that nalidixic acid had proved effective, but it was not available in Bunyole. So he was trying chloramphenicol on some patients and flagyl (metronidazole) on others.

3 Malaria is very probably overdiagnosed in rural health units. A study in Kabarole, western Uganda, found no malaria parasites in the blood of half of the patients who had received a clinical diagnosis of malaria (Barton and Wamai 1994: 87).

4 Particularly in the case of educated patients, this assumption is probably unfounded. Rose Asera and colleagues (1996) noted a sense of frustration among those who wrote to a Ugandan health advice column about the lack of information in clinical contexts.

5 I have not heard anyone speak of 'sent AIDS', as Paul Farmer (1992) described from Haiti. The Nyole idea seems to be that you can be afflicted either by sorcery or AIDS.

6 Persistent rumours suggested that health workers were seen as more than just negligent. It was said that 'victims' among them purposely contaminated injections and transfusions with their own blood. Like other rumours about 'victims', these were anonymous speculations about a worst possible scenario.

References

Abu-Lughod, Lila and Catherine A. Lutz. 1990. Introduction: emotion, discourse, and the politics of everyday life. In Catherine A. Lutz and Lila Abu-Lughod (eds.) *Language and the Politics of Emotion*. Cambridge: Cambridge University Press.

Akello, Margaret and Maria Bawubya. 1990. Development of Policies and Programmes on Women. Tororo District Profile. Project UGA/88/PO9. Republic of Uganda, Ministry of Women in Development.

Asera, Rose, Henry Bagarukayo, Dean Shuey, and Thomas Barton. 1996. Searching for solutions: health concerns expressed in letters to an East African newspaper column. *Health Transition Review* 6 (2): 169–78.

1997. An epidemic of apprehension: questions about HIV/AIDS to an East African newspaper health advice column. *AIDS Care* 9 (1): 5–12.

Augé, Marc. 1985. Introduction. *History and Anthropology* 2: 1–15.

Barth, Frederik. 1992. Towards greater naturalism in conceptualizing societies. In Adam Kuper (ed.) *Conceptualizing Society*. London: Routledge.

Barton, Tom and Gimono Wamai. 1994. *Equity and Vulnerability: A Situation Analysis of Women, Adolescents and Children in Uganda, 1994*. Kampala: Government of Uganda, National Council for Children.

Beattie, John. 1958. Nyoro marriage and affinity. *Africa* 28 (1): 1–22.

1967. Divination in Bunyoro, Uganda. In John Middleton (ed.) *Magic, Witchcraft and Curing*. Garden City, NY: Natural History Press.

1969. Spirit mediumship in Bunyoro. In John Beattie and John Middleton (eds.) *Spirit Mediumship and Society in Africa*. London: Routledge & Kegan Paul.

1980. Representations of the self in traditional Africa. *Africa* 50 (3): 313–20.

Behrend, Heike. 1991. Is Alice Lakwena a witch? The Holy Spirit Movement and its fight against evil in the north. In H. B. Hansen and M. Twaddle (eds.) *Changing Uganda: Dilemmas of Structural Adjustment and Revolutionary Change*. London: James Currey.

Beidelman, T. O. 1993 (orig. publ. 1986). *Moral Imagination in Kaguru Modes of Thought*. Bloomington: Indiana University Press.

Birungi, Harriet. 1994a. Injections as household utilities: injection practices in Busoga, eastern Uganda. In Nina Etikin and Michael Tan (eds.) *Medicines: Meanings and Contexts*. Manila: Health Action Information Network.

1994b. The domestication of injections: a study of social relations of health care in Busoga, Eastern Uganda. Ph.D. thesis. University of Copenhagen.

Bloch, Maurice. 1968. Astrology and writing in Madagascar. In Jack Goody (ed.) *Literacy in Traditional Societies*. Cambridge: Cambridge University Press.
1989. *Ritual, History and Power. Selected Papers in Anthropology*. London: Athlone Press.
Boddy, Janice. 1989. *Wombs and Alien Spirits. Women, Men, and the Zar Cult in Northern Sudan*. Madison: University of Wisconsin Press.
Bradley, D. J. 1975. Helminths. In S. A. Hall and B. W. Langlands (eds.) *Uganda Atlas of Disease Distribution*. Nairobi: East African Publishing House.
Brown, J. A. Kinnear. 1975. Leprosy. In S. A. Hall and B. W. Langlands (eds.) *Uganda Atlas of Disease Distribution*. Nairobi: East African Publishing House.
Burgess, H. J. L. 1962. Protein-calorie malnutrition in Uganda: III-Bukedi District. *East African Medical Journal* 39 (7): 375–85.
Campbell, James. 1995. *Understanding John Dewey*. Chicago: Open Court.
Cohen, Anthony P. 1994. *Self-Consciousness: An Alternative Anthropology of Identity*. London: Routledge.
Cohen, David William. 1972. *The Historical Tradition of Busoga: Mukama and Kintu*. Oxford: Clarendon Press.
1977. *Womunafu's Bunafu: A Study of Authority in a Nineteenth-Century African Community*. Princeton: Princeton University Press.
1986. *Towards a Reconstructed Past: Historical Texts from Busoga, Uganda*. Union Académique Internationale Fontes Historiae Africanae Series Veria III. Oxford: Oxford University Press for the British Academy.
Cohen, David William and E. S. Atieno Odhiambo. 1992. *Burying SM: The Politics of Knowledge and the Sociology of Power in Africa*. London: James Currey.
Colson, Elizabeth. 1971. *The Social Consequences of Resettlement*. Manchester: Manchester University Press.
Comaroff, Jean and John Comaroff. 1993. Introduction. In Jean Comaroff and John Comaroff (eds.) *Modernity and its Malcontents. Ritual and Power in Postcolonial Africa*. Chicago: University of Chicago Press.
Davis, John. 1992. Tense in ethnography: some practical considerations. In Judith Okely and Helen Callaway (eds.) *Anthropology and Autobiography*. London: Routledge.
Devisch, René. 1985. Perspectives on divination in contemporary Sub-Saharan Africa. In W. van Binsbergen and M. Schoffeleers (eds.) *Theoretical Explorations in African Religions*. London: Routledge & Kegan Paul.
Dewey, John. 1922. *Human Nature and Conduct*. New York: Random House Modern Library.
1981. Experience and nature. In Jo Ann Boydston (ed.) *John Dewey: The Later Works, 1925–1953. vol 1: 1925*. Carbondale, Ill: University of Southern Illinois Press.
1984. The quest for certainty. In Jo Ann Boydston (ed.) *John Dewey: The Later Works, 1925–1953. vol 4: 1929*. Carbondale, Ill: University of Southern Illinois Press.
Diggins, John Patrick. 1994. *The Promise of Pragmatism: Modernism and the Crisis of Knowledge and Authority*. Chicago: University of Chicago Press.

Dodge, Cole P. and Paul D. Wiebe. 1985. *Crisis in Uganda: The Breakdown of Health Services*. Oxford: Pergamon Press.

Douglas, Mary. 1966. *Purity and Danger: An Analysis of Concepts of Pollution and Taboo*. London: Routledge and Kegan Paul.

Eastman, Carol M. 1974. Lunyole of the Bamenya. *Journal of African Languages* (E. Lansing) 11: 63–78.

Engero ja Banyole. 1936. Mbale: N. Were Hamala.

Evans-Pritchard, E. E. 1937. *Witchcraft, Oracles and Magic among the Azande*. Oxford: Clarendon Press.

Fallers, Lloyd A. 1965 (orig. publ. 1956). *Bantu Bureaucracy: a Century of Political Evolution among the Basoga of Uganda*. Chicago: University of Chicago Press.

Farmer, Paul. 1992. *AIDS and Accusation. Haiti and the Geography of Blame*. Berkeley: University of California Press.

Fernandez, James. 1982. *Bwiti: An Ethnography of the Religious Imagination in Africa*. Princeton: Princeton University Press.

Fortes, Meyer. 1973. On the concept of the person among the Tallensi. In Colloques Internationaux du Centre National de la Recherche Scientifique No. 544: *La Notion de Personne en Afrique Noire*. Paris: Editions du Centre National de la Recherche Scientifique.

Foster, George. 1976. Disease etiologies in nonwestern medical systems. *American Anthropologist* 78: 773–82.

Gable, Eric. 1995. The decolonization of consciousness: local skeptics and the 'will to be modern' in a West African village. *American Ethnologist* 22 (2): 242–57.

Gale, H. P. 1959. *Uganda and the Mill Hill Fathers*. London: Macmillan.

Geertz, Clifford. 1966. Religion as a cultural system. In Michael Banton (ed.) *Anthropological Approaches to the Study of Religion*. London: Tavistock.

1983. *Local Knowledge*. New York: Basic Books.

Giddens, Anthony. 1979. *Central Problems in Social Theory*. London: Macmillan.

1987. *Social Theory and Modern Sociology*. Cambridge: Polity Press.

1990. *The Consequences of Modernity*. Stanford: Stanford University Press.

Gillies, Eva. 1976. Causal criteria in African classifications of disease. In J. B. London (ed.) *Social Anthropology and Medicine*. London: Academic Press.

Good, Byron. 1994. *Medicine, Rationality, and Experience: An Anthropological Perspective*. Cambridge: Cambridge University Press.

Good, Mary-Jo Delvecchio, Byron Good, Cynthia Schaffer, and Stuart Lind. 1990. American oncology and the discourse on hope. *Culture, Medicine and Psychiatry* 14 (1): 59–79.

Gray, Sir John. 1963. Kakunguru in Bukedi. *Uganda Journal* 27 (1): 31–59.

Grech, E. S., J. Galea, and R. R. Trussell. 1975. Pregnancy, childbirth and the puerperium. In S. A. Hall and B. W. Langlands (eds.) *Uganda Atlas of Disease Distribution*. Nairobi: East African Publishing House.

Hansen, Ann-Brit Eg. 1995. Cost-sharing initiatives in Tororo District: a study of user-charges for health service in Uganda. Denmark: Aarhus University, Department of Epidemiology and Social Medicine, report no. 14.

Hansen, Holger Bernt. 1984. *Mission, Church and State in a Colonial Setting. Uganda 1890–1925*. London: Heinemann.

Hansen, Holger Bernt and Michael Twaddle (eds.). 1995. *Religion and Politics in East Africa: The Period since Independence.* London: James Currey.

Harris, Grace Gredys. 1978. *Casting Out Anger. Religion among the Taita of Kenya.* Cambridge: Cambridge University Press.

1989. Concepts of individual, self, and person in description and analysis. *American Anthropologist* 91: 599–612.

Harwood, Alan. 1970. *Witchcraft, Sorcery and Social Categories among the Safwa.* London: Oxford University Press for the International African Institute.

Hastrup, Kirsten. 1992. Writing ethnography: state of the art. In Judith Okely and Helen Callaway (eds.) *Anthropology and Autobiography.* London: Routledge.

Heald, Suzette. 1989. *Controlling Anger. The Sociology of Gisu Violence.* Manchester: Manchester University Press.

1991. Divinatory failure: the religious and social role of Gisu diviners. *Africa* 61 (3): 299–317.

Hook, Sidney. 1981. Introduction. In Jo Ann Boydston (ed.) *John Dewey: The Later Works, 1925–1953. vol 1: 1925.* Carbondale, Ill: University of Southern Illinois Press.

Horton, Robin. 1967. African traditional thought and Western science. *Africa* 37: 50–71.

Jackson, Michael. 1978. An approach to Kuranko divination. *Human Relations* 31 (2):117–38.

1982. *Allegories of the Wilderness: Ethics and Ambiguity in Kuranko Narratives.* Bloomington: Indiana University Press.

1989. *Paths Toward a Clearing. Radical Empiricism and Ethnographic Inquiry.* Bloomington: Indiana University Press.

1995. *At Home in the World.* Durham: Duke University Press.

1996. Introduction: Phenomenology, radical empiricism, and anthropological critique. In Michael Jackson (ed.) *Things as They Are: New Directions in Phenomenological Anthropology.* Bloomington: Indiana University Press.

Jamal, Vali. 1991. The agrarian context of the Ugandan crisis. In H. B. Hansen and M. Twaddle (eds.) *Changing Uganda: Dilemmas of Structural Adjustment and Revolutionary Change.* London: James Currey.

James, Wendy. 1995. Introduction: whatever happened to the Enlightenment. In Wendy James (ed.) *The Pursuit of Certainty: Religious and Cultural Formulations.* London: Routledge.

James, William. 1974. (orig. publ. 1907, 1909). *Pragmatism and four essays from The Meaning of Truth.* New York: New American Library.

Kafuko, Jessica, Christine Zirabamuzaale, and Dan Bagenda. 1994. Rational Drug Use in the Rural Health Units of Uganda: Effect of National Standard Treatment Guidelines on Rational Drug Use. Uganda Essential Drugs Management Programme, Ministry of Health.

Kenny, Michael G. 1977. The powers of Lake Victoria. *Anthropos* 72: 717–33.

Ker, A. D. R. 1967. Agriculture in Bukedi District. Soroti: Arapai Agricultural College. Stencilled MS (144 pages).

Kleinman, Arthur. 1980. *Patients and Healers in the Context of Culture.* Berkeley: University of California Press.

Kleinman, Arthur and Joan Kleinman. 1991. Suffering and its professional transformation: toward an ethnography of interpersonal experience. *Culture, Medicine and Psychiatry* 15 (3): 275–301.

Ladefoged, Peter, Ruth Glick and Clive Criper. 1972. *Language in Uganda.* London: Oxford University Press.

La Fontaine, J. S. 1985. Person and individual: some anthropological reflections. In M. Carrithers, S. Collins and S. Lukes (eds.) *The Category of the Person.* Cambridge: Cambridge University Press.

Lambek, Michael. 1993. *Knowledge and Practice in Mayotte. Local Discourses of Islam, Sorcery, and Spirit Possession.* Toronto: University of Toronto Press.

1995. Choking on the Quran: and other consuming parables from the western Indian Ocean front. In Wendy James (ed.) *The Pursuit of Certainty: Religious and Cultural Formulations.* London: Routledge.

Langlands, B. W. 1971. The Population Geography of Bukedi District. Occ. paper no. 27, Kampala: Department of Geography, Makerere University.

Last, Murray. 1981. The importance of knowing about not-knowing. *Social Science and Medicine* 15B: 387–92.

Last, Murray and G. L. Chavunduka (eds.),1986. *The Professionalisation of African Medicine.* Manchester: Manchester University Press.

Lévi-Strauss, C. 1963. The bear and the barber. *Journal of the Royal Anthropological Institute* 93: 1–11.

Lewis, I. M. 1971. *Ecstatic Religion: An Anthropological Study of Spirit Possession and Shamanism.* Harmondsworth: Penguin.

Lienhardt, Godfrey. 1985. Self: public, private. Some African representations. In M. Carrithers, S. Collins and S. Lukes (eds.) *The Category of the Person.* Cambridge: Cambridge University Press.

Low, D. A. 1965. Uganda: the establishment of the Protectorate 1894–1919. In Vincent Harlow and E. M. Chilver (eds.) *History of East Africa vol. II.* Oxford: Clarendon Press.

McCrae, A. W. R. 1975. Malaria. In S. A. Hall and B. W. Langlands (eds.) *Uganda Atlas of Disease Distribution.* Nairobi: East African Publishing House.

Macrae, Joanna, Anthony B. Zwi, and Lucy Gilson. 1996. A triple burden for health sector reform: 'post'-conflict rehabilitation in Uganda. *Social Science and Medicine* 42 (87): 1095–108.

Middleton, John. 1960. *Lugbara Religion: Ritual and Authority among an East African People.* London: Oxford University Press.

1973. The concept of the person among the Lugbara of Uganda. In Colloques Internationaux du Centre National de la Recherche Scientifique No. 544: *La Notion de Personne en Afrique Noire.* Paris: Editions du Centre National de la Recherche Scientifique.

Middleton, John and E. H. Winter. 1963. Introduction. In *Witchcraft and Sorcery in East Africa.* John Middleton and E. H. Winter (eds.) London: Routledge and Kegan Paul.

Morris, H. F. 1963. A note on Lunyole. *Uganda Journal* 27 (1):127–34.

Mudoola, Dan. 1993. *Religion, Ethnicity and Politics in Uganda.* Kampala: Fountain Publishers.

Mutibwa, Phares. 1992. *Uganda since Independence: A Story of Unfulfilled Hopes.*

Trenton, NJ: Africa World Press.

Mwamula-Lubandi, E. D. 1978. Transitional Socio-economic Clan Relations among Basoga. Uppsala University, doctoral dissertation.

Mwesigye, Runumi Francis. 1995. Effects of user charges on quality of curative services: a perspective of Uganda's rural health units. Health Planning Unit, Ministry of Health, Entebbe.

Mwima-Mudeenya, Elijah and John Wafula. 1977. Bukedi. In Joel Barkan et al. (eds.) Uganda District Government and Politics 1947–1967. Madison: African Studies Program, University of Wisconsin-Madison and Uganda Institute of Public Administration.

Ngubane, Harriet. 1977. *Body and Mind in Zulu Medicine: An Ethnography of Health and Disease in Nyuswa-Zulu Thought and Practice.* London: Academic Press.

Nichter, Mark. 1989. *Anthropology and International Health. South Asian Case Studies.* Dordrecht: Kluwer.

Obbo, Christine. 1980. *African Women. Their Struggle for Economic Independence.* London: Zed Press.

Odoi Adome, Richard, S. R. Whyte and Anita Hardon. 1996. *Popular Pills: Community Drug Use in Uganda.* Amsterdam: Het Spinhuis.

Ogot, B. A. 1967. *History of the Southern Luo. Vol I. Migration and Settlement.* Nairobi: East African Publishing House.

1972. On the making of a sanctuary: being some thoughts on the history of religion in Padhola. In T. O. Ranger and Isaria Kimambo (eds.) *The Historical Study of African Religion.* Berkeley: University of California Press.

Oliver, Roland. 1952. *The Missionary Factor in East Africa.* London: Longman.

Ortner, Sherry B. 1984. Theory in anthropology since the sixties. *Comparative Studies in Society and History* 26: 126–66.

Packard, Randall. 1970. The significance of neighbourhoods for the collection of oral history in Padhola. *Uganda Journal* 34 (2): 147–62.

Park, George. 1967. Divination and its social contexts. In J. Middleton (ed.) *Magic, Witchcraft and Curing.* Garden City: Natural History Press.

Parkin, David. 1968. Medicines and men of influence. *Man* 3: 424–39.

1982. Straightening the paths from wilderness: simultaneity and sequencing in divinatory speech. *Paideuma* 28: 71–83.

1986. Violence and will. In David Riches (ed.) *The Anthropology of Violence.* Oxford: Basil Blackwell.

1995. Latticed knowledge: eradication and dispersal of the unpalatable in Islam, medicine and anthropological theory. In Richard Fardon (ed.) *Counterworks: Managing the Diversity of Knowledge.* London: Routledge.

Peek, Philip M. (ed.). 1991. *African Divination Systems: Ways of Knowing.* Bloomington: Indiana University Press.

Prins, Gwyn. 1992. A modern history of Lozi therapeutics. In Steven Feierman and John M. Janzen (eds.) *The Social Basis of Health and Healing in Africa.* Berkeley: University of California Press.

Ramløv, Kirsten 1986. On the limits of explanation. *Folk* 28: 125–40.

Ray, Benjamin C. 1972. Royal shrines and ceremonies of Buganda. *Uganda Journal* 36: 35–48.

1991. *Myth, Ritual and Kingship in Buganda*. New York: Oxford University Press.

Reeler, Anne. 1996. *Friend, Patient or Customer? Empowerment and Health Care in Thailand*. Amsterdam: Het Spinhuis.

Republic of Uganda. 1971. *Report on the 1969 Population Census*. Entebbe: Government Printer.

1991. *Provisional Results of the 1991 Population and Housing Census*. Entebbe: Government Printer.

Riesman, Paul. 1986. The person and the life cycle in African social life and thought. *African Studies Review* 29 (2): 71–138.

Robertson, A. F. 1978. *Community of Strangers: A Journal of Discovery at the Source of the Nile*. London: Scolar Press.

Rorty, Richard. 1991 (orig. publ. 1982). *Consequences of Pragmatism*. New York: Harvester Wheatsheaf.

Roscoe, John. 1909. Python worship in Uganda. *Man* 9

1924. *The Bagesu and other tribes of the Uganda Protectorate*. Cambridge: Cambridge University Press.

Rosen, Lawrence (ed.) 1995. *Other Intentions: Cultural Contexts and the Attribution of Inner States*. Santa Fe, NM: School of American Research Press.

Sachs, Lisbeth. 1989. Misunderstanding as therapy: doctors, patients and medicines in a rural clinic in Sri Lanka. *Culture, Medicine and Psychiatry* 8: 49–70.

Sahlins, Marshall. 1976. *Culture and Practical Reason*. Chicago: University of Chicago Press.

Sharman, Anne. 1970. Nutrition and social planning. In R. Apthorpe (ed.) *People, Planning and Development Studies*. London: Frank Cass.

1974. Land tenure and 'room for manoeuvre'. In J. Davis (ed.) *Choice and Change. Essays in Honour of Lucy Mair*. London: Athlone.

Southall, Aidan. 1970. The illusion of tribe. *Journal of Asian and African Studies* 5: (1–2): 28–50.

Southwold, Martin. 1973. The Baganda of central Uganda. In Angela Molnos (ed.) *Cultural Source Materials for Population Planning in East Africa. Vol. III. Beliefs and Practices*. Nairobi: East African Publishing House.

Steedly, Mary Margaret. 1993. *Hanging without a Rope: Narrative Experience in Colonial and Postcolonial Karoland*. Princeton: Princeton University Press.

Swantz, Lloyd. 1990. *The Medicine Man among the Zaramo of Dar es Salaam*. Uppsala: Scandinavian Institute of African Studies.

Taylor, John V. 1958. *The Growth of the Church in Buganda. An Attempt at Understanding*. London: SCM Press.

Thomas, H. B. and Robert Scott. 1935. *Uganda*. London: Oxford University Press.

Trimingham, J. Spencer. 1964. *Islam in East Africa*. Oxford: Clarendon Press.

Tuma, A. D. Tom. 1980. *Building a Ugandan Church. African Participation in Church Growth and Expansion in Busoga 1891–1940*. Nairobi: Kenya Literature Bureau.

Turner, Victor. 1964. Witchcraft and sorcery: taxonomy versus dynamics. *Africa* 34 (4): 314–25.

1975. *Revelation and Divination in Ndembu Ritual.* Ithaca, NY: Cornell University Press.

Twaddle, Michael. 1969. 'Tribalism' in Eastern Uganda. In P. H. Gulliver (ed.) *Tradition and Transition in East Africa.* London: Routledge & Kegan Paul.

1974. On Ganda historiography. *History in Africa* 1: 85–100.

1993. *Kakungulu and the Creation of Uganda.* London: James Currey.

Uganda Government. 1965. *Report on Uganda Census of Agriculture*, vol. I. Entebbe: Government Printer.

Uganda Protectorate. 1956. *Annual Report for Eastern Province.* Rhodes House Library, Oxford University.

1961. *Uganda Census, 1959.* African Population. Statistics Branch, Ministry of Economic Affairs.

Van der Geest, Sjaak and Susan Reynolds Whyte. 1989. The charm of medicines: metaphors and metonyms. *Medical Anthropology Quarterly* 3 (4): 345–367.

Van der Heijden, Thomas and Jessica Jitta. 1993. Economic survival strategies of health workers in Uganda. Kampala: Child Health and Development Centre, unpubl. MS.

Weiss, Brad. 1993. 'Buying her grave': money, movement and AIDS in northwest Tanzania. *Africa* 63 (1): 19–35.

Welbourn, F. B. 1961. *East African Rebels.* London: SCM Press.

1965. *Religion and Politics in Uganda 1952–62.* Nairobi: East African Publishing House.

Werbner, Richard. 1973. The superabundance of understanding: Kalanga rhetoric and domestic divination. *American Anthropologist* 75 (5): 1414–40.

Whyte, Michael A. 1983. Clan versus lineage: notes on the semantics of solidarity and conflict among the Ugandan Nyole. *Folk* 25: 129–45.

1988. Nyole economic transformation in eastern Uganda. In H. B. Hansen and M. Twaddle (eds.) *Uganda Now: Between Decay and Development.* London: James Currey.

1990a. The process of survival in southeastern Uganda. In Mette Bovin and Leif Manger (eds.) *Adaptive Strategies in African Arid Lands.* Uppsala: Scandinavian Institute of African Studies.

1990b. 'We have no cash crops anymore.' Agriculture as a cultural system in Uganda, 1969–1987. In Anita Jacobson-Widding and Walter van Beek (eds.) *The Creative Communion: African Folk Models of Fertility and the Regeneration of Life.* Uppsala: Almqvist & Wiksell.

1996. Talking about AIDS: the biography of a local AIDS organization within the Church of Uganda. In Inon Schenker, Francisco Sy and Galia Sabar Friedman (eds.) *AIDS Education: Interventions in Multi-Cultural Societies.* New York: Plenum.

Whyte, Michael A. and the Lunyole Language Committee (LLC) (compilers). 1994. *Lunyole-English and English-Lunyole Word Lists.* Kampala: The Lunyole Language Committee.

Whyte, Susan Reynolds. 1981. Men, women and misfortune in Bunyole. *Man* 16 (3): 350–66.

1982. Penicillin, battery acid and sacrifice: cures and causes in Nyole medicine. *Social Science and Medicine* 16: 2055–64.

1988. The power of medicine in East Africa. In S. van der Geest and S. R. Whyte (eds.) *The Context of Medicines in Developing Countries. Studies in Pharmaceutical Anthropology.* Kluwer: Dordrecht.

1990a. Uncertain persons in Nyole divination. *Journal of Religion in Africa* 20 (1): 41–62.

1990b. The widow's dream: sex and death in Western Kenya. In Michael Jackson and Ivan Karp (eds.) *Personhood and Agency: The Experience of Self and Other in African Cultures.* Uppsala Studies in Cultural Anthropology 14. Uppsala: Uppsala University.

1991a. Medicines and self-help. The privatization of health care in Eastern Uganda. In H. B. Hansen and M. Twaddle (eds.) *Changing Uganda: Dilemmas of Structural Adjustment and Revolutionary Change.* London: James Currey.

1991b. Power and knowledge in Nyole divination. In Philip M. Peek (ed.) *African Systems of Divination: Ways of Knowing.* Bloomington: Indiana University Press.

1992. Pharmaceuticals as folk medicine: transformations in the social relations of health care in Uganda. *Culture, Medicine and Psychiatry* 16: 163–86.

Whyte, Susan Reynolds and Michael A. Whyte. 1981. Cursing and pollution: supernatural styles in two Luyia-speaking groups. *Folk* 23: 133–46.

1985. Peasants and workers: the legacy of partition among the Luyia-speaking Nyole and Marachi. *Journal of the Historical Society of Nigeria* 12 (3 & 4): 139–58.

1987. Clans, brides and dancing spirits. *Folk* 29: 97–123.

1992. Boomtime in Busolwe: culture, trade and transformation in a rural Ugandan town. In Hermine G. De Soto (ed.) *Culture and Contradictions: Dialectics of Wealth, Power and Symbols.* San Francisco: Mellen Research University Press.

1997. The values of development: conceiving growth and progress in Bunyole. In Holger Bernt Hansen and Michael Twaddle (eds.) *Developing Uganda.* London: James Currey.

Wikan, Unni. 1990. *Managing Turbulent Hearts: A Balinese Formula for Living.* Chicago: Chicago University Press.

1992. Beyond the words: the power of resonance. *American Ethnologist* 19: 460–82.

Wilson, Monica. 1977. *For Men and Elders: Change in the Relation of Generations and of Men and Women among the Nyakyusa-Ngonde People 1875–1971.* London: International African Institute.

Zuesse, Evan M. 1979. *Ritual Cosmos: the Sanctification of Life in African Religions.* Athens, OH: Ohio University Press.

UNPUBLISHED MANUSCRIPTS ON NYOLE CULTURE

Higeny-Gabuni. n.d. Esiibuha ya Munyole oba Esiibuha ya Banyole (The Origin of Banyole). Files of the Lunyole Language Committee, Wilson Birikire, Secretary, Busolwe.

Higenyi, Erika. The history of the Banyole. (Original MS in Luganda 1936.

Translated into Lunyole by Higenyi 1964. Translated into English by E. Wesana-Chomi 1968.)

Mubene, Dan and Higenyi Gabuni. n.d. Ehitabo Ehidayi Mululimi Olunyole. (The First Book in the Lunyole Language.) Files of the Lunyole Language Committee, Wilson Birikire, Secretary, Busolwe.

Nyango, Y. Family life and custom in Bunyole. MS in Makerere University Library.

Wesana-Chomi, Elley. Traditional customs of the Banyole. MS.

Index

Abu-Lughod, Lila and Catherine Lutz, 23
Adhola, 35, 238n.8
adultery, 189–91, 240n.6
aetiological perspective, 25–28, 30, 192
  see also explanatory idiom
agents of misfortune, 26, 30–32
  feelings/disposition of, 80
  in divination, 63, 66
  motivation of, 80–1
  relationships, and, 32
  spirit and human, 31–2
  see also clan spirits, cursing, little spirits, shades, sorcery
agriculture, 39–42, 53, 125
AIDS, 24, 51, 59, 89, 92, 94, 129–30, 203, 205, 213–23, 227, 234n.6
  prevention, 220–1, 222–3
  responses to, 215
  and sorcery, 220–1, 241n.5
  suspicions, 220–2
  tests, 213, 214–15, 219
Akello, Margaret and Maria Bawubya, 47
amulets, 133–4, 149, 150, 151
anaemia, 50
ancestors, see shades
Asera, Rose et al., 214, 240n.4
Augé, Marc, 21

barrenness, 18, 51, 56, 69, 72, 146–7, 166, 187, 237n.6
Barton, Tom and Gimono Wamai, 49, 50, 240n.3
Beattie, John, 58, 63, 233n.5, 235n.2
Behrend, Heike, 53
Beidelman, T. O., 106
biomedicine, 26, 203, 205–13, 231, 232
  and childrens illness, 133, 150, 151, 177
  diagnoses, 212, 214
  history in Bunyole, 51–2, 205–6
  see also drug shops, health facilities,

health workers, pharmaceuticals
Birungi, Harriet, 221, 240n.1
blessings, 13, 14
blindness, 180
Bloch, Maurice, 20, 22, 64
Boddy, Janice, 235n.2
book diviners, see lamuli
Bradley, D. J., 50
bridewealth, 54, 56, 94, 121, 123, 162, 164
  amount 55, 167
  and cursing, 161, 166–7, 169, 171, 172
  in explanations of misfortune, 71, 75, 78–9, 80, 120
  and men's control, 56
  refund of, 59, 76, 129
Brown, J. A. Kinnear, 50
Buganda, 64, 65, 127, 174, 221, 234n.3, 234n.8
Bugisu, 234n.2
Bugwere, 127, 234n.2, 238n.8
Bungima, 111, 112, 237n.2
Bunyole County, 34, 35
Bunyoro, 140
Burgess, H. J. L., 50
burial, 93–4, 198–9, 237n.6
  and land rights, 93–4
  of women, 94–5
Busamia, 234n.2
Busoga, 65, 98, 101, 104, 127, 140, 158, 163, 177, 198, 234n.2, 234n.3
Busolwe, 42–3, 64

Campbell, James, 232
cash crops, 40
childbirth, 49–50, 74, 239n.6.1
children, 69, 119, 125, 127, 166
  and cursing, 156, 158, 168
  and little spirits, 132–52
  as extensions of parents, 32, 60, 169
  mortality of, 49, 132, 166, 191

252